Introducing Cultural Anthropology

Essential Readings

Revised Edition

cognella
San Diego, CA

First published in the United States of America in 2010 by Cognella, a division of University Readers, Inc.

Trademark Notice: Product or corporate names may be trademarks or registered trademarks, and are used only for identification and explanation without intent to infringe.

Photo Credits
Wikimedia Commons (GNU Free Documentation License): 10
Author: 188, 230

15 14 13 12 11   1 2 3 4 5

Printed in the United States of America

ISBN: 978-1-934269-97-8

www.cognella.com 800.200.3908

Contents

CHAPTER FIVE: CONTEMPORARY PERSPECTIVES AND ISSUES   153

Foreword

Anthropology is unique among disciplines because it is both a natural science and a social science. On the one hand, biological/physical anthropologists and archaeologists concern themselves with physical remnants, including fossils and other relics that provide clues about human and non-human artifacts of present and by-gone eras. These anthropologists analyze artifacts in laboratories. Their scientific endeavors cause the discipline to be classified as a natural science.

On the other hand, cultural anthropologists and linguistic anthropologists seek to understand how human beings across the world live together as "social" beings. These anthropologists discovered long ago that human beings are very much on the move. So, they've made no attempt to get them into laboratories or to study them under "controlled" conditions. The work and methods of cultural anthropologists and linguists are what cause anthropology to be termed a social science.

For the cultural anthropologist, the whole world is a laboratory, and human beings are studied in their own habitats by means of fieldwork or participant observation viz., studying every social aspect of human beings—their language, their families, their food, their art, their religion; in sum, their total way of life.

This textbook is a collection of articles that pertain to the social science realm of anthropology. It seeks to survey the kind of reading to which a cultural anthropology student of today should be exposed to for a first-rate introduction to the field. Students who are using this anthology are reading select articles, many of which are the best of the best. The articles go beyond didactic discussion and review of concepts, terms, theories, and principles—necessary though covering these matters may be—and invite the introductory student to explore how anthropologists think and conduct their research.

Many anthropologists whose articles are included in this anthology have names that are easily recognized as masters who helped pioneer the field of cultural anthropology. Every well-prepared student of introductory anthropology, upon completion of the course, should know many if not most of them. Other authors selected for this anthology are ones whose articles were selected because they are well-written or because they treat timely subject matter in a student-oriented manner. They too have a special role to play in introducing first-time students of cultural anthropology to the depth and range of the discipline. Such understanding is essential for the beginning student of anthropology to grasp a comprehension of the theory and method of cultural anthropology. Where better to acquire such an understanding than from the pen and perspective of anthropologists who have helped to define the field?

Fundamental to the study of cultural anthropology is the concept of culture. The culture concept is, appropriately, the essence of the field. To fully understand cultural anthropology, one must first grasp its essence. Thus, the first chapter of this collection devotes itself to this all-important concept. The articles in the first chapter are written by masters in the field of cultural anthropology whose writings changed the way people thought about the world and its people. Down through the decades, the culture concept has been useful in helping us to better understand those who were different. No matter where any of us may have been born, or in what society any of us may have acquired our way of life, there are other societies that provide a contrast; other societies that are different from our own.

Cultural anthropology, through the culture concept, prompts us to better understand those who are different, those who may live in distant lands, those who may eat foods with which we are not familiar, listen to music we consider strange, speak languages we cannot understand, and engage in customs or practices we consider odd or bizarre. The culture concept helps us understand the essence or the core of those differences.

Concurrently, the same concept that enables us to see and understand difference also prompts us to see and understand commonality; how much we share with those whose way of life differs from our own. Anthropologist Johnnetta Cole appropriately subtitled one of her books, "Lines That Divide, Ties That Bind."* This phrase effectively spells out the mission of cultural anthropology: viz., to provide a means of seeing and understanding both the lines that divide us from others, and the ties that bind us to them.

A major emphasis of cultural anthropology, then, is placed on cultural relativism, the notion that an anthropologist must seek to view another culture by reference to the values and perspectives of that culture, insofar as the anthropologist can ascertain them. How then does an anthropologist go about determining those perspectives?

Fieldwork is the anthropologist's reply, and the book's second and third chapters consider both the theory of anthropological field work—i.e., what issues anthropologists have found challenging as they have endeavored to immerse themselves in the ways of life of others, and a wide array of fieldwork examples drawn from sites as wide-ranging as an urban street corner to folk cultures representing the far corners of the globe. As noted above, the whole world is a laboratory for the cultural anthropologist. These articles provide a beginning student of cultural anthropology with a glimpse of what the fieldwork or participant observation of anthropologists has produced.

---

* Johnnetta B. Cole, *All American Women: Lines That Divide, Ties That Bind*, The Free Press, 1986.

Chapter 4 singles out one of the many cultural institutions that could have been selected to illustrate how widely human societies may vary. In this case, the institution selected is the family. The focus is on variations in marriage and family forms and practices. Alternately, we might have chosen cross-cultural variations, in art, religion, gender roles, or any number of other societal forms, patterns or institutions found across the world. Again, this illustrates the difference/commonality dichotomy, key to the mission of cultural anthropology (viz., seeking to understand those things that make us different as well as those things we have in common with others.)

Poet Susan Polis Schutz, extends this principle to an applied purpose:

We all hear the same sounds. We look up and see the same sky. We cry the same tears. Our feelings and emotions are the same. All mothers are sisters. All fathers are brothers. All children are one.

Yet there is hate. There is violence. There is intolerance. There is confusion among people. We don't try hard enough to understand each other. We don't seem to realize that we all have the same basic needs, no matter who we are or what part of the world we come from.

We must understand the differences among us and celebrate the sameness. We must make the world a place where love and friendship dominate our hearts. Equality, respect, compassion, and kindness must guide our actions. Only then will we all be able to peacefully and lovingly live the life we each choose.

—Susan Polis Schutz[*]

The anthology's final chapter explores a potpourri of contemporary issues and perspectives that may be used selectively to complement course discussions and basic textbook readings for the introductory student of cultural anthropology.

While cultural anthropology enables us to see and understand others, it also seeks to help us better understand ourselves. In so doing, we see that we may have similarities and commonalities with other cultures that we may not have seen or understood before. This self-reflection is considered an important trait of a cultural anthropologist. It requires that the anthropologist suspend judgments and assumptions about others in order to view them from the perspective of their own values, customs, and world view.

Anthropologist Ethel J. Alpenfels sees this perspective as not just an essential characteristic of a competent cultural anthropologist, but as a virtue that must be shared by all

---

[*] Stephen Schutz and Susan Polis Schutz, *One World, One Heart*, Blue Mountain Arts Publication, 2001.

human beings, if we are to find ways to live together harmoniously and democratically in an increasingly global existence:

> This is the sin of you, and me, and all of us
> To have more power than we have love,
> More knowledge, than we have understanding,
> More information about this earth, than we have
> about the people who live on it,
> More ability to fly off to faraway places,
> Than to stop for a moment, and to look within
> the secret spots of our own hearts
> For freedom can become a dreadful word,
> Unless it goes hand-in-hand with responsibility,
> And democracy could disappear from the face of the earth,
> Unless the hearts and the minds, and the souls
> of men and women grow mature.

Acknowledgments

D r. Ethel J. Alpenfels was my doctoral mentor at New York University. So it is appropriate here to express my great esteem for her and my profound indebtedness to her for her incomparable teaching, guidance, and inspiration. I have never known a teacher quite like Ethel Alpenfels. Few students who have taken any of my anthropology courses have left the course unaware of my keen admiration of my teacher, or unaware of the profound influence Dr. Alpenfels continues to have on my life and on my career as an anthropologist.

Among the many others to whom I must also express my appreciation is my colleague and fellow anthropologist, Dr. Joan Burroughs, who also received her doctorate from NYU. Her doctorate is in the anthropology of dance. She has been a constant source of inspiration and support in several projects I have undertaken as professor of anthropology at Hunter College.

I also thank Hunter College and the City University of New York for granting me the sabbatical time I've needed to complete this book and to complete other such projects that will enhance my work as a professor of anthropology. Hunter's president, provost, and my dean in the School of Arts and Sciences have all been strong in their support of my work. This kind of discerning support is what makes it possible for scholars and teachers to do well what we love to do.

My gratitude extends as well to my cherished colleagues in the department of anthropology, who were unanimous in their quest to recruit me into the department after I completed an administrative stint as dean of the School of Education a few years ago. Their welcome has been as constant as it has been warm and generous.

To the incomparable students of anthropology I've had the privilege of teaching, and from whom I have learned much more than I have taught, I am also deeply indebted. They have made me a better scholar and teacher than I could possibly have been without them. Some of them over the years—even when not formally in my classes—contributed implicitly to this project. I must mention specifically, Dayana Blandon, Vicky Chang, Imran Chowdhury, Kilrak Chung, Michael Kim, Elisabeth Manwiller, Mai Matsumura, Don Elio Robertson, Wadiyyah Salaam, and Allyshia West.

It is appropriate here to acknowledge once again, as I have in previous works published by them, the awesome expertise of University Readers in many areas, but especially their expertise in acquiring the copyright permissions that are so crucial to an anthology of this type. Each reading in this collection is a crucial component of the book's theme and foundation. What confidence it has been to know that I could rely upon University Readers to attend—diligently and successfully—to the all-important acquisition of permissions as the last "leg of the race" to get this book published, leaving me to be concerned solely with the tasks of editorship and writing. They are indeed, "copyright champions." I am especially grateful to Mieka Hemesath, Jessica Knott and their entire publishing team. The book's cover is the result of the skill and graphic arts expertise of Monica Hui who graciously and patiently allowed me to participate in her design.

Last but by no means least, I express my deepest appreciation to Terry Wykowski and Neil Douglas of the Oxford Consulting Group without whose unstinting support, encouragement, and caring this book might never have been started or completed.

David Julian Hodges

CHAPTER ONE:
THE CONCEPT OF CULTURE

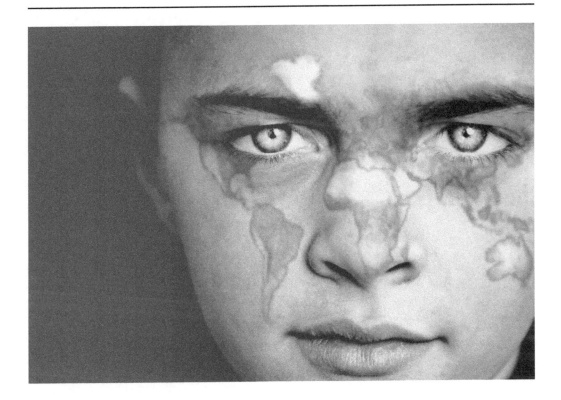

READINGS IN THIS SECTION

Introduction

By David Julian Hodges

T he idea of culture, the meaning and dynamics of culture, the methods of study of culture, and the primary constraint on understanding of culture are addressed in this chapter. The first article of this chapter is written by Sir Edward Burnett Tylor. If anyone may be said to be the founder of the discipline of social anthropology, as it is known in Europe, or cultural anthropology, as it is known in the United States, it is Tylor. According to Tylor, culture is "that complex whole, which includes knowledge, belief, art, morals, law, customs, and any other capabilities and habits acquired by man as a member of society." It is widely agreed among anthropologists that Tylor's definition of culture was the most important at the time it was coined, and remains today a most revered definition, often referred to as the classical definition.

Tylor, arguably the most important pioneer to shape the discipline in its early stages, is credited with the "backpack analogy" used to illustrate the value of anthropology as an integrative science, and a holistic discipline. Tylor used the backpack analogy to explain why still another subject should be added for students to study, given the fact that there are already so many. Tylor explained that as a backpack may actually add to the total weight of a person's load, it more than compensates for this, by making everything else contained inside the backpack so much easier to carry. This, for Tylor, was what the new field of anthropology, beginning to emerge in the 19th Century, would do. For him, it justified anthropology's existence as a new science. Though Tylor held the view of unilinear evolutionism, a theory later discredited by most anthropologists, his contributions to the development of the discipline were profound.

C.B. Tylor Aet 67
Shown a photograph by Hamll and Son

Portrait of Edward
Burnett Tylor

Culture means the total way of life of a people, the social legacy the individual acquires from his group; culture is a design for living. Culture reflects the acquired belief people use to interpret, experience, and to orient behavior. A culture constitutes a storehouse of the pooled learning of a group. While culture is perceived as existing apart and independently of people, culture is not a disembodied force. It is created and transmitted by people.

Although culture is a human construct, its study is undertaken by anthropology as a science. The science of cultural anthropology, however, is distinctly non-reductionist, i.e., it does not seek to simply apply the science of nature and matter to human phenomena. Culture cannot be explained solely in terms of the biological properties of the people involved, their individual past experience, and the immediate situation. Culture arises out of human nature and its forms are restricted by biology, natural law, and the collective human experience. Cultural determinism is as one-sided as biological determinism and the two factors are interdependent. Consistent with the scientific process, the first step in the study of culture is to "taxonomize" or to classify cultural details into proper groups, e.g., weapons, myths, rites, and ceremonies, etc. When the study of culture is undertaken, three fundamental aspects of human experience must be dealt with: what people do, what people believe and sometimes know, and the things people make and use.

The scientific method pertaining to the study of behavior, artifacts, and beliefs associated with culture is ethnography. Ethnography is the work of describing a culture and ethnographic fieldwork is the hallmark of cultural anthropology. The central aim of ethnography is to understand another way of life from the point of view of the native. The essential core of ethnography is concerned with the meaning of actions and events to the members of the culture about which understanding is sought. The ethnographer must take the role of student and begin with a conscious attitude of almost complete ignorance, avoiding ethnocentrism as a profound barrier to understanding culture. Ethnocentrism places the ethnographer's own culture as an exemplar of "good" and colors, as well as shapes what can be learned about other cultures.

The final two articles in this chapter illuminate how ethnocentrism is responsible for flawed cultural perspectives. "Magical Practices among the Nacirema" by Horace Miner describes the practices of the familiar-sounding people of Nacirema that seem to betray a strong underlying belief in magic and superstition. Miner, a professor at the University of Michigan for most of his career, was deeply interested in examining the cultural contexts in which the individual actions of people take place. In a surprising and humorous way, this reading puts side by side the anthropological perspective regarding indigenous cultures and what we take to be advanced, modern cultures.

The article by Linton takes aim at what we take to be unique and original in our own culture. We like to believe that the attributes of our own culture are unique and original. However the final reading in Chapter One, Ralph Linton's "One Hundred Percent American" illuminates the fundamental error of such a belief and, in addition, points to the need to apply cultural analysis to our own communities. Readers are encouraged to become aware of their beliefs about culture in general and their own cultures in particular, and to be prepared to challenge their assumptions and beliefs through the readings in Chapter One as well as the readings in the remaining parts of this anthology.

Culture: The Classical Definition

By Edward Burnett Tylor

Culture or Civilization, taken in its wide ethnographic sense, is that complex whole which includes knowledge, belief, art, morals, law, custom, and any other capabilities and habits acquired by man as a member of society. The condition of culture among the various societies of mankind, in so far as it is capable of being investigated on general principles, is a subject apt for the study of laws of human thought and action. On the one hand, the uniformity which so largely pervades civilization may be ascribed, in great measure, to the uniform action of uniform causes; while on the other hand its various grades may be regarded as stages of development or evolution, each the outcome of previous history, and about to do its proper part in shaping the history of the future. ...

Our modern investigators in the sciences of inorganic nature are foremost to recognize, both within and without their special fields of work, the unity of nature, the fixity of its laws, the definite sequence of cause and effect through which every fact depends on what has gone before it, and acts upon what is to come after it. They grasp firmly the Pythagorean doctrine of pervading order in the universal Kosmos. They affirm, with Aristotle, that nature is not full of incoherent episodes, like a bad tragedy. They agree with Leibnitz in what he calls "my axiom, that nature never acts by leaps," as well as in his "great principle, commonly little employed, that nothing happens without its sufficient reason." Nor, again, in studying the structure and habits of plants and animals, or in investigating the lower functions even of man, are these leading ideas unacknowledged. But when we come to talk of the higher processes of human feeling and action, of thought and language, knowledge and art, a change appears in the prevalent tone of opinion. The world at large is scarcely prepared to accept the general study of human life as a branch of natural science, and to carry out, in a large sense, the poet's injunction to "Account for moral as for natural things." To many educated minds there seems something presumptuous and repulsive in

Edward B. Tylor, "Culture: The Classical Definition," *Primitive Culture, Vol. 1*. New York: Henry Holt and Company, 1871, pp. 1–9. Reprinted in *Exploring the Ways of Mankind*, ed. Walter Goldschmidt. Holt, Rinehart, and Winston, 1960, pp. 21–23. Permission to reprint granted by the publisher.

the view that the history of mankind is part and parcel of the history of nature, that our thoughts, wills, and actions accord with laws as definite as those which govern the motion of waves, the combination of acids and bases, and the growth of plants and animals. ...

"One event is always the son of another, and we must never forget the parentage," was a remark made by a Bechuana chief to Casalis the African missionary. Thus at all times historians, so far as they have aimed at being more than mere chroniclers, have done their best to show not merely succession, but connection, among the events upon their record. Moreover, they have striven to elicit general principles of human action, and by these to explain particular events, stating expressly or taking tacitly for granted the existence of a philosophy of history. Should any one deny the possibility of thus establishing historical laws, the answer is ready with which Boswell in such a case turned on Johnson: "Then, sir, you would reduce all history to no better than an almanack." That nevertheless the labors of so many eminent thinkers should have as yet brought history only to the threshold of science, need cause no wonder to those who consider the bewildering complexity of the problems which come before the general historian. The evidence from which he is to draw his conclusions is at once so multifarious and so doubtful, that a full and distinct view of its bearing on a particular question is hardly to be attained, and thus the temptation becomes all but irresistible to garble it in support of some rough and ready theory of the course of events. The philosophy of history at large, explaining the past and predicting the future phenomena of man's life in the world by reference to general laws, is in fact a subject with which, in the present state of knowledge, even genius aided by wide research seems but hardly able to cope. Yet there are departments of it which, though difficult enough, seem comparatively accessible. If the field of inquiry is narrowed from History as a whole to that branch of it which is here called Culture, the history, not of tribes or nations, but of the condition of knowledge, religion, art, custom, and the like, among them the task of investigation proves to lie within far more moderate compass. We suffer still from the same kind of difficulties which beset the wider argument, but they are much diminished. The evidence is no longer so wildly heterogeneous, but may be more simply classified and compared, while the power of getting rid of extraneous matter, and treating each issue on its own proper set of facts, makes close reasoning on the whole more available than in general history. ...

A first step in the study of civilization is to dissect it into details, and to classify these in their proper groups. Thus, in examining weapons, they are to be classed under spear, club, sling, bow and arrow, and so forth; among textile arts are to be ranged matting, netting, and several grades of making and weaving threads; myths are divided under such headings as myths of sunrise and sunset, eclipse-myths, earthquake-myths, local myths which account for the names of places by some fanciful tale, eponymic myths which account for the parentage of a tribe by turning its name into the name of an imaginary ancestor; under rites and ceremonies occur such practices as the various kinds of sacrifice to the ghosts of the dead and to other spiritual beings, the turning to the east in worship, the purification of ceremonial or moral uncleanness by means of water or fire. Such are a few miscellaneous examples from a list of hundreds, and the ethnographer's business is to classify such details with a view to making out their distribution in geography and history, and the relations which exist among them.

Culture: Queer Customs

By Clyde Kluckhohn

W hy do the Chinese dislike milk and milk products? Why would the Japanese die willingly in a Banzai charge that seemed senseless to Americans? Why do some nations trace descent through the father, others through the mother, still others through both parents? Not because different peoples have different instincts, not because they were destined by God or Fate to different habits, not because the weather is different in China and Japan and the United States. Sometimes shrewd common sense has an answer that is close to that of the anthropologist: "because they were brought up that way." By "culture" anthropology means the total life way of a people, the social legacy the individual acquires from his group. Or culture can be regarded as that part of the environment that is the creation of man.

This technical term has a wider meaning than the "culture" of history and literature. A humble cooking pot is as much a cultural product as is a Beethoven sonata. In ordinary speech a man of culture is a man who can speak languages other than his own, who is familiar with history, literature, philosophy, or the fine arts. In some cliques that definition is still narrower. The cultured person is one who can talk about James Joyce, Scarlatti, and Picasso. To the anthropologist, however, to be human is to be cultured. There is culture in general, and then there are the specific cultures such as Russian, American, British, Hottentot, Inca. The general abstract notion services to remind us that we cannot explain acts solely in terms of the biological properties of the people concerned, their individual past experience, and the immediate situation. The past experience of other men in the form of culture enters into almost every event. Each specific culture constitutes a kind of blueprint for all of life's activities.

One of the interesting things about human beings is that they try to understand themselves and their own behavior. While this has been particularly true of Europeans in recent times, there is no group which has not developed a scheme or schemes to explain man's

Clyde Kluckhohn, "Culture: Queer Customs," *Readings in the Socio-Cultural Foundations of Education*, eds. John H. Chilcott, Norman C. Greenberg, and Herbert B. Wilson. Wadsworth Publishing, 1968, pp. 29–39. Permission to reprint granted by the publisher.

actions. To the insistent human query "why?" the most exciting illumination anthropology has to offer is that of the concept of culture. Its explanatory importance is comparable to categories such as evolution in biology, gravity in physics, disease in medicine. A good deal of human behavior can be understood, and indeed predicted, if we know a people's design for living. Many acts are neither accidental nor due to personal peculiarities nor caused by supernatural forces nor simply mysterious. Even those of us who pride ourselves on our individualism follow most of the time a pattern not of our own making. We brush our teeth on arising. We put on pants—not a loincloth or a grass skirt. We eat three meals a day—not four or five or two. We sleep in a bed—not in a hammock or on a sheep pelt. I do not have to know the individual and his life history to be able to predict these and countless other regularities, including many in the thinking process, of all Americans who are not incarcerated in jails or hospitals for the insane.

To the American woman a system of plural wives seems "instinctively" abhorrent. She cannot understand how any woman can fail to be jealous and uncomfortable if she must share her husband with other women. She feels it "unnatural" to accept such a situation. On the other hand, a Koryak woman of Siberia, for example, would find it hard to understand how a woman could be so selfish and so undesirous of feminine companionship in the home as to wish to restrict her husband to one mate.

Some years ago I met in New York City a young man who did not speak a word of English and was obviously bewildered by American ways. By "blood" he was as American as you or I, for his parents had gone from Indiana to China as missionaries. Orphaned in infancy, he was reared by a Chinese family in a remote village. All who met him found him more Chinese than American. The facts of his blue eyes and light hair were less impressive than a Chinese style of gait, Chinese arm and hand movements, Chinese facial expression, and Chinese modes of thought. The biological heritage was American, but the cultural training had been Chinese. He returned to China.

Another example of another kind: I once knew a trader's wife in Arizona who took a somewhat devilish interest in producing a cultural reaction. Guests who came her way were often served delicious sandwiches filled with a meat that seemed to be neither chicken nor tuna fish yet was reminiscent of both. To queries she gave no reply until each had eaten his fill. She then explained that what they had eaten was not chicken, not tuna fish, but the rich, white flesh of freshly killed rattlesnakes. The response was instantaneous—vomiting, often violent vomiting. A biological process is caught in a cultural web.

A highly intelligent teacher with long and successful experience in the public schools of Chicago was finishing her first year in an Indian school. When asked how her Navaho pupils compared in intelligence with Chicago youngsters, she replied, "Well, I just don't know. Sometimes the Indians seem just as bright. At other times they just act like dumb animals. The other night we had a dance in the high school. I saw a boy who is one of the best students in my English class standing off by himself So I took him over to a pretty girl and told them to dance. But they just stood there with their heads down. They wouldn't even say anything." I inquired if she knew whether or not they were members of the same clan. "What difference would that make?"

"How would you feel about getting into bed with your brother?" The teacher walked off in a huff: but, actually, the two cases were quite comparable in principle. To the Indian the type of bodily contact involved in our social dancing has a directly sexual connotation. The incest taboos between members of the same clan are as severe as between true brothers and sisters. The shame of the Indians at the suggestion that a clan brother and sister should dance and the indignation of the white teacher at the idea that she should share a bed with an adult brother represent equally nonrational responses, culturally standardized unreason.

All this does not mean that there is no such thing as raw human nature. The very fact that certain of the same institutions are found in all known societies indicates that at bottom all human beings are very much alike. The files of the Cross-Cultural Survey at Yale University are organized according to categories such as "marriage ceremonies," "life crisis rites," "incest taboos." At least seventy-five of these categories are represented in every single one of the hundreds of cultures analyzed. This is hardly surprising. The members of all human groups have about the same biological equipment. All men undergo the same poignant life experiences such as birth, helplessness, illness, old age, and death. The biological potentialities of the species are the blocks with which cultures are built. Some patterns of every culture crystallize around focuses provided by the inevitables of biology: the difference between the sexes, the presence of persons of different ages, the varying physical strength and skill of individuals. The facts of nature also limit culture forms. No culture provides patterns for jumping over trees or for eating iron ore.

There is thus no "either-or" between nature and that special form of nurture called culture. Culture determinism is as one-sided as biological determinism. The two factors are interdependent. Culture arises out of human nature, and its forms are restricted both by man's biology and by natural laws. It is equally true that culture channels biological processes—vomiting, weeping, fainting, sneezing, the daily habits of food intake and waste elimination. When a man eats, he is reacting to an internal "drive," namely, hunger contractions consequent upon the lowering of blood sugar, but his precise reaction to these internal stimuli cannot be predicted by physiological knowledge alone. Whether a healthy adult feels hungry twice, three times, or four times a day and the hours at which this feeling recurs is a question of culture. What he eats is of course limited by availability, but is also partly regulated by culture. It is a biological fact that some types of berries are poisonous; it is a cultural fact that, a few generations ago, most Americans considered tomatoes to be poisonous and refused to eat them. Such selective, discriminative use of the environment is characteristically cultural. In a still more general sense, too, the process of eating is channeled by culture. Whether a man eats to live, lives to eat, or merely eats and lives is only in part an individual matter, for there are also cultural trends. Emotions are physiological events. Certain situations will evoke fear in people from any culture. But sensations of pleasure, anger, and lust may be stimulated by cultural cues that would leave unmoved someone who has been reared in a different social tradition.

Except in the case of newborn babies and of individuals born with clear-cut structural or functional abnormalities we can observe innate endowments only as modified by cultural training. In a hospital in New Mexico where Zuñi Indian, Navaho Indian, and white American babies are born, it is possible to classify the newly arrived infants as unusually active, average, and quiet. Some babies from each "racial" group will fall into each category, though a higher proportion of the white babies will fall into the unusually active class. But if a Navaho baby, a Zuñi baby, and a white baby—all classified as unusually active at birth—are again observed at the age of two years, the Zuñi baby will no longer seem given to quick and restless activity—as compared with the white child—though he may seem so as compared with the other Zuñis of the same age. The Navaho child is likely to fall in between as contrasted with the Zuñi and the white, though he will probably still seem more active than the average Navaho youngster.

It was remarked by many observers in the Japanese relocation centers that Japanese who were born and brought up in this country, especially those who were reared apart from any large colony of Japanese, resemble in behavior their white neighbors much more closely than they do their own parents who were educated in Japan.

I have said "culture channels biological processes." It is more accurate to say "the biological functioning of individuals is modified if they have been trained in certain ways and not in others." Culture is not a disembodied force. It is created and transmitted by people. However, culture, like well-known concepts of the physical sciences, is a convenient abstraction. One never sees gravity. One sees bodies falling in regular ways. One never sees an electromagnetic field. Yet certain happenings that can be seen may be given a neat abstract formulation by assuming that the electromagnetic field exists. Similarly, one never sees culture as such. What is seen are regularities in the behavior or artifacts of a group that has adhered to a common tradition. The regularities in style and technique of ancient Inca tapestries or stone axes from Melanesian islands are due to the existence of mental blueprints for the group.

Culture is a way of thinking, feeling, believing. It is the group's knowledge stored up (in memories of men; in books and objects) for future use. We study the products of this "mental" activity: the overt behavior, the speech and gestures and activities of people, and the tangible results of these things such as tools, houses, cornfields, and what not. It has been customary in lists of "culture traits" to include such things as watches or law books. This is a convenient way of thinking about them, but in the solution of any important problem we must remember that they, in themselves, are nothing but metals, paper, and ink. What is important is that some men know how to make them, others set a value on them, are unhappy without them, direct their activities in relation to them, or disregard them.

It is only a helpful shorthand when we say "The cultural patterns of the Zulu were resistant to Christianization." In the directly observable world of course, it was individual Zulus who resisted. Nevertheless, if we do not forget that we are speaking at a high level of abstraction, it is justifiable to speak of culture as a cause. One may compare the practice of saying "syphilis caused the extinction of the native population of the island." Was it "syphilis" or "syphilis germs" or "human beings who were carriers of syphilis?"

"Culture," then, is "a theory." But if a theory is not contradicted by any relevant fact and if it helps us to understand a mass of otherwise chaotic facts, it is useful. Darwin's contribution was much less the accumulation of new knowledge than the creation of a theory which put in order data already known. An accumulation of facts, however large, is no more a science than a pile of bricks is a house. Anthropology's demonstration that the most weird set of customs has a consistency and an order is comparable to modern psychiatry's showing that there is meaning and purpose in the apparently incoherent talk of the insane. In fact, the inability of the older psychologies and philosophies to account for the strange behavior of madmen and heathens was the principal factor that forced psychiatry and anthropology to develop theories of the unconscious and of culture.

Since culture is an abstraction, it is important not to confuse culture with society. A "society" refers to a group of people who interact more with each other than they do with other individuals—who cooperate with each other for the attainment of certain ends. You can see and indeed count the individuals who make up a society. A "culture" refers to the distinctive ways of life of such a group of people. Not all social events are culturally patterned. New types of circumstances arise for which no cultural solutions have as yet been devised.

A culture constitutes a storehouse of the pooled learning of the group. A rabbit starts life with some innate responses. He can learn from his own experience and perhaps from observing other rabbits. A human infant is born with fewer instincts and greater plasticity. His main task is to learn the answers that persons he will never see, persons long dead, have worked out. Once he has learned the formulas supplied by the culture of his group, most of his behavior becomes almost as automatic and unthinking as if it were instinctive. There is a tremendous amount of intelligence behind the making of a radio, but not much is required to learn to turn it on.

The members of all human societies face some of the same unavoidable dilemmas, posed by biology and other facts of the human situation. This is why the basic categories of all cultures are so similar. Human culture without language is unthinkable. No culture fails to provide for aesthetic expression and aesthetic delight. Every culture supplies standard-ized orientations toward the deeper problems, such as death. Every culture is designed to perpetuate the group and its solidarity, to meet the demands of individuals for an orderly way of life and for satisfaction of biological needs.

However, the variations on these basic themes are numberless. Some languages are built up out of twenty basic sounds, others out of forty. Nose plugs were considered beautiful by the predynastic Egyptians but are not by the modern French. Puberty is a biological fact. But one culture ignores it, another prescribes informal instructions about sex but no ceremony, a third has impressive rites for girls only, a fourth for boys and girls. In this culture, the first menstruation is welcomed as a happy, natural event; in that culture the atmosphere is full of dread and supernatural threat. Each culture dissects nature according to its own system of categories. The Navaho Indians apply the same word to the color of a robin's egg and to that of grass. A psychologist once assumed that this meant a difference in the sense organs, that Navahos didn't have the physiological equipment to distinguish "green" from "blue." However, when he showed them objects of the two colors and asked them if they were exactly the same colors, they looked at him with astonishment. His dream of discovering a new type of color blindness was shattered.

Every culture must deal with the sexual instinct. Some, however, seek to deny all sexual expression before marriage, whereas a Polynesian adolescent who was not promiscuous would be distinctly abnormal. Some cultures enforce lifelong monogamy, others, like our own, tolerate serial monogamy; in still other cultures, two or more women may be joined to one man or several men to a single woman. Homosexuality has been a permitted pat-tern in the Greco-Roman world, in parts of Islam, arid in various primitive tribes. Large portions of the population of Tibet, and of Christendom at some places and periods, have practiced completely celibacy. To us marriage is first and foremost an arrangement between two individuals. In many more societies marriage is merely one facet of a complicated set of reciprocities, economic and otherwise, between two families or two clans.

The essence of the cultural process is selectivity. The selection is only exceptionally conscious and rational. Cultures are like Topsy. They just grew. Once, however, a way of handling a situation becomes institutionalized, there is ordinarily great resistance to change or deviation. When we speak of "our sacred beliefs," we mean of course that they are beyond criticism and that the person who suggests modification or abandonment must be punished. No person is emotionally indifferent to his culture. Certain cultural premises may become totally out of accord with a new factual situation. Leaders may recognize this and reject the old ways in theory. Yet their emotional loyalty continues in the face of reason because of the intimate conditionings of early childhood.

A culture is learned by individuals as the result of belonging to some particular group, and it constitutes that part of learned behavior which is shared with others. It is our social legacy, as contrasted with our organic heredity. It is one of the important factors which permits us to live together in an organized society, giving us ready-made solutions to our problems, helping us to predict the behavior of others, and permitting others to know what to expect of us.

Culture regulates our lives at every turn. From the moment we are born until we die there is, whether we are conscious of it or not, constant pressure upon us to follow certain types of behavior that other men have created for us. Some paths we follow willingly, others we follow because we know no other way, still others we deviate from or go back to most unwillingly. Mothers of small children know how unnaturally most of this comes to us—how little regard we have, until we are "culturalized," for the "proper" place, time, and manner for certain acts such as eating, excreting, sleeping, getting dirty, and making loud noises. But by more or less adhering to a system of related designs for carrying out all the acts of living, a group of men and women feel themselves linked together by a powerful chain of sentiments. Ruth Benedict gave an almost complete definition of the concept when she said, "Culture is that which binds men together."

It is true any culture is a set of techniques for adjusting both to the external environment and to other men. However, cultures create problems as well as solve them. If the lore of a people states that frogs are dangerous creatures, or that it is not safe to go about at night because of witches or ghosts, threats are posed which do not arise out of the inexorable facts of the external world. Cultures produce needs as well as provide a means of fulfilling them. There exists for every group culturally defined, acquired drives that may be more powerful in ordinary daily life than the biologically inborn drives. Many Americans, for example, will work harder for "success" than they will for sexual satisfaction.

Most groups elaborate certain aspects of their culture far beyond maximum utility or survival value. In other words, not all culture promotes physical survival. At times, indeed, it does exactly the opposite. Aspects of culture which once were adaptive may persist long after they have ceased to be useful. An analysis of any culture will disclose many features which cannot possibly be construed as adaptations to the total environment in which the group now finds itself. However, it is altogether likely that these apparently useless features represent survivals, with modifications through time, of cultural forms which were adaptive in one or another previous situation.

Any cultural practice must be functional or it will disappear before long. That is, it must somehow contribute to the survival of the society or to the adjustment of the individual. However, many cultural functions are not manifest but latent. A cowboy will walk three miles to catch a horse which he then rides one mile to the store. From the point of view of manifest function this is positively irrational. But the act has the latent function of maintaining the cowboy's prestige in the terms of his own subculture. One can instance the buttons on the sleeve of a man's coat, our absurd English spelling, the use of capital letters, and a host of other apparently nonfunctional customs. They serve mainly the latent function of assisting individuals to maintain their security by preserving continuity with the past and by making certain sectors of life familiar and predictable.

Every culture is a precipitate of history. In more than one sense history is a sieve. Each culture embraces those aspects of the past which, usually in altered form and with altered meanings, live on in the present. Discoveries and inventions, both material and ideological, are constantly being made available to a group through its historical contacts with other peoples or being created by its own members. However, only those that fit the total immediate situation in meeting the group's needs for survival or in promoting the psychological adjustment of individuals will become part of the culture. The process of culture building may be regarded as an addition to man's innate biological capacities, an addition providing instruments which enlarge, or may even substitute for, biological functions, and to a degree compensating for biological limitations—as in ensuring that death does not always result in the loss to humanity of what the deceased has learned.

Culture is like a map. Just as a map isn't the territory but an abstract representation of a particular area, so also a culture is an abstract description of trends toward uniformity in the words, deeds, and artifacts of a human group. If a map is accurate and you can read it, you won't get lost; if you know a culture, you will know your way around in the life of a society. Many educated people have the notion that culture applies only to exotic ways of life or to societies where relative simplicity and relative homogeneity prevail. Some sophisticated missionaries, for example, will use the anthropological conception in discussing the special modes of living of South Sea Islanders, but seem amazed at the idea that it could be applied equally to inhabitants of New York City. And social workers in Boston will talk about the culture of a colorful and well-knit immigrant group but boggle at applying it to the behavior of staff members in the social-service agency itself.

In the primitive society the correspondence between the habits of individuals and the customs of the community is ordinarily greater. There is probably some truth in what an old Indian once said, "In the old days there was no law; everybody did what was right." The primitive tends to find happiness in the fulfillment of intricately involuted cultural patterns; the modern more often tends to feel the pattern as repressive to his individuality. It is also true that in a complex stratified society there are numerous exceptions to generalizations made about the culture as a whole. It is necessary to study regional, class, and occupational subcultures. Primitive cultures have greater stability than modern cultures; they change—but less rapidly.

However, modern men also are creators and carriers of culture. Only in some respects are they influenced differently from primitives by culture. Moreover, there are such wide variations in primitive cultures that any black-and-white contrast between the primitive and the civilized is altogether fictitious. The distinction which is most generally true lies in the field of conscious philosophy.

Magical Practices Among the Nacirema

By Horace Miner

T he anthropologist has become so familiar with the diversity of ways in which different peoples behave in similar situations that he is not apt to be surprised by even the most exotic customs. In fact, if all of the logically possible combinations of behavior have not been found somewhere in the world, he is apt to suspect that they must be present in some yet undescribed tribe. This point has, in fact, been expressed with respect to clan organization by Murdock. In this light, the magical beliefs and practices of the Nacirema present such unusual aspects that it seems desirable to describe them as an example of the extremes to which human behavior can go.

Professor Linton first brought the ritual of the Nacirema to the attention of anthropologists twenty years ago, but the culture of this people is still very poorly understood. They are a North American group living in the territory between the Canadian Cree, the Yaqui and Tarahumare of Mexico, and the Carib and Arawak of the Antilles. Little is known of their origin, although tradition states that they came from the east. ...

Nacirema culture is characterized by a highly developed market economy which has evolved in a rich natural habitat. While much of the people's time is devoted to economic pursuits, a large part of the fruits of these labors and a considerable portion of the day are spent in ritual activity. The focus of this activity is the human body, the appearance and health of which loom as a dominant concern in the ethos of the people. While such a concern is certainly not unusual, its ceremonial aspects and associated philosophy are unique.

The fundamental belief underlying the whole system appears to be that the human body is ugly and that its natural tendency is to debility and disease. Incarcerated in such a body, man's only hope is to avert these characteristics through the use of the powerful influences of ritual and ceremony. Every household has one or more shrines devoted to this purpose. The more powerful individuals in the society have several shrines in their

Horace Miner, "Magical Practices Among the Nacirema," *Exploring the Ways of Mankind*, ed. Walter Goldschmidt. Holt, Rinehart, and Winston, 1960, pp. 335–338. Permission to reprint granted by the publisher.

houses and, in fact, the opulence of a house is often referred to in terms of the number of such ritual centers it possesses. Most houses are of wattle and daub construction, but the shrine rooms of the more weathly are walled with stone. Poorer families imitate the rich by applying pottery plaques to their shrine walls.

While each family has at least one such shrine, the rituals associated with it are not family ceremonies but are private and secret. The rites are normally only discussed with children, and then only during the period when they are being initiated into these mysteries. I was able, however, to establish sufficient rapport with the natives to examine these shrines and to have the rituals described to me.

The focal point of the shrine is a box or chest which is built into the wall. In this chest are kept the many charms and magical potions without which no native believes he could live. These preparations are secured from a variety of specialized practitioners. The most powerful of these are the medicine men, whose assistance must be rewarded with substantial gifts. However the medicine men do not provide the curative potions for their clients, but decide what the ingredients should be and then write them down in an ancient and secret language. This writing is understood only by the medicine men and by the herbalists who, for another gift, provide the required charm.

The charm is not disposed of after it has served its purpose, but is placed in the charm-box of the household shrine. As these magical materials are specific for certain ills, and the real or imagined maladies of the people are many, the charm-box is usually full to overflowing. The magical packets are so numerous that people forget what their purposes were and fear to use them again. While the natives are very vague on this point, we can only assume that the idea in retaining all the old magical materials is that their presence in the charm-box, before which the body rituals are conducted, will in some way protect the worshipper.

Beneath the charm-box is a small font. Each day every member of the family, in succession, enters the shrine room, bows his head before the charm-box, mingles different sorts of holy water in the font, and proceeds with a brief rite of ablution. The holy waters are secured from the Water Temple of the community, where the priests conduct elaborate ceremonies to make the liquid ritually pure.

In the hierarchy of magical practitioners, and below the medicine men in prestige, are specialists whose designation is best translated "holy-mouth-men." The Nacirema have an almost pathological horror of and fascination with the mouth, the condition of which is believed to have a supernatural influence on all social relationships. Were it not for the rituals of the mouth, they believe that their teeth would fall out, their gums bleed, their jaws shrink, their friends desert them, and their lovers reject them. They also believe that a strong relationship exists between oral and moral characteristics. For example, there is a ritual ablution of the mouth for children which is supposed to improve their moral fiber.

The daily body ritual performed by everyone includes a mouth-rite. Despite the fact that these people are so punctilious about care of the mouth, this rite involves a practice which strikes the uninitiated stranger as revolting. It was reported to me that the ritual consists of inserting a small bundle of hog hairs into the mouth, along with certain magical powders, and then moving the bundle in a highly formalized series of gestures.

In addition to the private mouth-rite, the people seek out a holy-mouth-man once or twice a year. These practitioners have an impressive set of paraphernalia, consisting of a variety of augers, awls, probes, and prods. The use of these objects in the exorcism of the evils of the mouth involves almost unbelievable ritual torture of the client. The holy-mouth-man opens the client's mouth and, using the above mentioned tools, enlarges any holes which decay may have created in the teeth. Magical materials are put into these holes. If there are no naturally occurring holes in the teeth, large sections of one or more teeth are gouged out so that the supernatural substance can be applied. In the client's view, the purpose of these ministrations is to arrest decay and to draw friends. The extremely sacred and traditional character of the rite is evident in the fact that the natives return to the holy-mouth-men year after year, despite the fact that their teeth continue to decay.

It is to be hoped that, when a thorough study of the Nacirema is made, there will be careful inquiry into the personality structure of these people. One has but to watch the gleam in the eye of a holy-mouth-man, as he jabs an awl into an exposed nerve, to suspect that a certain amount of sadism is involved. If this can be established, a very interesting pattern emerges, for most of the population shows definite masochistic tendencies. It was to these that Professor Linton referred in discussing a distinctive part of the daily body ritual which is performed only by men. This part of the rite involves scraping and lacerating the surface of the face with a sharp instrument. Special women's rites are performed only four times during each lunar month, but what they lack in frequency is made up in barbarity. As part of this ceremony women bake their heads in small ovens for about an hour. The theoretically interesting point is that what seems to be a preponderantly masochistic people have developed sadistic specialists.

The medicine men have an imposing temple, or latipso, in every community of any size. The more elaborate ceremonies required to treat very sick patients can only be performed at this temple. These ceremonies involve not only the thaumaturge but a permanent group of vestal maidens who move sedately about the temple chambers in distinctive costume and headdress.

The latipso ceremonies are so harsh that it is phenomenal that a fair proportion of the really sick natives who enter the temple ever recover. Small children whose indoctrination is still incomplete have been known to resist attempts to take them to the temple because "that is where you go to die." Despite this fact, sick adults are not only willing but eager to undergo the protracted ritual purification, if they can afford to do so. No matter how ill the supplicant or how grave the emergency, the guardians of many temples will not admit a client if he cannot give a rich gift to the custodian. Even after one has gained admission and survived the ceremonies, the guardians will not permit the neophyte to leave until he makes still another gift.

The supplicant entering the temple is first stripped of all his or her clothes. In everyday life the Nacirema avoids exposure of his body and its natural functions. Bathing and excretory acts are performed only in the secrecy of the household shrine, where they are ritualized as part of the body-rites. Psychological shock results from the fact that body secrecy is suddenly lost upon entry into the latipso. A man, whose own wife has never seen him in an excretory act, suddenly finds himself naked and assisted by a vestal maiden while he performs his natural functions into a sacred vessel. This sort of ceremonial treatment is necessitated by the fact that the excreta are used by a diviner to ascertain the course and nature of the client's sickness. Female clients, on the other hand, find their naked bodies are subjected to the scrutiny, manipulation and prodding of the medicine men.

Few supplicants in the temple are well enough to do anything but lie on their hard beds. The daily ceremonies, like the rites of the holy-mouth-men, involve discomfort and torture. With ritual precision, the vestals awaken their miserable charges each dawn and roll them about on their beds of pain while performing ablutions, in the formal movements of which the maidens are highly trained. At other times they insert magic wands in the supplicant's mouth or force him to eat substances which are supposed to be healing. From time to time the medicine men come to their clients and jab magically treated needles into their flesh. The fact that these temple ceremonies may not cure, and may even kill the neophyte, in no way decreases the people's faith in the medicine men.

There remains one other kind of practitioner, known as a "listener." This witchdoctor has the power to exorcise devils that lodge in the heads of people who have been bewitched. The Nacirema believe that parents bewitch their own children. Mothers are particularly suspected of putting a curse on children while teaching them the secret body rituals. The counter-magic of the witchdoctor is unusual in its lack of ritual. The patient simply tells the "listener" all his troubles and fears, beginning with the earliest difficulties he can remember. The memory displayed by the Nacirema in these exorcism sessions is truly remarkable. It is not uncommon for the patient to bemoan the rejection he felt upon being weaned as a babe, and a few individuals even see their troubles going back to the traumatic effects of their own birth.

In conclusion, mention must be made of certain practices which have their base in native esthetics but which depend upon the pervasive aversion to the natural body and its functions. There are ritual fasts to make fat people thin and ceremonial feasts to make thin people fat. Still other rites are used to make women's breasts larger if they are small, and smaller if they are large. General dissatisfaction with breast shape is symbolized in the fact that the ideal form is virtually outside the range of human variation. A few women afflicted with almost inhuman hyper-mammary development are so idolized that they make a handsome living by simply going from village to village and permitting the natives to stare at them for a fee.

Reference has already been made to the fact that excretory functions are ritualized, routinized, and relegated to secrecy. Natural reproductive functions are similarly distorted. Intercourse is taboo as a topic and scheduled as an act. Efforts are made to avoid pregnancy by the use of magical materials or by limiting intercourse to certain phases of the moon. Conception is actually very infrequent. When pregnant, women dress so as to hide their condition. Parturition takes place in secret, without friends or relatives to assist, and the majority of women do not nurse their infants.

Our review of the ritual life of the Nacirema has certainly shown them to be a magic-ridden people. It is hard to understand how they have managed to exist so long under the burdens which they have imposed upon themselves. But even such exotic customs as these take on real meaning when they are viewed with the insight provided by Malinowski when he wrote:

"Looking from far and above, from our high places of safety in the developed civilization, it is easy to see all the crudity and irrelevance of magic. But without its power and guidance early man could not have mastered his practical difficulties as he has done, nor could man have advanced to the higher stages of civilization."

100% American

By Ralph Linton

Our solid American citizen awakens in a bed built on a pattern which originated in the Near East but which was modified in Northern Europe before
it was transmitted to America. He throws back covers made from cotton,
domesticated in India, or linen, domesticated in the Near East, or wool from sheep, also
domesticated in the Near East, or silk, the use of which was discovered in China. All of
these materials have been spun and woven by processes invented in the Near East. He
slips into his moccasins invented by the Indians of the Eastern woodlands, and goes to
the bathroom, whose fixtures are a mixture of European and American inventions, both
of recent date. He takes off his pajamas, a garment invented in India, and washes with
soap invented by the ancient Gauls. He then shaves, a masochistic rite which seems to
have been derived from either Sumer or ancient Egypt.

Returning to the bedroom, he removes his clothes from a chair of southern European
type and proceeds to dress. He puts on garments whose form originally derived from
the skin clothing of the nomads of the Asiatic steppes, puts on shoes made from skins
tanned by a process invented in ancient Egypt and cut to a pattern derived from the classical civilizations of the Mediterranean, and ties around his neck a strip of bright-colored
cloth which is a vestigial survival of the shoulder shawls worn by the seventeenth-century
Croatians. Before going out for breakfast he glances through the window, made of glass
invented in Egypt, and if it is raining puts on overshoes made of rubber discovered by the
Central American Indians and takes an umbrella, invented in southeastern Asia. Upon his
head he puts a hat made of felt, a material invented in the Asiatic steppes.

On his way to breakfast he stops to buy a paper, paying for it with coins, an ancient
Lydian invention. At the restaurant a whole new series of borrowed elements confronts
him. His plate is made of a form of pottery invented in China. His knife is of steel, an

Ralph Linton, "100% American," *The Study of Man.* D. Appleton-Century Co., 1936, pp. 326–327.
Reprinted in *Readings in the Socio-Cultural Foundations of Education*, eds. John H. Chilcott, Norman C.
Greenberg, Herbert B. Wilson. Wadsworth Publishing, 1968, pp. 425–426. Permission to reprint granted
by the publisher.

alloy first made in southern India, his fork a medieval Italian invention, and his spoon a derivative of a Roman original. He begins breakfast with an orange, from the eastern Mediterranean, a cantaloupe from Persia, or perhaps a piece of African watermelon. With this he has coffee, an Abyssinian plant, with cream and sugar. Both the domestication of cows and the idea of milking them originated in the Near East, while sugar was first made in India. After his fruit and first coffee he goes on to waffles, cakes made by a Scandinavian technique from wheat domesticated in Asia Minor. Over these he pours maple syrup, invented by the Indians of the Eastern woodlands. As a side dish he may have the egg of a species of bird domesticated in Indo-China, or thin strips of the flesh of an animal domesticated in Eastern Asia which have been salted and smoked by a process developed in Northern Europe.

When our friend has finished eating he settles back to smoke, an American Indian habit, consuming a plant domesticated in Brazil in either a pipe, derived from the Indians of Virginia, or a cigarette, derived from Mexico. If he is hardy enough he may even attempt a cigar, transmitted to us from the Antilles by way of Spain. While smoking he reads the news of the day, imprinted in characters invented by the ancient Semites upon a material invented in China by a process invented in Germany. As he absorbs the accounts of foreign troubles he will, if he is a good conservative citizen, thank a Hebrew deity in an Indo-European language that he is 100 per cent American.

CHAPTER TWO:
FIELDWORK

READINGS IN THIS SECTION

Introduction

By David Julian Hodges

ieldwork is the hallmark of cultural anthropology. The purpose, nature, methods, and patterns of learning associated with fieldwork are addressed by the readings in this chapter. In seeking to learn about the human family and what it means to be human, the cultural anthropologist is confronted with the reality of her own culture in the process of seeking to know about other or foreign cultures. What counts as "other or foreign" is that which is not the native culture of the investigator. A foreign culture, therefore, may exist on the other side of the planet or just a few blocks from the campus or working context of the anthropologist. The culture shock brought about by extreme contrasts and the requirement to leave preconceptions and value judgments behind are two sides of the same ethnographic coin. Culture shock tends to be inevitable and, as described in chapter one, the preconceptions embedded in ethnocentric perspectives will doom the work of the anthropologist to failure.

The readings in chapter two speak to fieldwork in diverse settings, from the Trobriand Island people of the southwest Pacific to the native people of Barbados to the male population of a ghetto in a major American city. Malinowski describes the relationships among Trobriand kinsmen: the roles and divisions of functions among the residents of villages and members of families; and the details of domestic, communal, and economic life. In seeking to mitigate the effect of overlaying our own cultural norms, the author is careful to point out that our understanding of the word and concept "father" is not in accordance with the facts of life in this matrilineal society. In "Lessons from the Field," anthropology students participating in a field-based university term, learned about how the culture of Barbados differed from their own in positive as well as negative ways. Some students were permanently changed, especially with regard to materialism. They also learned something about what it means to be a member of a minority group. What they learned about doing fieldwork included inquisitiveness, how to probe sensitively into the villager's knowledge of events and culture, how to concentrate, to listen, and to recall in the recording of field notes.

Fieldwork on an Urban Street Corner is a cultural examination of the meaning of jobs to men in the urban ghetto. Our preconceptions, unmitigated, would leave us unable to understand the beliefs and behaviors of the "streetcorner" man. To the outsider, the man appears to treat the job in a cavalier fashion, working and not working as the spirit moves him, as if all that matters is the immediate satisfaction of his present appetites. To the middle class observer, this behavior reflects laziness and a present-time orientation—an inability to defer gratification. In truth, when the man squanders a week's pay in two days and turns down other work, it is not because he is present-time oriented, unaware of or unconcerned about the future. Rather, he does so precisely because he *is* aware of the future and the hopelessness of it all.

Franz Boas: A Natural History Approach to Fieldwork

By Marian Smith

In 1938, looking back on his life, Boas wrote: "An early intense interest in nature and a burning desire to see everything that I heard or read about dominated my youth" (Boas 1938:19). He goes on to speak of his "intensive, emotional interest in the phenomena of the world" (1938:20), and it is this active, almost devotional, attitude to "the surrounding world" which gave his fieldwork its distinctive character.

Born in the same year which saw publication of the Origin of Species, Boas could profit from the first great intellectual response which greeted man's entrance into the world of nature. The preceding years had seen the foundation in France, Britain, and the United States of anthropological societies formed to encourage the "study of man in all his varieties" (Constitution, American Ethnological Society, 1842) and the prevailing, forward-looking view was incorporated in the title of a book published in London in 1850: The Natural History of the Varieties of Man (Latham 1850). For the first time since the days of Athens, mankind was the legitimate subject of the kind of research which could be given to the other orders of creation. The museums of natural history included man and his products in their exhibits of the earth's wonders, extending their coverage to men of many times and many areas, but the universities had not yet caught up with the new surge of interest and the youthful Boas had to turn to geography as a formal study. He says, in contrast, that it was on account of his "intellectual interest" (Boas 1938:20) that he studied mathematics and physics. It has been pointed out many times that Boas' later work in anthropology combined his training in the diverse disciplines of geography and physics, but perhaps his unique contribution lay in the direction of his interest in natural phenomena—and it is that side of his work on which this paper will concentrate.

Boas more than any other person first brought the very mind of man into the natural world. As early as 1902 he recognized that the philosopher himself adopts much of the current thought of his environment (Boas 1902:872–74). Conceptualization and

Marian Smith, "Franz Boas: A Natural History Approach to Fieldwork," *The Anthropology of Franz Boas: Essays on the Centennial of His Birth*. American Anthropological Association, 1959, pp. 46–60. Permission to reprint granted by the publisher.

philosophy no longer breathed a finer air. They could be studied by the same techniques and approached by the same attitudes as other human characteristics, and consequently lost much of their aura of revealed truth. Man was now to be studied not only in all his varieties, but in all his activities.

The complete emergence of man into the natural world could only be achieved if men everywhere were equally deserving of study. The doctrine of social evolution which isolated certain cultural phenomena as superior to others effectually prohibited adequate classification. Behavior must be studied in its own terms, classified according to its own features. The thought processes of the investigator must therefore be subjected to similarly rigid examination.

Toward the end of his life, Boas wrote "... I fought 'the old speculative theories' as I am now fighting the new speculative theories based on the imposition of categories derived from our culture upon foreign cultures. ..." (Boas 1940:311, from a section that was apparently added to the original text of "History and Science in Anthropology: A Reply" when the paper was reprinted.) In one of his final papers, he returned to this methodological problem and there placed it in direct relation to the problem of classification (Boas 1943:314).

The continuity in Boas' thought which I have here chosen for emphasis is thus marked by two aspects: a distrust of traditional ideas, and faith in the natural world. He was fully conscious of both, and cites them in that retrospect of his early life to which reference has already been made. Having been "spared the struggle against religious dogma that besets the lives of so many young people," he suffered two shocks which he regarded as of "permanent influence" on his life:

> As I remember it now, my first shock came when one of my student friends, a theologian, declared his belief in the authority of tradition and his conviction that he had not the right to doubt what the past had transmitted to us. The shock that this outright abandonment of the freedom of thought gave me is one of the unforgettable moments of my life. I had been taught in home and school that it is our duty to think out our problems according to the best of our ability. The denial of this duty, or rather the claim that what I considered a duty was a wrong, seemed unbelievable to me. A second shock was a series of conversations with an artistically gifted elder sister to whom my materialistic world seemed unendurable (Boas 1938:19–20).

Many people share a distrust of traditional ideas and authority, and faith in the natural world. But the implications of these two attitudes, which Boas spent so much effort in developing, have not yet been fully realized. The position which Boas assumed may be conveniently characterized as the natural history approach to the social sciences. Because this position seems to me to be the foundation of Boas' ethnographic method, I shall elaborate it in contrast to another, equally prevalent among social scientists, which can be referred to as the social philosophy approach. In the United States, anthropology and sociology typically represent these two approaches. Within anthropology, British social anthropology, which aligns itself with sociology—and frequently defines itself as "comparative sociology"—has in the last two decades drawn apart by emphasizing its aim of achieving a comprehensive social theory. In consequence a distinction is sometimes drawn between social and cultural anthropology. The latter is recognized as owing many of its emphases to Boas and would, according to the terms used in this paper, be characterized by the natural history approach. This is still the broad discipline first outlined by such men as Tylor and Waitz, and is referred to here as anthropology, without qualification. Social anthropology, in contrast, delimits its field more strictly and is characterized by the social philosophy approach.

In characterizing Boas' thought and field method as distinguished by the natural history approach, it is difficult to know to what extent my own position, learned in part from Boas, influences the contrast being made. It would be fascinating to analyze his writings for a full statement of his own concept of man, but this task cannot be attempted here. Boas has meant many things to many people, and his influence is still hardly to be separated from his work. My awareness of the contrast has been sharpened by six years of close contact with certain British social anthropologists, and I owe a great debt to these British colleagues. Much that has been written concerning the two positions now seems to me to be peripheral to the essential differences in approach. The contrast as I present it may well suffer from over-generalization, but it seems to me fundamental to an understanding of Boas.

First, it is necessary to point out that one or the other approach is to be found in all the social sciences. They are often fused, or partially adapted, in the writings of a single social scientist, who may take first one position and then the other. It is only in the exceptional thinker that either position becomes clear and relatively self-contained, with its full implications realized. Because the approaches are generally implicit, they have little to do with the acceptance or rejection of explicit theories. When a position has been articulated it can be accepted for purposes of argument, and discussions concerning it can be exceedingly fruitful. When distinctions are implicit, on the other hand, communication becomes difficult and discourse on matters concerning them tends to evaporate in a haze of misunderstanding.

When such misunderstanding appears in anthropology, the difficulties are not due to differences in subject matter. It is not a question of knowing American Indian rather than, say, African data. Anthropologists are able to switch from one area to another and they have also been able to transfer their attention from primitive societies to modern industrial communities. Whether or not the anthropologist engages personally in research, he can foresee many of the problems which will arise, and discuss methods for dealing with them and the probable value of the results. Neither does the confusion arise from the importance which data as such are accorded. All anthropologists are empiricists in this sense, and all insist on the absolute importance of fieldwork; they also demand intensive studies carried out in anticipation of eventual comparison. Nor do differences in the recognition given to certain areas of investigation seem to me to constitute the main blocks to communication: the difficulties are not mainly due to such factors as the omission of linguistic data or a fondness for archeology.

Both in Great Britain and the Americas, anthropology continues its tradition of covering more than purely social phenomena. It includes archeology and physical anthropology and, outside of Britain, linguistics as well. In the United States, it is the only discipline to be included in the Social Science Research Council, the National Research Council (because of several of its aspects, including the biological), and the American Council of Learned Societies (because of its relations to the humanities). In Britain, it is always a moot point whether anthropology belongs with the disciplines of the Royal Society or those of the British Academy. Anthropology is becoming even wider with the current interest in cross-disciplinary studies. Despite criticisms to the effect that the fields are becoming too specialized for one person to be able to control several of them, and that he who attempts more than one "is spreading himself too thin," the general scope seems still to be expanding.

Although many sciences have retained the evolutionary type of approach, that of anthropology was considerably modified by Boas. His anti-evolutionary emphasis need not be reviewed here in detail. It is obvious that his rejection did not apply to the facts of evolution, which he and his students continued to document in physical anthropology as well as in technological fields. Rather, it was directed against evolution as a doctrine. The acceptance of evolution had become so general that there was a predisposition to view field data in its terms. Boas' arguments were directed against this use of evolution as a basic premise capable of coloring observation and interpretation.

Distrust is easily voiced, but such a doctrine cannot be readily replaced. Social scientists have been hard-pressed to find suitable substitutes for traditional concepts. It is frequently said, for example, that the self and society may be considered aspects of a single whole. Social scientists are aware that the interactions they study may preclude or render meaningless the opposition between the individual and society, but analyses are generally made in terms of one or the other of these units, and cross-cultural comparisons tend to perpetuate the dichotomy. Boas himself seems to have accepted this particular tradition, although he demanded that the interaction be studied. His general position in regard to tradition was plain: the only corrective was to allow conclusions to follow from the data without the introduction of preconceived philosophical positions.

Distrust of authority takes a different form in the social philosophy approach. Although this approach follows the long and firmly established path of philosophy itself, it grew up in the atmosphere of anticlericalism. It was an assertion of independence from clerical, even from divine, control. Whether or not its exponents accepted the extreme position of cognito ergo sum, they looked for the essential quality of man in his own faculties rather than in those derived from outside himself. The social philosophy approach was attracted to evolutionary theory in part because this made the progress of society dependent upon only those forces which were internal to the social system itself. Unilineal social evolution has never been wholly abandoned by such thinkers. Man's confidence could be centered in man; and in today's terms, both rationalism and humanism belong in this tradition. Perhaps a more significant development is the recently heightened importance of logic. If reason is to be one of the principal analytical tools, it must be honed down to a fine edge; its own analysis becomes essential.

Exponents of the social philosophy approach follow Durkheim in concentrating on the relationships which exist between phenomena. This is where the challenge and the accomplishment lie. It is thus a matter of small moment that many of Durkheim's facts are inadequate or inaccurate. The system of relationships he has constructed transcends details. Such men insist that phenomena be isolated, examined, and then related to each other. It is this threefold process to which their energies are applied, and the dexterity of their performance is in large part the measure which determines its acceptance. Validity thus derives less from verification than from the skillful manipulation of concepts.

The contrast between the two approaches is often described as though it boiled down to the significance of definition. A single issue of a recent publication carried two examples of contrasting attitudes toward the value of refinements in definition. One quotes the phrase of Trilling on the "useful ambiguity which attends the meaning of the word culture" (Lerner and Riesman 1955:67); the other speaks of the social anthropologist's endeavor "to employ a terminology which is completely unambiguous" (Leach 1955:82). The first centers attention on the descriptive material, and is content to leave the terminology fluid. The other emphasizes that science is discourse and must be precise in order to be valid. The first, or natural history, attitude is criticized for its lack of precision: "How can you talk about something when you cannot even say what it is?" And the social philosophy approach of the second is said by its critics to lead to a taxonomy which becomes more and more divorced from reality.

Boas' interest in classification was also reflected in attention to taxonomic systems. As he saw it, the problem was related to distrust of traditional concepts—in his case less a distrust of authority, for that he never accepted, than a deep suspicion of tradition as reflected in one's own thought processes.

> In natural sciences we are accustomed to demand a classification of phenomena expressed in a concise and unambiguous terminology. The same term should have the same meaning everywhere. We should like to see the same in anthropology. As long as we do not overstep the limits of one culture we are able to classify its features in a clear and definite terminology. We know what we mean by the terms family, state, government, etc. As soon as we overstep the limits of one culture we do not know in how far these may correspond to equivalent concepts. If we choose to apply our classification to alien cultures we may combine forms that do not belong together. The very rigidity of definition may lead to a misunderstanding of the essential problems involved. ... If it is our serious purpose to understand the thoughts of a people the whole analysis of experience must be based on their concepts, not ours (Boas 1943:314).

To Boas, man was preeminently a thinking creature. Reliance on an outer world never led him to the position that culture exists of and by itself, but rather that thought be subjected to the same treatment as other phenomena. An exponent of the natural history approach once wrote me: "I argue all the time with people who are oriented in terms of social theory as to the need of having theory develop out of data and of constantly referring theory to data." And the key to the contrast in approaches is often described in different postulated relations between data and theory. But if one glances at the work in any area of anthropology—or of the other social sciences—one is impressed by the fact that all aim at precision in definition, and all relate theory to data. The distinction seems to lie instead in the amount of care taken to preclude preconceived notions.

Boas' effort to preclude traditional concepts had immediate effects on his ethnographic method. Perhaps his most typical contributions are the phonetic texts which he produced in quantity and which he urged others to produce. They were taken down verbatim, and the interlinear translations were made with the assistance of the informant. These come close to being exact samples of a people's thought. Boas was conscious of distortions which could occur through the introduction of a foreign or a sophisticated collector (Boas 1916. Introduction), but the texts supplied a nearly perfect record of a people's language and of the organization and style of their connected discourse. The value of the texts lies in part in the fact that they preserve literary patterns which are fast disappearing under white contact, but their greatest value, and the one on which Boas was most insistent, lay in their character as raw data. Once they were published, conclusions drawn from them could be checked, and they also furnished material for other investigators to use in analyses not envisaged by their collector. The texts were objective in the sense that they were always available for reanalysis. Boas stressed that information should be collected and presented in as great detail and as free of outside bias as possible. The first duty was to give field data in the people's own terms: "… the whole analysis of experience must be based on their concepts, not ours."

Both approaches draw on the philosophy of science for validation and clarification. Thus exponents of the natural history approach are apt to think of field situations as counterparts of the laboratories of other scientists: the social scientist in contact with his data is paralleling the work of the laboratory technician. They know he works under conditions which make direct experimentation impossible, but he attempts to make his observations accurate and in his comparisons he finds factors which may be effectively employed as controls. The social philosopher, on the other hand, thinks of scientific activity primarily in terms of the testing of hypotheses. He conceives his first task to be the careful consideration of alternative hypotheses: data are then brought to bear on them so that they may be accepted or rejected, modified or refined. The field situation or his collection of facts is thus a testing ground, and its value is proportional to the pertinence of the hypothesis he checks with it. A worker in the one approach may be happy in amassing data, with a minimum of generalization; a worker in the other may be equally content to elaborate his hypotheses. One believes his methods are leading toward an accurate, or scientific, picture of actuality; the other may say, "scientifically, that is, hypothetically." As a matter of fact, the total demands of both positions include data and generalization, hypothesis and observation, but the extremes cited here occur with amazing regularity.

When one asks that theory be referred to data, or that conclusions follow as they will from data, this is often construed as a process similar to that involved in testing an hypothesis. Actually this is not a very accurate description of what is intended. Boas taught his students statistics and phonetics as tools for handling biological series and language, but the greatest lesson we learned was that data had an order of their own. This came out most clearly in the classes he conducted in the Eskimo and Kwakiutl languages. Part of the time he acted as informant and let the class work out a grammatical structure by questioning. The grammar was there and it rested with us to ask for translations which would reveal it. By giving only the raw data of speech, without formulation, Boas made us aware that our task was to discover the order we knew to be there. I well remember Boas' delight when I finally worked out the pattern of an Inca textile which at first sight had seemed to be only a jumble of elements with no pattern at all. This was not in itself important, but it could only be done by working with the materials in their own terms. The series of hypotheses which had to be tested could arise only as one worked with the data; none of them could have been formulated beforehand. It should also be recognized that once the data were arranged in the proper order, like the forms of a pronoun or the positions of a locative, the structure became self-evident.

A curious result of this view is to smudge over many common distinctions. For example, the opposition between abstract and concrete almost completely disappears. Whatever the research worker may claim to be his own beliefs concerning the nature of reality, he faces his data, whether abstract or concrete, as though they were equally susceptible to the same treatment. If firearms and sanctions against homicide are introduced simultaneously, the firearms may not be omitted from consideration because they are of a different order of being from sanctions. Both items are innovations due to contact, both may influence economic pursuits or social structure. It may be difficult to assess their relative importance in the new situation which they combine to create. Coming on the situation late in time, therefore, the research worker may have to abandon any preference as to the choice of material, and embark on a study of the relative efficiency of bows and arrows and guns, which was entirely beyond the original plan of his project.

A frequent cause of lack of communication is this apparently indiscriminate acceptance of fact. The social philosophy approach is deeply concerned with the nature of the material it is called upon to examine. It may make preliminary judgments as to the relative validity of sources of information. The natural history approach, on the contrary, begins by treating all fact as commensurable. It mistrusts judgments as to validity and is deeply concerned with the precision of interpretation. Thus, the one approach refers the expressed opinion of an informant to standards of veracity: Why did he say this, rather than that? Is what he said true? The other tends to take the opinion as given, compares it with another opinion expressed under similar circumstances, and asks questions about the significance of their similarity or dissimilarity. Exponents of the two approaches must be conscious of this difference. Otherwise, the social philosophy approach seems to have a naive obsession with "truth," and the natural history approach is thought of as naively gullible. Whereas the first accepts its premises as secure and questions its material, the other finds its security in the inviolability of its data and believes that if data are completely described they can be treated on one plane as hard fact.

One of the great bugaboos of the natural history approach is ethnocentrism. In contrast, social philosophy is little concerned with this factor. Suspicion of ethnocentricism is a natural concomitant of Boas' position, as outlined above, and its presence in modern thought is due in large part to him. This is perhaps not the least of his contributions, but it needs further elaboration here in relation to his ethnographic method. If I understand his position correctly, interpretation should enter the picture only after data have been collected. Raw data must be kept as free of outside interpretation as possible. It therefore followed that information gathered for a particular purpose became suspect, for selection in itself suggested distortion.

This does not mean that Boas never had problems in mind when he collected material. For instance, he wrote in 1920:

> One of the greatest obstacles to a clear understanding of the social organization of the Kwakiutl is the general confusion caused by the reduction in numbers of the tribe. I have tried to clear up the situation by recording the histories of a number of families in all possible detail (Boas 1920:111).

The interesting point here is the choice of the data selected for concentrated effort. The "histories of a number of families" constitute in themselves a block of information which can be used for as many purposes as can a collection of phonetic texts. They are raw data in the same sense. It would be useful to have such data included in any field study, but the selection here was determined by the local situation and was tailored to fit the demands of the particular inquiry. It did not grow out of hypotheses conceived in the culture of the investigator, and it did not overstep cultural boundaries. Selection of data, therefore, is suspect only if it does either of these things.

Systematic work was essential for obtaining the material needed to illuminate any problem. Boas never believed in the haphazard collection of field data. So far as I know, he left no explicit statement of his field techniques, but the nature of much of his field material suggests that he allowed informants a great deal of freedom in discussing topics of their own choice. This would be thoroughly consistent with his position as described here. Many of his data probably could not have been collected in response to direct questions. His effort to free thought from its traditional aspects would alert him to the fact that, coming from another culture, he might be unable to phrase the proper questions. At the start of work with an unfamiliar culture the research worker simply does not know enough for that, but he can begin with the most general inquiries and remain wholly systematic.

Boas' insistence on the integration of culture has direct bearing on this point, and it may not be irrelevant to recall an incident which occurred at one of my first attendances at the famous Wednesday afternoon seminars at Columbia. I do not remember what the paper had been, but discussion centered on the impossibility of foreseeing the ways in which one part of culture would be integrated with any other. In order to study art, therefore, one would have also to sample economics, the position of the artist in the prestige system, ritual, and so on. Furthermore, the integration of culture was such that the study of art would not be complete until all the other aspects of culture had been thoroughly investigated. Although I agreed with this in principle, I ventured to suggest that if the main problem was art, the investigator would concentrate on artistic matters such as techniques, style, and design elements. None of the students would allow this, and I was properly squelched. Afterward, going down in the elevator, Boas happened to stand near me, and he leaned over and said, "There is a thing called art." Nothing more was needed. The young student had been encouraged, and perspective had been reestablished.

The position seems actually to be that although both the investigator's previous unfamiliarity with the culture and his anticipation of its integration lead toward free interviews, concentration on particular problems is not only permissible but may be expected, particularly in the later stages of fieldwork. Once the problems have been seen in terms of the new culture, fields for study may be isolated. Systematic work can then be devoted to accumulation of the relevant raw data. Experience has also shown that certain topics such as kinship systems must always be investigated, and a fieldworker in a new area would therefore expect to do systematic work along these lines. In addition, Boas' emphasis on systematic fieldwork led to the collection of whatever data became available. If one found an informant to be particularly well versed in a subject, one concentrated on that subject, getting everything possible from him and following through with other informants, observations, and the like, even though the immediate usefulness of the material might not be apparent. Precision could come only from data systematically gathered "… in all possible detail."

This exhaustive collection of data which seems at the time to have little or no connection with any specific problem is peculiarly a feature of the natural history approach. Interest lies not mainly in systems per se, but in "the surrounding world." There is a fascination in following the details of a subject just for its intrinsic interest, and there is also the knowledge that, once accumulated, such systematic data will have value—sometimes in wholly unexpected directions. Masses of data may therefore be worked over with no clear knowledge of what is to be gained at the end. A new hypothesis or a new slant on an old problem will "emerge" or be "revealed" or "suggested." The data will "speak for themselves." This is the procedure by which the exponent of the natural history approach prefers to arrive at hypotheses: they do not come from systematic thought but from systematically ordered data.

The integration of culture may be thought of as a typical hypothesis of the natural history approach. The "conclusion" that cultures form more or less integrated wholes derives not from thoughtful analyses of our own cultural materials but from data collected over many years on a number of cultures. Comparison then "establishes" similarities which occur widely, and the hypothesis is ready for reexamination and refinement. It is not hypothetical in any usual sense of the word. It is rather a scientific generalization on regularities, similar to any which might be formulated in, say, astronomy. Boas always emphasized that the data of anthropology were different in many respects from those of the natural sciences, notably because of the presence of historical factors. He was equally clear, however, in stating that a people's actions would be the same whether or not they knew anything of the historical background. Dialects are spoken without the speakers being aware of the phonetic shifts which have occurred over time. Although culture change is therefore of great importance for ethnological analysis, I do not see that consideration of such change directly affected Boas' ethnographic method.

The same objections which can be made to selection of field data according to a preconceived scheme can also be brought to bear on a number of favorite sociological techniques. For example, the questionnaire is designed to sample opinion and to elicit responses on topics deeply imbedded in cultural values. It presupposes knowledge of the culture, and is pertinent to problems arising in the solution of imbalances. To transfer such instruments of investigation unchanged to other cultures is obviously unsound. But to construct similarly useful sets of questions for an alien culture, it would be necessary to have the same careful background analyses which the sociologist has been building up over the years; to attempt to devise a truly cross-cultural questionnaire would add tremendously to the difficulties. Questionnaires thus grow out of the investigator's own culture, and they overstep cultural boundaries. The second of these objections really constitutes the main point because, although Boas could have devised a questionnaire for Kwakiutl potlatch procedures, he would clearly have regarded it as inappropriate for administration to men who hold seats on the New York Stock Exchange. Investigation of the common features in these two cultural situations would demand a third, specially devised questionnaire—or other techniques—and it could follow only on parallel, prior investigation. Actually, Boas followed earlier anthropologists in using lists of questions. In his case the lists were small, but a fieldworker going to any part of the Northwest Coast would be asked, for instance, to supply the local word for "seal." These questions, far from overstepping cultural boundaries, were designed to help discover exactly where they lay.

The social anthropologist is apt to stress the importance of observation in his fieldwork; he tends to suspect informants' statements and to rely largely on those data which derive from his personal observation. This emphasis is foreign to Boas' approach. First, one of his prime interests was in meaning: he wanted to know not only what was done but why the persons thought they were doing it. Second, he was acutely aware of the extent to which perception is influenced by personal factors; people see what they expect o see, and interpret what they have seen in the light of their own previous experiences. All the arguments against ethnocentricism here come into play. Even the trained observer has constantly to be on guard against possible inaccuracies and omissions in his own records. Boas was always too self-critical to rely completely on his own observations. He needed the documentation of the text, the family history, to test his own precision. His half century of work with the Kwakiutl was increasingly intensive, but it was marked by constant reference back to early materials, checking and rechecking. Of course he depended on observation, but he took that for granted; it was typical of him that he expressed the limitations of a method more clearly than its values, which he took to be self evident.

The same demand for raw data determined Boas' relationship to such fieldworkers as Henry W. Tate, who collected the texts for Tsimshian Mythology, George Hunt and James A. Teit. It required the trained anthropologist to work with and analyze field data, but valuable material could be gathered by someone trained in a few relatively simple techniques. These men were technicians in the sense that the laboratory sciences have technicians. When so much has to be done, some of the tasks can be delegated. Hunt was a Kwakiutl; Teit had close ties with the people from whom he began to collect information, but later he also worked with relative strangers. Part of their value to anthropology lay in the fact that each man spoke the native language and had connections which enabled him to make personal contacts readily. But Teit's importance, especially in his later work, lay principally in the fact that here was a man on the spot, able and willing to continue the anthropologist's work. Folklore was naturally adapted to this, since a great deal of its collection could be described as relatively routine, but Teit's work was not limited to folklore.

It is interesting that this aspect of Boas' ethnographic method has not been more widely adopted. I suspect that this is partially because of the labor involved in editing material gathered by technicians, in going over it with the care necessary to make it part of one's own data. Most anthropologists find it difficult enough to go through their own notes. But I suspect also that as anthropology became an increasingly important university subject, students were employed more and more to augment earlier work. This served the dual purpose of adding information and giving students field experience. Some students, such as Ella Deloria, were as well fitted for fieldwork among their people as Hunt had been, but her work with the Sioux is not comparable to his among the Kwakiutl because she brings to her research the full training of the anthropologist. Remarkably little attention has been given to the development of field technicians who are not themselves training to become anthropologists.

From the time of The Central Eskimo, Boas always included with his own data any facts available from other sources. This did not imply that his use of such sources was uncritical. He felt that the more information one had, the more correct could be one's conclusions, and he often corrected a statement or an opinion earlier expressed in the literature.

> From observations made by Captain Spicer, of Groton, Conn., and information obtained from the Eskimo, we learn that the whole of the eastern part of Fox basin is extremely shallow ... (Boas 1888:416).

But one judges each statement on its own merits, and this acceptance of supported Eskimo testimony is followed by:

> Though the Eskimo assert that the discovery of Lake Nettelling is of recent date … this assertion is not trustworthy, for with them almost every historical tradition is supposed to have originated comparatively short time ago. I was told, for instance, … (Boas 1888:430).

Boas regarded data from others as critically as he did his own observations, and his criticism in each case was based on the same reasons.

Had Boas reached the eastern part of Fox basin, he would have been able to verify its depth; lacking first hand observation, he came to a decision on the information available. It is strange that Boas is sometimes said to have failed in the formulation of hypotheses. Every page of his descriptive work is full of such conclusions drawn from data. Each was viewed as subject to correction, and each was therefore regarded as tentative until fresh evidence came to hand. As his work became more intensive, fewer facts gathered by others could be brought in as relevant. But his work was extensive as well, and his conclusions in theoretical matters were based on information drawn from a variety of sources. It is true, however, that these conclusions led only to accuracy and precision in description and to depth of understanding. Interest in an abstract and universal truth which lay outside of the material world was foreign to Boas' thought, and hypotheses which aimed at establishment of such truth were absent from his ethnographic approach.

Although Boas was critical of information supplied by local residents, his attitude toward informants was not generally suspicious. In no other phase of their research are the extreme positions of the natural history and social philosophy approaches more distinct than in their relations to informants. During and just after the last war, several efforts were made to substitute some other word for "informant" because of the implied relation between it and "informing," with its unpleasant connotations. The close tie between an anthropologist and his informants is of such a special kind, however, that other words with other overtones of meaning already established failed to express what was intended, and the term has continued in use. Although the anthropologist is learning from his informant, the relation is clearly not that of pupil and teacher. Nor is the anthropologist asking for secret information; he considers important everyday matters which the informant would not ordinarily think about. Once the relationship is established, both an anthropologist and informant work together on the material—one contributing his skills, the other his knowledge and personal experience.

A study of ethnographic method could dwell at length on the various methods of conducting interviews. The kinds of personal interactions involved appear to influence directly the nature of the information obtained. The various interviewing techniques may all find a place at one time or another in the anthropologist's repertoire, and he may be more or less aware of their effects. They are of particular importance with supplementary informants who are used for comparatively short periods. Boas' own fieldwork, however, is distinguished by concentrated work with a few informants. This might continue over months or even years, and interviewing techniques lose much of their significance in the light of such protracted contact. Work with informants means work of this intensive kind and it is not generally comparable to ordinary interviewing.

Boas had early recognized that some types of information do not lend themselves to mathematical treatment (Boas 1938:22). This was particularly true of ideas and concepts, and to the extent that Boas' work was devoted to establishing a people's own concepts he was not interested in applying the statistical criteria he used so effectively in his studies of growth. To get the depth of understanding he required meant submerging his thinking in that of another. It meant learning to think in another's terms and to view the world through another's eyes. The most intimate knowledge of an informant's thought processes was mandatory and could only be obtained by intensive work over a long period. Important concepts and strange viewpoints had to be checked with other material and with a number of informants; supplementary information had to be obtained elsewhere. But Boas conceived of his main task as the adoption of an informant's mode of thought while retaining full use of his own critical faculties. For this, sampling and other semi-mathematical techniques were of no immediate assistance, and they played little part in his ethographic method.

The custom of concentrating on a few informants may have arisen in work with American Indians in part because of the urgent need felt by many early anthropologists to obtain and preserve information before it was too late. Conditions seemed to be changing so rapidly that in a few years the old ways would be gone forever. There was also the practical consideration that most people are too busy to spend much time with an anthropologist, however willing they may be, and one is obliged to work with the few who already have time on their hands or to create circumstances which make time available. But neither the imminence of change nor practical considerations lay behind Boas' choice of method; it was determined by his whole approach. He could obtain the kind of knowledge he wanted only by concentrating his work with a few persons.

Boas was little concerned whether an informant was "typical" or not; this was a pseudo-statistical concept which he disposed of most effectively in his discussions of race. Surely any active participant in a society must be thinking and generally behaving in ways appropriate to that society. Boas' interest lay in uncovering the premises on which such a person operated, and if it were not possible to work with a representative of every specialized role in a society, at least every person had ideas as to what those roles were. Intensive work with an informant means reviewing with him every aspect of his culture, retaining his emphases, noting his omissions, and maintaining the relationships he establishes. Work should be done with such precision that one could construct a house from the informant's description of a house. Although one can generally see a house, observation must be combined with data from informants, for what an informant sees in a house—designs and ritual association, symbols and values—will be quite different from what the untutored anthropologist will see in it. This ideal of complete work with an informant may seldom be realized in practice, yet the method is clear-cut and applicable to any society of any complexity. Of course data obtained in this way must be augmented by many other kinds of information, but there is no substitute for exhaustive and intensive work with informants.

A misstatement of fact can be serious in an interview. The person being interviewed may intentionally distort the true picture for any one of a number of reasons and the investigator must allow for such factors in assessing his results. Falsehood of this sort is impossible to maintain in the protracted anthropologist-informant relationship. The complexity of fully recorded data goes far beyond any tests of veracity. Thus, if an informant says that something happens, whereas the anthropologist observes the opposite, this cannot simply be disposed of as a lie; it poses a problem which must be given further attention. In the same way, consistent distortion may be a clue to important facets of behavior, to be noted and given their appropriate weight. Boas' field material gives no evidence of moral judgments of his informants or of the customs of their societies.

Many anthropologists who studied under Boas have relied heavily on "main" informants. Their thinking has been conditioned by intensive work with one or two persons with whom they could establish rapport, and with whom it was possible to work for long periods. Although it seems a natural outgrowth of Boas' work, this type of relationship does not seem characteristic of it. Boas himself seems always to have retained considerable objectivity. He worked with informants in order to obtain a particular kind of information, and the data themselves remained foremost in his interest. This lends his work a curious detachment which is slightly repellent to social scientists who are absorbed in people. But it must be remembered that it was the whole world with which Boas was fascinated. People were part of it, but they were not the reason for its being. They represented no culmination of creative effort, no end point of development.

Another aspect of this same broad view of all phenomena underlay Boas' attitude to individuals.

> The habit of identifying an individual with a class, owing to his bodily appearance, language, or manners, has always seemed to me a survival of barbaric, or rather of primitive, habits of mind. ... There are too few among us who are willing to forget completely that a particular person is a Negro, a Jew, ... and to judge him as an individual (Boas 1938:24).

Acceptance of class standards and national stereotypes naturally seemed to him a form of subservience to traditional concepts. I believe that his whole position on race was determined not only by the factual aspects of scientific inquiry but also by his conviction that obedience to the dictates of racial prejudice constituted a violation of freedom of thought. One must determine for oneself the attributes of individuals.

Boas carried this attitude with him in the field. Not only did he refrain from preconceived judgments but he also met each man without condescension, with no sense of the absolute superiority of the Western culture which he himself represented. His standards were high, but they were for individuals, and it is particularly to be noted that he found individuals in the field who met those standards, whom he could meet on his own intellectual terms. The experience of other anthropologists confirms this, and one of the best documented facts in cross-cultural work is the presence in many cultures of persons capable of clear judgments and dispassionate opinions on matters close to their own and their society's interests. Cultural differences may remain, but such persons must be judged on a par with the investigator. Although Boas felt no hesitation in attributing positive value to certain actions and modes of thought, his work was not normative; it was given its unique force by his refusal to abide by cultural prejudices and by his recognition of the universal occurrence of human qualities. His capacity for maintaining both these positions relates directly to the natural history approach which he so well represented, and which seems as pertinent as ever to the problems of the social sciences.

THE REFERENCES CITED

Boas Franz

1888 The Central Eskimo.

1902 The ethnological significance of esoteric doctrines. Science, 16:872–874.

1916 Tsimshian mythology. 31st Annual Report, Bureau of American Ethnology, Washington, D.C.

1920 The social organization of the Kwakiutl. American Anthropologist, 22:111–126.

1938 Franz Boas. In I believe, Clifton Fadiman, ed. New York, Simon & Shuster, pp. 19–29. Reprinted from The Nation 147:201–204.

1940 Race, language and culture. New York, Macmillan Co.

1943 Recent anthropology. Science, 98:311–314, 334–337.

Latham Robert Gordon

1850 Natural history of the varieties of man. London, John Van Vorst.

Leach Edmund R.

1955 He wasn't there again today. Explorations #5.

Lerner Daniel, and David Riesman

1955 Self and society. Explorations #5.

Fieldwork Among the Trobrianders

By Bronislaw Malinowski

W e find in the Trobriands a matrilineal society, in which descent, kinship, and every social relationship are legally reckoned through the mother only, and in which women have a considerable share in tribal life, even to the taking of a leading part in economic, ceremonial, and magical activities—a fact which very deeply influences all the customs of erotic life as well as the institution of marriage. It will be well, therefore, first to consider the sexual relation in its widest aspect, beginning with some account of those features of custom and tribal law which underlie the institution of mother-right, and the various views and conceptions which throw light upon it; after this, a short sketch of each of the chief domains of tribal life—domestic, economic, legal, ceremonial, and magical—will combine to show the respective spheres of male and female activity among these natives.

The idea that it is solely and exclusively the mother who builds up the child's body, the man in no way contributing to its formation, is the most important factor in the legal system of the Trobrianders. Their views on the process of procreation, coupled with certain mythological and animistic beliefs, affirm, without doubt or reserve, that the child is of the same substance as its mother, and that between the father and the child there is no bond of physical union whatsoever.

That the mother contributes everything to the new being to be born of her is taken for granted by the natives, and forcibly expressed by them. "The mother feeds the infant in her body. Then, when it comes out, she feeds it with her milk." "The mother makes the child out of her blood." "Brothers and sisters are of the same flesh, because they come of the same mother." These and similar expressions describe their attitude towards this, their fundamental principle of kinship.

This attitude is also to be found embodied, in an even more telling manner, in the rules governing descent, inheritance, succession in rank, chieftainship, hereditary offices, and magic—in every regulation, in fact, concerning transmission by kinship. Social position is handed on in the mother-line from a man to his sister's children, and this exclusively matrilineal conception of kinship is of paramount importance in the restrictions and regulations of marriage, and in the taboos on sexual intercourse. The working of these ideas of kinship can be observed, breaking out with a dramatic intensity, at death. For the social rules underlying burial, lamentation, and mourning, together with certain very elaborate ceremonies of food distribution, are based on the principle that people joined by the tie of maternal kinship form a closely knit group, bound by an identity of feelings, of interests, and of flesh. And from this group, even those united to it by marriage and by the father-to-child relation are sharply excluded, as having no natural share in the bereavement.

These natives have a well-established institution of marriage, and yet are quite ignorant of the man's share in the begetting of children. At the same time, the term "father" has, for the Trobriander, a clear, though exclusively social, definition: it signifies the man married to the mother, who lives in the same house with her, and forms part of the household. The father, in all discussions about relationship, was pointedly described to me as tomakava, a "stranger," or even more correctly, an "outsider." This expression would also frequently be used by natives in conversation, when they were arguing some point of inheritance or trying to justify some line of behavior, or again when the position of the father was to be belittled in some quarrel.

It will be clear to the reader, therefore, that the term "father," as I use it here, must be taken, not as having the various legal, moral, and biological implications that it holds for us, but in a sense entirely specific to the society with which we are dealing. It might have seemed better, in order to avoid any chance of such misconception, not to have used our word "father" at all, but rather the native one tama, and to have spoken of the "tama relationship" instead of "fatherhood"; but, in practice, this would have proved too unwieldy. The reader, therefore, when he meets the word "father" in these pages, should never forget that it must be defined, not as in the English dictionary, but in accordance with the facts of native life. I may add that this rule applies to all terms which carry special sociological implication, that is to all terms of relationship, and such words as "marriage," "divorce," "betrothal," "love," "courtship," and the like.

What does the word tama (father) express to the native? "Husband of my mother" would be the answer first given by an intelligent informant. He would go on to say that his tama is the man in whose loving and protecting company he has grown up. For, since marriage is patrilocal in the Trobriands, since the woman, that is to say, moves to her husband's village community and lives in his house, the father is a close companion to his children; he takes an active part in the cares which are lavished upon them, invariably feels and shows a deep affection for them, and later has a share in their education. The word tama (father) condenses, therefore, in its emotional meaning, a host of experiences of early childhood, and expresses the typical sentiment existing between a boy or girl and a mature affectionate man of the same household; while socially it denotes the male person who stands in an intimate relation to the mother, and who is master of the household.

So far tama does not differ essentially from "father" in our sense. But as soon as the child begins to grow up and take an interest in things outside the affairs of the household and its own immediate needs, certain complications arise, and change the meaning of tama for him. He learns that he is not of the same clan as his tama, that his totemic appellation is different, and that it is identical with that of his mother. At the same time he learns that all sorts of duties, restrictions, and concerns for personal pride unite him to his mother and separate him from his father. Another man appears on the horizon, and is called by the child kadagu ("my mother's brother"). This man may live in the same locality, but he is just as likely to reside in another village. The child also learns that the place where his kada (mother's brother) resides is also his, the child's, "own village"; that there he has his property and his other rights of citizenship; that there his future career awaits him; that there his natural allies and associates are to be found. He may even be taunted in the village of his birth with being an "outsider" (tomakava), while in the village he has to call "his own," in which his mother's brother lives, his father is a stranger and he a natural citizen. He also sees, as he grows up, that the mother's brother assumes a gradually increasing authority over him, requiring his services, helping him in some things, granting or withholding his permission to carry out certain actions; while the father's authority and counsel become less and less important.

Thus the life of a Trobriander runs under a two-fold influence—a duality which must not be imagined as a mere surface play of custom. It enters deeply into the existence of every individual, it produces strange complications of usage, it creates frequent tensions and difficulties, and not seldom gives rise to violent breaks in the continuity of tribal life. For this dual influence of paternal love and the matrilineal principle, which penetrates so far into the framework of institutions and into the social ideas and sentiments of the native, is not, as a matter of fact, quite well adjusted in its working. ...

* * *

In entering the village we had to pass across the street between the two concentric rows of houses. This is the normal setting of the everyday life of the community, and thither we must return in order to make a closer survey of the groups of people sitting in front of their dwellings. As a rule we find that each group consists of one family only—man, wife, and children—taking their leisure, or engaged in some domestic activity which varies with the time of day. On a fine morning we would see them hastily eating a scanty breakfast, and then the man and woman preparing the implements for the day's work, with the help of the bigger children, while the baby is laid out of the way on a mat. Afterwards, during the cool hours of the forenoon, each family would probably set off to their work, leaving the village almost deserted. The man, in company with others, may be fishing or hunting or building a canoe or looking for timber. The woman may have gone collecting shell-fish or wild fruits. Or else both may be working in the gardens, or paying a visit. The man often does harder work than the woman, but when they return in the hot hours of the afternoon he will rest, while the woman busies herself with household affairs. Towards evening, when the descending sun casts longer, cooler shadows, the social life of the village begins. At this time we would see our family group in front of their hut, the wife preparing food, the children playing, the husband, perhaps, seated amusing the smallest baby. This is the time when neighbors call on one another, and conversation may be exchanged from group to group.

The frank and friendly tone of intercourse, the obvious feeling of equality, the father's domestic helpfulness, especially with the children would at once strike any observant visitor. The wife joins freely in the jokes and conversation; she does her work independently, not with the air of a slave or a servant, but as one who manages her own department. She will order the husband about if she needs his help. Close observation, day after day, confirms this first impression. The typical Trobriand household is founded on the principles of equality and independence of function: the man is considered to be the master, for he is in his own village and the house belongs to him, but the woman has, in other respects, a considerable influence; she and her family have a great deal to do with the food supply of the household; she is the owner of separate possessions in the house; and she is—next to her brother—the legal head of her family.

The division of functions within the household is, in certain matters, quite definite. The woman has to cook the food, which is simple, and does not require much preparation. The main meal is taken at sunset, and consists of yams, taro, or other tubers, roasted in the open fire—or, less frequently, boiled in a small pot, or baked in the ground—with the occasional addition of fish or meat. Next morning the remains are eaten cold, and sometimes, though not regularly, shell-fish, or some other light snack may be taken at mid-day.

In some circumstances, men can and do prepare and cook the food: on journeys, oversea voyages, fishing or hunting expeditions, when they are without their women folk. Also, on certain occasions, when taro or sago dumplings are cooked in the large clay pots, men are required by tradition to assist their wives. But within the village and in normal daily life the man never cooks. It would be considered shameful for him to do so. "You are a he-cook" would be said tauntingly. The fear of deserving such an epithet, or being laughed at or shamed, is extreme. It arises from the characteristic dread and shame, found among savages, of not doing the proper thing, or, worse still, of doing something which is intrinsically the attribute of another sex or social class.

There are a number of occupations strictly assigned by tribal custom to one sex only. The manner of carrying loads is a very noteworthy example. Women have to carry the special feminine receptacle, the bell-shaped basket, or any other kind of load upon their heads; men must carry only on the shoulder. It would be with a real shudder, and a profound feeling of shame, that an individual would regard carrying anything in the manner proper to the opposite sex and nothing would induce a man to put any load on his head, even in fun.

An exclusively feminine department is the water supply. The woman has the water bottles of the household in her charge. These are made out of the woody shell of a mature coconut, with a stopper of twisted palm-leaf. In the morning or near sunset she goes, sometimes a full half-mile, to fill them at the water-hole: here the women foregather, resting and chatting, while one after the other fills her water-vessels, cleans them, arranges them in baskets or on large wooden platters, and, just before leaving, gives the cluster a final sprinkling of water to cover it with a suggestive gloss of freshness. The water-hole is the woman's club and centre of gossip, and as such is important, for there is a distinct woman's public opinion and point of view in a Trobriand village, and they have their secrets from the male, just as the male has from the female.

We have already seen that the husband fully shares in the care of the children. He will fondle and carry a baby, clean and wash it, and give it the mashed vegetable food which it receives in addition to the mother's milk almost from birth. In fact, nursing the baby in the arms or holding it on the knees, which is described by the native word kopo'I, is the special role and duty of the father (tama). It is said of the children of unmarried women who, according to the native expression, are "without a tama" (that is, it must be remembered, without a husband to their mother), that they are "unfortunate" or "bad" because "there is no one to nurse and hug them." Again, if anyone inquires why children should have duties toward their father, who is a "stranger" to them, the answer is invariably: "because of the nursing, because his hands have been soiled with the child's excrement and urine."

The father performs his duties with genuine natural fondness: he will carry an infant about for hours, looking at it with eyes full of such love and pride as are seldom seen in those of a European father. Any praise of the baby goes directly to his heart, and he will never tire of talking about and exhibiting the virtues and achievements of his wife's offspring. Indeed, watching a native family at home or meeting them on the road, one receives a strong impression of close union and intimacy between its members. Nor, as we have seen, does this mutual affection abate in later years. Thus, in the intimacy of domestic life, we discover another aspect of the interesting and complicated struggle between social and emotional paternity, on the one hand, and the explicitly acknowledged legal mother-right on the other.

It will be noticed that we have not yet penetrated into the interior of a house, for in fine weather the scene of family life is always laid in front of the dwelling. Only when it is cold and raining, at night, or for intimate uses, do the natives retire into the interior. On a wet or windy evening in the cooler season we would find the village streets deserted, dim lights flickering through small interstices in the hut walls, and voices sounding from within in animated conversation. Inside, in a small space heavy with dense smoke and human exhalation, the people sit on the floor round the fire or recline on bedsteads covered with mats.

Lessons from the Field

By George Gmelch

S ara, Eric, and Kristen heave their backpacks and suitcases—all the gear they'll need for the next ten weeks—into the back of the Institute's battered Toyota pick-up. Sara, a tense grin on her face, gets up front with me, the others climb in the back and try to make themselves comfortable on the luggage.

Leaving Bellairs Research Institute on the west coast of Barbados, we drive north past the island's posh resorts. Their names—Cobblers Cove, Coral Reef Club, Coconut Creek, and Glitter Bay—evoke images of tropical paradise. The scene changes abruptly once we leave the coast and move from tourism to agriculture. Here amid the green and quiet of rolling sugar cane fields, there are no more white faces. Graceful cabbage palms flank a large plantation house, one of the island's former "great houses." On the edge of its cane fields is a tenantry, a cluster of small board houses whose inhabitants are the descendants of the slaves who once worked on the plantation.

Two monkeys emerge from a gully and cross the road. I tell Sara that they came to Barbados aboard slave ships 300 years ago, but she is absorbed in her own thoughts and doesn't seem to hear me. I've taken enough students to the field to have an idea of what's on her mind. What will her village be like—the one we just passed through looked unusually poor. Will the family she is going to live with like her? Will she like them? Will she be up to the challenge? Many people are walking along the road; clusters of men sit outside a rum shop shouting loudly while slamming dominoes on a wobbly plywood table.

Earlier in the day, Eric told me that many of the ten students on the field program thought they had made a mistake coming to Barbados. If they had chosen to go on the term abroad to Greece or England or even Japan, they mused, they would be together on a campus, among friends. They wouldn't have to live in a village. They wouldn't have to go out and meet people and try to make friends with all these strangers. To do it all alone now seemed more of a challenge than many wanted.

George Gmelch, "Lessons from the Field," *Annual Editions: 06/07*. McGraw Hill, Contemporary Learning Series, 2006, pp. 14–19. Permission to reprint granted by the publisher.

We continue driving toward the northeastern corner of the island to the village of Pie Corner, where Sara will live. Several miles out we can see huge swells rolling in off the Atlantic, beating against the cliffs. This is the unsheltered side of the island. The village only has a few hundred people but six churches. Marcus Hinds and his family all come out to the truck to welcome Sara. Mrs. Hinds gives her a big hug, as though she were a returning relative, and daughter Yvette takes her into the yard to show her the pigs and chickens, and then on a tour of the small house. The bedroom is smaller than Sara imagined, barely larger than the bed. She puzzles over where to put all her stuff, while I explain to the Hinds, again, the nature of the program. Sara, I tell them, will be spending most of her time in the village talking to people and participating as much as possible in the life of the community, everything from attending church to cutting sugar cane. My description doesn't fit their conception of what a university education is all about. The everyday lives of people in their community are probably not something they think worthy of a university student's attention.

Back in the truck Eric and Kristen ask me anxiously how their villages compare to Sara's. Kristen begins to bite her nails.

* * *

For twenty years I have been taking students to the field with my colleague and wife, Sharon Gmelch, and we have acquired a great deal of knowledge about what students have learned from the foreign cultures in which they live. But it wasn't until serving on a committee that was evaluating my college's international study programs, that I ever thought much about what my students learned about their own culture by living in another. The belief that you have to live abroad before you can truly understand your own culture has gained wide acceptance on college campuses today. But what exactly is it students learn?

I questioned other anthropologists who also took students to the field and they too were unclear about its lessons. A search through the literature didn't help. All the research on the educational outcomes of foreign study had been on students who study at universities abroad, not in more immersive, anthropology field schools.

My curiosity aroused, I decided to examine the experiences of our students in Barbados. Through a questionnaire, interviews, and analysis of their field notes and journals, I looked at their adjustment to Bajan village life and what they learned about themselves and their culture by living on a Caribbean island.

RURAL LIFE

Living in a Barbadian village brings many lessons in the differences between rural and urban. About 90% of our students come from suburbs or cities and have never lived in the countryside before. For them a significant part of their experience in Barbados is living with people who are close to the land. Their host families, like most villagers, grow crops and raise animals. Each morning, before dawn, the students wake to the sounds of animals in the yard. They quickly begin to learn about the behavior of chickens, pigs, sheep, and cows. They witness animals giving birth and being slaughtered. They see the satisfaction families get from consuming food they have produced themselves.

Even inside their village, homes the students live close to "nature." They may share their bedrooms with green lizards, mice, cockroaches, and sometimes a whistling frog. They become aware of how different are the sounds of the countryside, and they are struck by the darkness of the sky and the brightness of the stars at night with no city lights to diminish their intensity. A student from Long Island said it was "like living in a planetarium."

The social world of the village is quite unlike the communities they come from. In doing a household survey, they discover that people know virtually everyone in the village. And they often know them in more than one context, not just as neighbors but perhaps also as members of the same church, and as teammates on the village cricket or soccer team. Relationships are not single-stranded as they often are in suburban America.

Most students have never known a place of such intimacy, where relationships are also embedded with so many different meanings and a shared history. In their journals, some students reflect upon and compare the warmth, friendliness, and frequent sharing of food and other resources that occurs in the village with the impersonality, individualism, and detachment of suburban life at home. But they also learn the drawbacks to living in a small community: there is no anonymity. People are nosy and unduly interested in the affairs of their neighbors. The students discover that they too may be the object of local gossip. Several female students learned from village friends that there were stories afoot that they were either mistresses to their host fathers or sleeping with their host brothers. The gossip hurt, for the students, like any anthropologist, had worked hard to gain acceptance and worried about the damage such rumors might do to their reputations.

One of the biggest adjustments students must make to village life is the absence of the diversions and entertainment that they are accustomed to at home. Early in their stay there seems little to do apart from their research. At times they are bored, lonely and desperate to escape the village, but they are not allowed to leave except on designated days. (All students initially hate this restriction, but by the end of the term they understand the rationale behind it.) This isolation forces students to satisfy their needs for recreation and companionship within their communities which they do by hanging out with the villagers, a practice which strengthens friendships and results in a good deal of informal education about Bajan life and culture.

PACE OF LIFE

Students discover that the pace of life is slower than home. Much slower. As her host mother explained to Sara, "There are only two speeds in Barbados: slow and dead stop." Languor is an accommodation to the hot, tropical climate. But also, compared to Americans, Bajans are in less of a hurry to get things done. At the shop or post office in town customers wait to be served until the clerk finishes chatting with others. Bajans think little of being late for appointments. Accustomed to the punctuality and hectic pace of North American life, our students are often impatient and frustrated. But as they socialize more with village friends, their compulsive haste begins to dissipate. They sense a different time, one that is unhurried and attuned to the place. They begin to see things they didn't notice before, the bit of earth they're sitting on, the cane fields, the blue sky, and the palm trees. As the term passes, students come to value this unhurried way of life, and by the time they leave the island most are determined to maintain a more tranquil, relaxed lifestyle when they return home.

RACE

In Barbados our students become members of a racial minority for the first time in their lives. During their first few weeks in the field they become acutely aware of their own "race," of their being white while everyone around them is dark. Students are often called "white girl" or "white boy" by people in the village until they get to know one another. Village children have sometimes asked to touch a student's skin, marveling at the blue veins which show through it. They sometimes ask students with freckles if they have a skin disease. Others want to feel straight hair. Characteristically, one student during the second week wrote:

> I have never been in a situation before where I was a minority purely due to the color of my skin, and treated differently because of it. When I approach people I am very conscious of having white skin. Before I never thought of myself as having color.

The students are surprised that Barbadians speak so openly about racial difference, something which is not done at home in the United States. A few students become hypersensitive to race during the early weeks of their stay. When leaving their villages, they travel on a crowded bus on which they are the only whites. Often they are stared at (as the bus heads into the countryside, the passengers may worry that the student has missed his or her stop or has taken the wrong bus). Students notice that as the bus fills up, the seat next to them is often the last to be taken.

Concerns about race, even the very awareness of race, diminish rapidly, however, as the students make friends and become integrated into their villages. In fact, by the end of the term most said they were "rarely" aware of being white. Several students described incidents in which they had become so unaware of skin color that they were shocked when someone made a remark or did something to remind them of their being different. Kristen was startled when, after shaking her hand, an old woman from her village remarked that she had never touched the hand of a white person before. Several students reported being surprised when they walked by a mirror and got a glimpse of their white skin. One student wrote that although she knew she wasn't black, she no longer felt white.

What is the outcome of all this? Do students now have an understanding of what it means to be a minority, and does this translate into their having more empathy at home? I think so. All the students from the previous Barbados programs whom I questioned about the impact of their experiences mentioned a heightened empathy for African-Americans, and some included other minorities as well. Several said that when they first returned home, they wanted to go up to any black person they saw and have a conversation. "But I kept having to remind myself," reported Megan when I saw her on campus later, "that most blacks in America are not West Indians and they wouldn't understand where I am coming from."

GENDER

Female students quickly learn that gender relations are quite different in Barbados. Often, the most difficult adjustment for women students is learning how to deal with the frequent and aggressive advances of Bajan men. At the end of her first week in the field, Jenny described a plight common to the students:

> When I walk through the village, the guys who hang out at the rum shop yell comments. I have never heard men say some of the things they tell me here. My friend Andrew tells me that most of the comments are actually compliments. Yet I still feel weird. ... I am merely an object that they would like to conquer. I hate that feeling, so I am trying to get to know these guys. I figure that if they

know me as a person and a friend, they will stop with the demeaning comments. Maybe it's a cultural thing they do to all women.

Indeed, many Bajan men feel it is their right as males to accost women in public with hissing, appreciative remarks, and offers of sex. This sexual bantering is tolerated by Bajan women who generally ignore the men's comments. Most women consider it harmless, if annoying; some think it flattering. Students like Jenny, however, are not sure what to make of it. They do not know whether it is being directed at them because local men think white girls are "loose" or whether Bajan men behave in this fashion towards all women. Anxious to be accepted and not wanting to be rude or culturally insensitive, most female students tolerate the remarks the best they can, while searching for a strategy to politely discourage them. Most find that as people get to know them by name, the verbal harassment subsides.

But they still must get accustomed to other sexual behavior. For example, when invited to their first neighborhood parties most are shocked at the sexually explicit dancing, in which movements imitate intercourse. One female student wrote, after having been to several fetes or parties:

> I was watching everyone dance when I realized that even the way we dance says a lot about culture. We are so conservative at home. Inhibited. In the U.S. one's body is a personal, private thing, and when it is invaded we get angry. We might give a boyfriend some degree of control over our bodies, but no one else. Bajans aren't nearly as possessive about their bodies. Men and women can freely move from one dance partner to the next without asking, and then grind the other person—it's like having sex with your clothes on.

Students discover that even more than in the U.S., women are regarded by men as both subordinates and sexual objects. Masculinity is largely based on men's sexual conquest of women and on their ability to give them pleasure. Being sexually active, a good sex partner, and becoming a father, all enhance young men's status among their male peers. As time passes, the students see male dominance in other areas of Barbadian life as well: that women earn less than men, are more likely to be unemployed, and are less likely to attain political office, all despite their doing better and going further in school. They conclude that though U.S. society is sexist, Barbados is far more so.

MATERIALISM AND CONSUMPTION

Many students arrive at a new awareness of wealth and materialism. One of the strongest initial perceptions the students have of their villages is that the people are poor: most of their houses are tiny, their diets are restricted, and they have few of the amenities and comforts the students are accustomed to. Even little things may remind them of the difference in wealth, as Betsy recounted after her first week in the field:

> At home [Vermont] when I go into a convenience store and buy a soda, I don't think twice about handing the clerk a 20 dollar bill. But here when you hand a man in the rum shop a 20 dollar bill [equals $10 USD], they often ask if you have something smaller. It makes me self conscious of how wealthy I appear, and of how little money the rum shop man makes in a day.

The initial response of the students to the poverty they perceive around them is to feel embarrassed and even guilty that they have and consume so much. However as the students get to know families better, they no longer see poverty. Even the houses no longer seem so small. They discover that most people not only manage quite well on what they have but are also reasonably content. In fact, most students eventually come to believe that the villagers are more satisfied with their lives than are most Americans. Whether or not this is true, it's an important perception for students, whose ideas about happiness have been shaped by an ethos which measures success and satisfaction materially. About his host family, Dan said:

> I ate off the same plate and drank from the same cup every night. We only had an old fridge, an old stove, and an old TV, and a few dishes and pots and pans. But that was plenty. Mrs. H. never felt like she needed any more. And after awhile I never felt like I needed any more either.

Ellen recounted her reactions to a car that her host father had just purchased.

> He was thrilled, talking about how great this car was. When he pulled up in a used Toyota Corolla, I laughed to myself. It was the exact same car that I had just bought at home, the only car that a poor student could afford, and by American standards certainly nothing flashy. But to my host father it was top of the line, and he was ecstatic. To me it was a reminder that everything is relative. ...

Many said that when they returned home from Barbados they were surprised at the number of their possessions. Compared to Barbadians, their middle-class parents' lifestyle seemed incredibly extravagant and wasteful. When the students return to campus they don't bring nearly as many things with them as they had before. Some go through their drawers and closets and give the things they don't really need to the Good Will or Salvation Army. Most said they would no longer take luxuries like hot showers for granted. Amy wrote:

> When I came back I saw how out of control the students here are. It's just crazy. They want so much, they talk about how much money they need to make, as if these things are necessities and you'll never be happy without them. Maybe I was like that too, but now I know I don't need those things; sure I'd like a great car, but I don't need it.

When alumni of the program were asked in a survey how they had been changed by their experience in Barbados, most believed they were less materialistic today. For example, Susan said, "I remember bringing some perfume to Barbados because I was used to wearing it every day. But when I got there I only wore it once, it just seemed unnecessary, and I haven't really worn perfume since. Even now, ten years later, I don't mind wearing the same clothes often. I just think Barbados taught me how to find comfort in simple things."

SOCIAL CLASS

American students, particularly compared to their European counterparts, have little understanding of social class. Even after several weeks in Barbados, most students are fairly oblivious to class and status distinctions in their villages. The U.S. suburbs that most grow up in are fairly homogenous in social composition and housing. Most homes fall in the same general price range. In contrast, the Barbadian villages the students live in exhibit a broad spectrum, ranging from large two-story masonry homes usually built by returning migrants to tiny board houses owned by farmers who eke out a living from a few acres. The students are slow to translate such differences in the material conditions of village households into class differences. Also, Barbadians' well-developed class consciousness, fostered by three centuries of British rule, is foreign to U.S. students steeped in a culture that stresses, at least in its rhetoric, egalitarianism.

Students gradually become aware of status distinctions from the comments that their host families make about other people. But they also learn about class and status by making mistakes, by violating norms concerning relationships between different categories of people. After Kristen walked home through the village carrying a bundle on her head, she learned that there are different standards of behavior for the more affluent families. "Mrs C. told me never to do that again, that only poor people carry things on their heads, and that my doing it reflected badly on her family."

As in most field situations, the first villagers to offer the student friendship are sometimes marginal members of the community and this creates special problems because the students are usually guests in the homes of respectable and often high-status village families. Host parents become upset when they discover their student has been seeing a disreputable man or woman. Most serious is the occasional female student who goes out with a lower-class local man or "beach boy." She enters into this relationship oblivious to what the local reaction might be, and equally oblivious to how little privacy there is in a village where everyone knows everyone else's business. Amy said she wrongly assumed that people would look favorably upon her going out with a local guy because it would show that she wasn't prejudiced and that she found Blacks just as desirable as whites. Johanna was befriended by some Rastafarians living nearby—orthodox Rastas who wore no clothes, lived off the land, and slept in caves in the hills above her village. When villagers discovered she had been seeing the Rastas, her home stay mother nearly evicted her and others gave her the cold shoulder. Johanna wrote in her field notes, "I have discovered the power of a societal norm: nice girls don't talk to Rastas. When girls who were formerly nice talk to Rastas, they cease to be known as nice. Exceptions none."

NEW PERSPECTIVES ON BEING AMERICAN

In learning about Barbadian society, students inevitably compare Barbadian customs to the way things are done at home in the U.S. The students are often assisted in such comparisons by villagers who are curious and ask questions. Most villagers already have opinions about the U.S., mostly formed from watching American television and movies, from observing visiting tourists and, for some, from their own travel. The students are surprised at how much Bajans, even the lesser educated, know about the U.S. They discover, however, that the villagers' perspectives are often at odds with their own. Jay put it best: "They have a love/hate attitude towards the U.S. They think of the U.S. as a great place to shop, and that we have good movies and good fashion. But, they also think we are dumb, too talkative, too full of ourselves, too patriotic, and that our government is dangerous." Indeed, most students learn that Bajans like the open friendliness and sunny optimism of individual Americans, and they admire the economic opportunities and freedoms the society affords. But they also think middle class Americans are pampered and overly materialistic. Bajans are puzzled about why such a wealthy nation has so many people living in poverty and in prisons, and why, unlike poor Caribbean islands, there is not good health care for everyone. They also don't think black people get a fair shake in America.

Early in the term, students often find themselves defending the United States from criticism and stereotypes. Jay described in his journal getting very annoyed when a guest at his host family's dinner table railed against the U.S. and talked about the chemical adulteration of American chicken. He knew this to be true, but later he said, "I couldn't take it anymore and fought back. I felt like an idiot afterward, defending American chicken."

Over time the students become less defensive, and more sympathetic to the criticisms, particularly to the notion of Americans as pampered and wastefully materialistic, and that the U.S. government is somewhat of an international bully. What makes our students question their own society after a few months in Barbados? Part of the answer is found in their growing appreciation of Bajan life and local people. They begin to see things from the perspective of their village friends. They begin to understand the degree to which American culture, especially its media, music, entertainment, and consumer goods, overwhelms local cultures. They see that many Bajans, for example, know more about the American President than their own Governor General or Prime Minister, and that they know Tiger Woods and Kobe Bryant better than their own cricket stars. Some students become quite critical of the U.S. government, especially its often unilateral and self-interested policies, as when it refused to sign international treaties on global warming, on land mines, and on a World Criminal Court.

The students' exposure to North Americans vacationing in Barbados also influences their perceptions of themselves as Americans. When they go to the beach or town they often encounter tourists and are reminded of villagers' criticisms. They are sometimes embarrassed by what they see and hear—Americans who are loud, demanding, and even condescending, in their dealings with locals. Some tourists (though not just Americans) enter shops and walk the streets in skimpy beach attire never thinking that it may be offensive to local people. Students are appalled that tourists can come all the way to Barbados to vacation and hardly know anything about the place or its people. They are irritated that many tourists only view Barbados as a playground—a place to lounge on the beach, swim, snorkel, dive, sail, dance, and drink—and have little curiosity about its geography, history of colonization and slavery, or current underdevelopment. They are horrified when they themselves are mistaken for tourists, since they take pride in their knowledge of local culture. One outcome of this, say the alumni of the field programs, is that when they travel today they believe they are more curious and sensitive than other tourists. Some even try to pass themselves off as Canadian.

EDUCATION

Most students return home from Barbados with a more positive attitude towards education. I believe this stems both from their experiences in doing research and from seeing the high value that villagers place on formal education, which is their chief means of upward mobility. Students are accorded respect and adult status largely because they are working toward a university degree. Also, as the weeks pass, most students become deeply involved in their own research. They are surprised at how much satisfaction they get from doing something that they previously regarded as "work." Students from past terms have said they didn't see education as an end in itself, something to be enjoyed, until doing fieldwork in Barbados. Emily wrote about her attitude change after returning from the field:

> I feel isolated from many of my old friends on campus, and I no longer feel guilty missing social events. … I appreciate my education more and I do much more work for my own understanding and enjoyment rather than just for the exam or grades. I find myself on a daily basis growing agitated with those who don't appreciate what is being offered to them here. Several of my classmates blow off class and use other peoples' notes. A lot of what I feel is from seeing how important education was to my Bajan friends in Barbados compared to the lax attitude of my friends here.

Students spend much of their time in the field talking to people; a good part of each day is spent in conversations which they must direct onto the topics that they are investigating. To succeed at their studies, they learn to be inquisitive, to probe sensitively into the villager's knowledge of events and culture. They learn to concentrate, to listen to what they are being told, and later to recall it so that they can record it in field notes. They become proficient at maintaining lengthy conversations with adults and at asking pertinent questions. These are interpersonal and communication skills they bring back with them and make use of in many aspects of their own lives, and in their future work.

Clearly, getting to know another culture is to look in the proverbial mirror and get a glimpse of oneself and of what it means to be American. As the world's economies intertwine and its societies move closer to becoming a "global village," it is more imperative than ever that we seek to understand other peoples and cultures. Without understanding there can be neither respect, mutual prosperity, nor lasting peace. "The tragedy about Americans," noted Mexican novelist Carlos Fuentes, "is that they understand others so little." Students who study abroad not only enrich themselves but in countless small ways help bridge the gulf between "them" and "us."

Fieldwork on an Urban Street Corner

By Elliot Liebow

A pickup truck drives slowly down the street. The truck stops as it comes abreast of a man sitting on a cast-iron porch and the white driver calls out, asking if the man wants a day's work. The man shakes his head and the truck moves on up the block, stopping again whenever idling men come within calling distance of the driver. At the Carry-out corner, five men debate the question briefly and shake their heads no to the truck. The truck turns the corner and repeats the same performance up the next street. In the distance, one can see one man, then another, climb into the back of the truck and sit down. It starts and stops, the truck finally disappears.

What is it we have witnessed here? A labor scavenger rebuffed by his would-be prey? Lazy, irresponsible men turning down an honest day's pay for an honest day's work? Or a more complex phenomenon marking the intersection of economic forces, social values, and individual of mind and body?

Let us look again at the driver of the truck. He has been able to recruit only two or three men from each twenty or fifty he contacts. To him, it is clear that the others simply do not choose to work. Singly or in groups, belly-empty or belly-full, sullen or gregarious, drunk or sober, they confirm what he has read, heard and knows from his own experience: these men wouldn't take a job if it were handed to them on a platter.[*]

---

[*] By different methods, perhaps, some social scientists have also located the problem in the men themselves, in their unwillingness or lack of desire to work: "To improve the underprivileged worker's performance, one must help him to learn to want ... higher social goals for himself and his children. ... The problem of changing the work habits and motivation of [lower class] people ... is a problem of changing the goals, the ambitions, and the level of cultural and occupational aspiration of the underprivileged worker." (Emphasis in original.) Allison Davis, "The Motivation of the Underprivileged Worker," p. 90.

Elliot Liebow, "Fieldwork on an Urban Street Corner," *Conformity & Conflict: Readings in Cultural Anthropology*. Little Brown and Company, Inc., 1971, pp. 229–231. Permission to reprint granted by the publisher.

Quite apart from the question of whether or not this is true of some of the men he sees on the street, it is clearly not true of all of them. If it were, he would not have come here in the first place; or having come, he would have left with an empty truck. It is not even true of most of them, for most of the men he sees on the street this weekday morning do, in fact, have jobs. But since, at the moment, they are neither working nor sleeping, and since they hate the depressing room or apartment they live in, or because there is nothing to do there,* or because they want to get away from their wives or anyone else living there, they are out on the street, indistinguishable from those who do not have jobs or do not want them. Some, like Boley, a member of a trash-collection crew in a suburban housing development, work Saturdays and are off on this weekday. Some, like Sweets, work nights cleaning up middle-class trash, dirt, dishes, and garbage, and mopping the floors of the office buildings, hotels, restaurants, toilets, and other public places dirtied during the day. Some men work for retail businesses such as liquor stores which do not begin the day until ten o'clock. Some laborers, like Tally, have already come back from the job because the ground was too wet for pick and shovel or because the weather was too cold for pouring concrete. Other employed men stayed off the job today for personal reasons: Clarence to go to a funeral at eleven this morning and Sea Cat to answer a subpoena as a witness in a criminal proceeding.

Also on the street, unwitting contributors to the impression taken away by the truck driver, are the halt and the lame. The man on the cast-iron steps strokes one gnarled arthritic hand with the other and says he doesn't know whether or not he'll live long enough to be eligible for Social Security. He pauses, then adds matter-of-factly, "Most times, I don't care whether I do or don't." Stoopy's left leg was polio-withered in childhood. Raymond, who looks as if he could tear out a fire hydrant, coughs up blood if he bends or moves suddenly. The quiet man who hangs out in front of the Saratoga apartments has a steel hook strapped onto his left elbow. And had the man in the truck been able to look into the wine-clouded eyes of the man in the green cap, he would have realized that the man did not even understand he was being offered a day's work.

Others, having had jobs and been laid off, are drawing unemployment compensation (up to $44 per week) and have nothing to gain by accepting work which pays little more than this and frequently less.

Still others, like Bumdoodle the numbers man, are working hard at illegal ways of making money, hustlers who are on the street to turn a dollar any way they can: buying and selling sex, liquor, narcotics, stolen goods, or anything else that turns up.

Only a handful remains unaccounted for. There is Tonk, who cannot bring himself to take a job away from the corner, because, according to the other men, he suspects his wife

---

* The comparison of sitting at home alone with being in jail is commonplace.

will be unfaithful if given the opportunity. There is Stanton, who has not reported to work for four days now, not since Bernice disappeared. He bought a brand new knife against her return. She had done this twice before, he said, but not for so long and not without warning, and he had forgiven her. But this time, "I ain't got it in me to forgive her again." His rage and shame are there for all to see as he paces the Carry-out and the corner, day and night, hoping to catch a glimpse of her.

And finally, there are those like Arthur, able-bodied men who have no visible means of support, legal or illegal, who neither have jobs nor want them. The truck driver, among others, believes the Arthurs to be representative of all the men he sees idling on the street during his own working hours. They are not, but they cannot be dismissed simply because they are a small minority. It is not enough to explain them away as being lazy or irresponsible or both because an able-bodied man with responsibilities who refuses work is, by the truck driver's definition, lazy and irresponsible. Such an answer begs the question. It is descriptive of the facts; it does not explain them.

CHAPTER THREE:
ETHNOGRAPHIC PROFILES

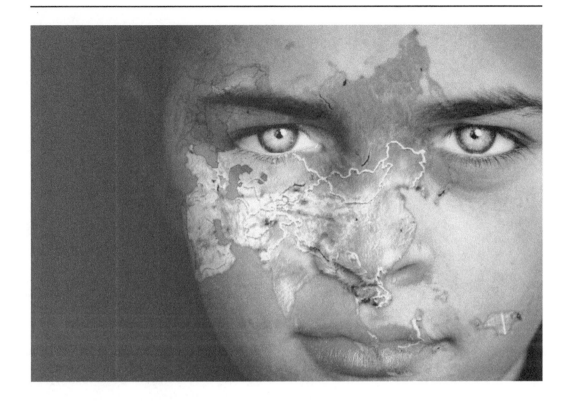

READINGS IN THIS SECTION

Introduction

By David Julian Hodges

T he ethnographic profiles of four traditional cultures are surveyed in this chapter. These include the Hopi of the American southwest, the Amish, the Inuit or Eskimo people, and the Forest People or the BaMbuti of the central African rain forest. While there are profound differences in patterns and content of belief and behavior among these cultures, areas of commonality are strikingly apparent. Although differences among cultures help explain how we fail to understand each other and bring about conflict and sometimes violence, we tend to be more alike than we are different. All cultures have some supernatural, religious, or spiritual tradition and behavior influencing myths. These traditions seek to explain creation and how the world and the body of people in question came into existence. They also serve to mitigate the anxiety associated with random misfortune and the uncertainty of life.

These cultures function to provide social organization and control, whether through religious tradition or some other set of beliefs, and they embody at least a basic system of material or economic life encompassing trade, exchange, and division of labor. These cultures exhibit features associated with stages of life, life cycle, and stratification of roles and define kinship and patterns of marriage, family life, and childrearing. It also seems to be a common feature of all cultures that they tend to be stereotyped by outsiders. Such stereotypes, while usually embodying some aspect or trace of truth, fail to grasp the whole of the reality of "other" cultures. As the articles in this collection remind us, virtually all cultures help us understand our own patterns of belief and behavior. We should also be prepared to learn from some traditional cultures that express unique and beneficial knowledge.

The Inuit people give evidence to a profound knowledge of the environment expressed as the nexus of mind and nature. This is expressed as a familiar commitment to the empirical method. They acquire their knowledge of the natural world through gradual collection and assimilation of naturalistic observations, year after year, generation after generation. In contrast, much of the experience of the past several million years of human evolution lies beyond our grasp as "advanced" cultures. It is also surprising to learn how the Inuit people thrive on a high protein, high fat diet. Wild animal fats are different from other fats. Farm animals typically have lots of highly saturated fats. Wild animals that range freely and eat what nature intended have fat that is far more healthful. The negative health effects of our food, as science is broadly beginning to fully understand and as study of cultures like the Inuit validate, are the price we pay for too little exercise and too much mass-produced food.

The difference between an orientation to community and the individual is dramatically expressed in the concept of gift in the Hopi culture. The Hopi idea of gift embraces friendship and intercommunication. The essential element in Hopi gift giving is the establishment of a substantive link between giver and receiver. The Hopi concept establishes kinship for the purpose of extending community and contrasts with Western ideas of exchange underpinned by competition and individualistic social relations. Social organization and control is an unmistakable dimension of life in Amish society. A person passes through a series of six distinct age categories or stages of socialization. The collective beliefs of the Amish are so unambiguous and so consistently reinforced throughout all stages of life, including the discouragement of intellectual curiosity, that the result is relatively uniform if isolated behavior.

The BaMbuti live and thrive in the Ituri Forest, a vast expanse of dense, damp darkness in The Republic of the Congo. The Ituri Forest is generally perceived as a profoundly hostile and frightening place, except by these inhabitants of many thousand years. The BaMbuti are a pygmy people, averaging less than four and half feet in height, with a unique culture that defied reliable characterization until the twentieth century. Their material well-being seems to be based on a blend of affection, trust, and care for the forest that supplies them with what they need and a symbiotic if highly eccentric coexistence with the tribes that live in forest clearings and on its edges. The BaMbuti roam the forest at will without fear because for them there is no danger. They have no need for belief in evil spirits because they experience little hardship. For the BaMbuti, it is a good world and they are a joyous people who express their religion, to the extent that it can be called that, by dancing and singing to their god.

The Hopi

By Peter M. Whiteley

In 1852, shortly after the United States had nominally annexed Hopi country, in northern Arizona, the Hopi people arranged for a diplomatic packet to reach President Millard Fillmore at the White House. Part message and part magical gift, the packet was delivered by a delegation of five prominent men from another Pueblo tribe, the Tewas of Tesuque Pueblo in New Mexico, who wanted to gain legal protection from Anglo and Hispanic settlers who were encroaching on their lands. The delegation traveled for nearly three months, on horseback, steamboat, and train, from Santa Fe to Washington, D.C., more than 2,600 miles away. The five men spoke fluent Spanish, the dominant European language of the region at the time—which made them ideally suited to convey the gift packet and its message to the president.

At the time, no U.S. government official had visited the Hopi (and few would do so before the 1890s). Their "unique diplomatic pacquet," in the words of the nineteenth-century ethnologist Henry Rowe Schoolcraft, offered "friendship and intercommunication … opening, symbolically, a road from the Moqui [Hopi] country to Washington." The packet was in two parts. The first part comprised two pahos, or prayer-sticks, at either end of a long cotton cord, dyed for part of its length. Separating the dyed from the undyed part of the cord were six varicolored feathers, knotted into a bunch. The pahos "represent the Moqui [Hopi] people and the President [respectively]," Schoolcraft wrote; "the cord is the road which separates them; the [bunch of feathers] tied to the cord is the meeting point."

As well as encoding a message, the pahos were an offering of a kind that Hopi deities such as Taawa, the Sun god, traditionally like to receive. By giving the president pahos worthy of the Sun, the Hopi signaled their expectation that he would reciprocate. Just as the Sun, on receiving the appropriate offerings, would send rain clouds for sustaining life and growth, so, too, the president would send protection for Hopi lives and lands—in this instance, protection from assaults by neighboring tribes such as the Navajo.

Peter M. Whiteley, "The Hopi," *Natural History*, November 2004, pp. 26–31. Permission to reprint granted by the publisher.

The second part of the packet comprised a cornstalk cigarette filled with tobacco ("to be smoked by the president") and a small cornhusk package that enclosed honey-soaked cornmeal. According to the Tesuque delegation, the honey-meal package was "a charm to call down rain from heaven." When the president smoked the cigarette, he would exhale clouds of smoke, which would sympathetically attract the clouds of the sky. Then, when he chewed the cornmeal and spat the wild honey on ground that needed rain, the Tesuque statement concluded, "the Moquis assure him that it [the rain] will come."

In sum, the packet was three things at once: message, offering, and gift of magical power. In conveying those elements, the Hopi sought to open diplomatic relations with the U.S.

But their intent appears to have been lost on their recipient. As so often happens when two cultures make contact, deep misunderstandings can arise: What does a gift mean? What, if anything, does the gift giver expect in return? Do the giver and the recipient both assign the same value to the gift? In twenty-five years of ethnographic fieldwork with the Hopi, it has been my goal to learn something of their history and culture. Recently I turned my attention to certain important events, such as the Millard Fillmore episode, that might shed light on how Hopi society changed as the U.S. developed. In that context Hopi gift giving and the ways it functions as a pillar of Hopi social organization have been central to my studies. One lesson of my work shines through: When nations exchange gifts, all the parties would do best to keep in mind the old adage, "It's the thought that counts."

* * *

Given the differences between Hopi and Western traditions and culture, perhaps it is not surprising that the Hopi idea of "gift" is only loosely equivalent to the Western one. In 1852 the Hopi people were still little affected by outside populations, and Hopi land use spread across much of northern Arizona and even into southern Utah. At that time, the Hopi lifestyle was traditional, based on farming, foraging, and some pastoralism. Even today, important elements of the subsistence economy persist, though wage labor and small business provide supplemental income.

The Hopi typically divide their work according to gender. Work done by men (such as farming and harvesting of crops) is perceived as a gift to the women; work done by women (such as gardening, gathering of pinion nuts, grasses, wild fruits, berries, and the like) is perceived as a gift to the men. Women also own and manage the distribution of their household's goods and crops. In fact, Hopi women control most of the material economic life, whereas Hopi men largely control the ritual and spiritual aspects.

The Hopi take part in an elaborate cycle of religious ceremonies, to which a range of specialized offices and privileges is attached. But individuals gain those distinctive social positions not through material wealth but rather through gender and kinship relations, which are ordered in a matrilineal manner. In fact, clan heads and chiefs of religious societies are typically worse off materially than the average member of the clan. Hopi leaders are supposed to be materially poor, and a wealthy individual is often criticized as qahopi, un-Hopi, for failing to share. Wealth and status among the Hopi is thus phrased in ritual terms: a poor person is one without ceremonial prerogatives, not one without money. So averse are the Hopi to material accumulation that in May 2004, for the second time, they voted against casino gambling, despite substantial poverty on the reservation.

Does such a primacy of value placed on ceremonial roles explain the evanescent nature of the gift given to President Fillmore? In what world of meaning did the packet represent great value? Indeed, what's in a gift?

* * *

Anthropologists have been making hay of that last question ever since 1925, when the French anthropologist Marcel Mauss published his groundbreaking Essai sur le Don (translated into English as "The Gift"). Mauss convincingly argued that in small-scale societies (10,000 or fewer persons) gifts are "total social facts." What he meant is that, in gift- or barter-based social systems, divisions of social life into discrete domains—such as economy, politics, law, or religion—are meaningless; each sphere interpenetrates and overlaps the others.

As in strict barter, an exchange in Hopi culture that begins by making a gift to someone does not involve money, but it does require reciprocity. Thus goods, services, or knowledge "given" to an individual or a group are answered with something of equivalent value. "Gifts" develop an interconnectedness between Hopi individuals in a way that outright purchases cannot. Furthermore, the Hopi offer girls in a much broader range of circumstances than people in Western cultures do, and the value of those gifts extends to the religious realm, tying individuals and groups to each other and to the realm of the spirits.

Probably the key to understanding a gift-based system such as that of the Hopi is to recognize that such systems are built on kinship. "Kinship"—the godzilla that has driven multitudes of college students screaming from anthropology 101—is, in this regard at least, straightforward. It means simply that the great majority of human social activity is framed in terms of reciprocal family ties. Where all personal relationships are cast within the "kinship idiom" there are no members of the society who are not kin to me, nor I to them.

Kinship terms encode behavioral expectations as well as familial role. As anthropologists never tire of saying, such terms are primarily social, not biological: obviously if I call fifteen women "mother," as the average Hopi can do, I do not assume that each woman physically gave birth to me. But my "mothers" all have rights and duties in relation to me. And, reciprocally, I have duties and rights with respect to them: in fact, their duties are my rights, and my duties are their rights in the relationship. That is what reciprocity is all about. You give me food, I plant your cornfield, to give a crude example. But, in a kinship society, such a basic structure of mutual expectations forms the foundation for an entire apparatus of courtesy and manners, deference and respect, familiarity or distance. Those expectations are concretely expressed by gifts—spontaneous and planned, routine and special, trivial and grand. Gifts are thus communications in a language of social belonging.

* * *

So-called gift economies entail a certain kind of sociality, or sense of what it means to belong to a community. In such an economy, one gives a gift to mark social relations built on kinship and altruism, but without the expectation of direct repayment. According to some arguments, gifts are also given to foster a sense of community, as well as sustainable interrelations with the local environment. In fact, in some respects the giver still "owns" some part of the gift, and it is the intangible connection between the two parties, mediated by the gift, that forms the basis of interpersonal relationships.

In contrast, in exchange economies, commodities dominate social interchange. Competitive markets, governed by the profit motive, connect buyer and seller, and social relations are characterized by individualism. A gift, once given, belongs entirely to the recipient; only when the item given has sentimental value does it keep the bond between giver and recipient alive.

That is not to say the Hopi did not engage in the more impersonal, "Western" forms of material exchange. In the Hopi language, as in English, several words describe how an item is transferred from one person to another: maqa ("to give"); hùuya ("to barter or trade"); and tu'i ("to buy"). Those words all antedate the arrival of Europeans—and anthropological classifications. Barter and purchase, as well as gifts, have all long been present in Hopi life. Furthermore, gift exchange in the West can also function as it does among the Hopi, as part of kinship obligations or ordinary social life.

What is distinctive about Hopi custom is the fact that the gift economy is responsible for the great majority of exchanges. Furthermore, there is no such thing as a free gift. The strong interpersonal bonds created by a gift make giving almost de rigueur at ceremonial events. Gifts, particularly gifts of food or utensils, are transmitted during ceremonies of personal milestones (at a birth or a marriage), as well as at public gatherings.

For example, at the annual so-called basket dances, girls and women distribute a variety of objects they have collected for the occasion. The dances illustrate the Hopi lack of acquisitiveness. The women form a semicircle and dance and sing; after each song two girls fling gifts into the crowd of men assembled outside the circle. Among the gifts are valuable baskets and buckskins, though inexpensive utensils and manufactured items are also popular. Each man zealously grabs for the flying objects, and if two men happen to catch the same item, both wrestle with the object, often until it has been totally destroyed.

Although gift giving has been a pillar of Hopi society, trade has also flourished in Hopi towns since prehistory, with a network that extended from the Great Plains to the Pacific Coast, and from the Great Basin, centered on present-day Nevada and Utah, to the Valley of Mexico. Manufactured goods, raw materials, and gems drove the trade, supplemented by exotic items such as parrots. The Hopis were producers as well, manufacturing large quantities of cotton cloth and ceramics for the trade. To this day, interhousehold trade and barter, especially for items of traditional manufacture for ceremonial use (such as basketry, bows, cloth, moccasins, pottery, and rattles), remain vigorous.

For hundreds of years, at least, the Hopi traded with the Rio Grande Pueblos to acquire turquoise, heishi (shell necklaces), and buckskins; one long string of heishi, for instance, was worth two Hopi woven cotton mantas. Similarly, songs, dances, and other ritual elements were often exchanged for an agreed-upon equivalent.

The high value the Hopi placed on the items they acquired by trade correlate, in many respects, with the value Europeans placed on them. Silver, for instance, had high value among both Westerners and Native Americans as money and as jewelry. Siiva, the Hopi word both for "money" and for "silver jewelry" was borrowed directly from the English word "silver" Paper money itself was often treated the way traditional resources were: older Hopi men bundled it and stored it in trunks, stacked by denomination.

It was not until the 1890s, however, that silver jewelry began to be produced by the Hopi. A man named Sikyatala learned silversmithing from a Zuni man, and his craftsmanship quickly made silver jewelry into treasured adornments. Those among the Hopi who cared for it too much, though, were criticized for vanity; one nickname, Siisiva ("[wearing] a lot of silver"), characterized a fop.

Some jewels, such as turquoise, traditionally had a sacred value, beyond adornment. Even today, flakes of turquoise are occasionally offered to the spirits in religious ceremonies. Turquoise and shell necklaces appear in many ritual settings, frequently adorning the costumes of katsinas (ceremonial figures) and performers in the social dances.

How much the Hopi value turquoise becomes apparent toward the close of a ritual enactment known as the Clown Ceremony. The "clowns"—more than mere entertainers—represent unbridled human impulses. Warrior katsinas arrive to punish the clowns for licentious behavior and teach them good Hopi behavior: modest and quiet in conduct, careful and decorous in speech, abstemious and sharing about food, and unselfish about other things. The clowns fail miserably (and hilariously) at their lessons. Eventually the warrior chief presents an ultimatum: stop flaunting chaos or die. The clown chief then offers him a turquoise necklace as a "mortgage" on the clowns' lives. The warrior chief accepts, the downs receive a lesser punishment, and community life goes on—not with perfection, but with a human mixture of the virtuous and the flawed.

* * *

In Hopi tradition, the first clan among the Hopi, and the one that supplied the kikmongwi, or village chief, was Bear. When other clans arrived, their leaders approached the kikmongwi to request entry into the village. He asked what they had to contribute, such as a beneficial ceremony. So challenged, each clan performed its ceremony, and if successful, say, in producing rain, its members were invited to live in the village, assigned an area for housing, and granted agricultural lands to work in the valley below. In return, the clan agreed to perform its ceremony, as part of a cycle of ceremonies throughout the year, and to intermarry with the other clans of the community, a practice called exogamous marriage. In that way, the Snake clan brought the Snake Dance, the Badger clan introduced principal katsina ceremonies, and the Fire clan brought the Warriors' society to the Hopi village. The villages thus came to be made up of mutually interdependent clans.

One of the essential principles expressed here, and the very cornerstone of Hopi society and sociality, is the exchange of mutually beneficial gifts—ceremonies for land, people in exogamous marriage—and the relationships reconfigured by those exchanges. And the same model is extended to the supernatural world: the gods must be propitiated with offerings of ritual gifts, and thus reminded of their dependence upon and obligations to mortal people.

The items sent to President Fillmore conform to the archetypal Hopi offering. Seeking to incorporate the president into the Hopi world, the appropriate strategy was to give him valuable presents that sought something in return, and to make sure he understood what that meant. Addressing him with prayer-sticks the way they might address the Sun father, the delegation sought to engage him within the gifting and kinship idiom. The instructions delivered with the packet—even across a succession of translations—spoke clearly of the Hopi intent. As with the turquoise mortgage of the katsina clowns, the idea of reciprocity is central. If the president wants more of, say, rain-magic, he must give back: he must receive the gift and its political proposal, and provide something in return.

* * *

Alas, the magico-religious sensibility of the Hopi worldview and the offer of serial reciprocity clashed with Manifest Destiny and the assimilationist ideology of Fillmore's presidency. Historical records make it clear that he did not smoke the cigarette, nor chew nor spit

Hopi pueblo cliff homes

the honey-meal, and, so far as we know, he sent no formal reply. None of the objects has survived.

What the five men of the Tesuque delegation received no doubt perplexed them as much as the packet they delivered perplexed the president: Each man was given a Millard Fillmore peace medal, a Western-style business suit, and a daguerreotype portrait (all now lost, as well). They also got a tour of standard destinations in Washington, including the Patent Office and the Smithsonian Institution, where they were introduced to the "wonders of electricity," according to a contemporary newspaper account in the Daily National

Intelligencer. In their meeting with Fillmore they heard the president say he "hoped the Great Spirit would bless and sustain them till they again returned to the bosom of their families."

Certainly Fillmore expressed the goodwill of the U.S. toward the Pueblos in general and to the Tesuque party in particular—who, in all probability, conveyed that sentiment to the Hopi. But the dissonance between gift and exchange economies helps explain why the Hopis did not achieve their goals. (The U.S. did not protect the Hopi from intrusions by the Navajo or by anyone else.)

The Hopi sought to embrace the president in their own sphere of sociality and mutuality—to extend kinship to him. But in a social system like the president's, where gifts are not total social facts, the political belongs in a separate domain from the religious or the economic, and kinship is secondary. The gift of a jeweled sword, for instance, might have impressed Fillmore more, but for the Hopi, its strictly symbolic value—as an item for display, but with no political, religious, or social value—would not have ensured a return, a social connection built on mutual exchange. More, by Hopi standards, presenting such a gift might have seemed inhospitable and materialistic, indeed, undiplomatic and even selfish. Thus does understanding fail between nations.

The Amish

By John Hostetler and Gertrude Enders Huntington

I n all societies occupations are ascribed on the basis of age and sex. Knowledge, values, and attitudes are differentially attributed to each age classification. An individual must recognize the age category to which another person belongs in order to respond properly to him and to expect an appropriate response. Age stages differ from one society to another, but at least seven age-sex categories, according to Linton (1945:66), are universally recognized; Erikson (1950) lists eight. The Amish recognize six age categories, with several less well-defined subcategories, within their culture. The stages in the Amish life cycle are not as sharply delineated as in many cultures, and although each stage tends to correspond to a biological phase, the social functions of each group are culturally determined. Some knowledge of the age structure of Amish society is essential to understanding Amish socialization patterns and the Amishman's participation in his culture.

THE AGE STAGES

In Amish society a person passes through a series of six distinct age categories or stages of socialization as he progresses through life. Different behavior is demanded of him at each stage. The stages, from birth to death, are as follows:

Infancy The first stage covers the period from birth until the child walks. Children of this age are generally referred to as "babies."

Preschool children The second stage covers the period between walking and entrance into school, generally at the age of six or seven. Children of this stage are referred to as little children. Sometimes they are spoken of as children at home, although that phrase more often refers to all children who are unmarried and still eat and sleep under the parental roof.

John Hostetler and Gertrude Enders Huntington, "The Amish," *Children in Amish Society: Socialization and Community Education*. Holt, Rinehart and Winston, 1971, pp. 12–33. Permission to reprint granted by the publisher.

School children Children attending school are referred to as scholars by the Amish. These children are fulfilling the eight years of elementary schooling required by the state. They attend either public schools or Amish schools and are between the ages of 6 and 16.

Young people Young people or youth are those who have completed eight years of schooling and can therefore do a full day's work. Young people participate in the social life of their peers as distinct from the family-centered social activity that characterizes the other age stages in Amish culture. Young people are between the ages of 14 or 16 and marriage, which usually takes place in the early twenties. There are several subdivisions within this age stage: Those young people who have finished elementary school but are not yet 16 are generally not full participants in the social life of this group. Those young, people who have been baptized are, in many communities, no longer full participants in this age group for they have voluntarily chosen to abide by the rules of the church and are no longer testing the boundaries of their culture. The draft, which removes Amish young men from the community for two years of alternative service, has not become integrated into the age patterning of Amish culture. It can affect either young people or adults.

Adulthood Baptism signifies religious adulthood, but marriage and the birth of the first child brings social adulthood. Generally the time interval between baptism and marriage is relatively short. The major activity during adulthood is childrearing.

Old folks Adults generally retire sometime after their youngest child has married and started to raise a family. They move from the big house into the grandfather house or to the edge of a village. They are cared for by their children and exert a conservative influence as they fulfill their accepted role of admonishing the young.

ADULTHOOD

Age grading in Amish society must begin with a discussion of adults, for the family is the basic unit of Amish culture. The most important family activity is childrearing. Household size may vary from those married pairs who have no children to those having 14 children or more. Studies of family size show that for completed families the average number of children is slightly over seven. Ask an Amishman how big his church district is and he will answer you with the number of families, not with the number of individuals. An Amish schoolteacher will tell you how many families attend the school, and when she introduces the children, she will often introduce them by family rather than by grade.

The Amish family is marked by its stability. Theologically the Amish believe that the commitment to one's spouse is second only to the commitment to God. Husband and wife become one flesh, a single unit separable only by God. For the Amishman, the question of sacrificing his family for his profession never comes up. The family comes first. A job is of no intrinsic importance; it is necessary, because it supplies the economic basis for the family. The work of the household should provide vocational education for the children and fulfill the biblical standard, "In the sweat of thy face shalt thou eat bread." Although the Amish family is patriarchal and the husband is the head of the wife, the wife has an immortal soul and is therefore not merely an extension of her husband, nor wholly subservient to him. Her relative position is illustrated by her position in church, where she has an equal vote but not an equal voice.

Parents are expected to serve as examples for the child. An Amish minister admonishes, "Our lives should, by all means, be separated from the world, and be so consecrated, that our children can see by our words and deeds. ..." Parents do not have individual rights; they have responsibilities and obligations for the correct nurture of their children. An Amishman says, "I am a father. ... I must teach, train, admonish, chasten, love, and guide my children, and all this with patience and wisdom." In his final admonition before his death, an Amish preacher wrote to his sons, "The responsibility to teach your children lies fully upon you [parents]." Parents are believed to be accountable to God for their children's spiritual welfare. The Amish quote Menno Simons, the sixteenth-century founder of the Mennonites, who says, "Watch over their [your children's] souls as long as they are under your care, lest you lose also your own salvation on their account."

Amish parents act as a single unit when dealing with their children and reinforce one another. Referring to repeated misbehavior of one of her children, an Amish woman said, "We finally decided we would have to spank him if he did it again. He was late again so Amos took him into the bedroom to spank him. I went too because I should help by being there. The boy must know that both of us are concerned." Admonitions to parents in the sermons and in Amish writings are directed not to fathers as such or to mothers alone, but to parents. Parents are taught that if there is a difference of opinion between them, they should discuss it privately and prayerfully and always be of one mind when disciplining the child. The wife is expected to support her husband in all things, especially in his relationship with other people, whether it be their children, parents, or friends and neighbors. The husband in turn should be considerate of his wife on a physical, emotional, and spiritual level. The ideal is to be individuals to one another, but of one mind to all others.

Amish parents are remarkably consistent in the demands they make on their children and in the behavior they expect of them. They constantly reinforce one another and there is general consensus within the community as to how children ought to be raised and how they ought to behave at different stages.

Children function as socializing agents for their parents in a variety of ways. As parents strive to be good examples for their children, they modify their own behavior. In their efforts to teach their children to become good Amishmen, they become better Amishmen themselves. The birth of a child enhances the status of his parents in the community; they attain full adulthood with parenthood. Children take up so much time and energy that the parents are not likely to have time for other interests. Today, because most doctors refuse to come to the house, the large majority of Amish babies are born in the hospital. Medically this is advantageous, but culturally it is not. Home births have a positive value in uniting the family. They demonstrate the wife's unique, dramatic contribution and strengthen her position in the patriarchal family. The husband and wife grow closer by sharing the experience of childbirth. Amish women do not see childbirth as threatening, but as status-enhancing. The most traditional Amish have continued to oppose hospital deliveries and with the help of sympathetic doctors or midwives some of them still quietly give birth at home. Birth control is not practiced among the conservative Amish.

INFANCY

Babyhood is the stage between birth and walking. The Amish believe a baby is a pleasure. He may be enjoyed without fear of self-pride, for the baby is a gift from God and not primarily an extension of the parents. At this tender age a baby can do no wrong. If he cries he is in need of comfort, not discipline. It is believed that a baby can be spoiled by wrong handling, especially by nervous, tense handling, but the resultant irritability is the fault of the environment, not the baby; he remains blameless. An Amish baby is born into the community. He is never spoken of as "a little stranger," but is welcomed as a "new woodchopper" or a "little dishwasher." Future sex roles are recognized, but there is little difference in the care given a boy or girl. Each baby is greeted happily as a contribution to the security of the family and the church.

Amish babies are rarely alone. They sleep in their parents' room, are moved around the house during the day, and in a large family are held during most of their waking hours. They are diapered and bathed on their mother's lap, not on a hard, cold table or tub; it is a time of happy sociability. Babies are rarely fed on a strict time schedule, but in relation to their own pattern of hunger and the work pattern of the family. Solid food is given at the family table during family meals. The family attitude is one of sharing its good food with the baby. Babies as young as five or six months don't eat well if fed alone, they believe. It is generally thought that everyone eats better in a group; eating is an important social activity. When parents are visiting, at church, traveling, or ill, friends and members of the extended family help with one another's babies. During the first year of life the baby receives solicitous care from a large number of Amish of all ages.

The relaxed handling of Amish babies within the home or the community is quite different from the care taken of them when mother and baby make an excursion into the world. The baby is tightly wrapped and covered, often hidden in his mother's shawl. Even his face may be covered in order to protect him from the "bad air." Passing strangers would probably not realize that the mother was carrying a baby. The traditional Amish dislike having their babies cared for by outsiders or even noticed by them. The way the baby is handled when the mother is shopping or traveling shows the Amish distrust of the outside world and the parents' efforts to protect the baby from its malevolent influence. Old Order Amish parents give generous attention to their babies' needs, both physical and social. This care equips the baby to trust himself and those around him (Erikson 1950:247). Babies are enjoyed by the Amish; they are believed to be gentle, responsive, and secure within the home and the Amish community, but vulnerable when out in the world. Babies are not scolded or punished, and there is no such thing as a bad baby, although there may be a difficult baby.

LITTLE CHILDREN

The preschool stage lasts from walking until entrance into elementary school. During his preschool years the Amish child is taught to respect and obey those in authority, to care for those younger and less able than he, to share with others and to help others, to do what he is taught is right and to avoid that which is wrong, to enjoy work and to fulfill his work responsibilities pleasantly. The parents' task in these years is to create a safe environment for their children. The parents live separated from the world, maintaining the boundary for their children and striving always to protect them from both physical and moral danger.

The children are taught to respect authority, and respect is shown by obedience. The Amish do not strive for blind obedience, but for obedience based on love and on the belief that those in authority have deep concern for one's welfare and know what is best. Children learn this relationship between authority and responsibility very early. The four-year-old child is expected to hand over his toy to the three-year-old if the three-year-old cries for it, but in the parents' absence the three-year-old should do what the four-year-old tells him to. However, the older child may not make arbitrary demands of the younger, and he is expected to cajole rather than force him into cooperation. The children learn in this way that authority is closely linked to responsibility for others. Those in authority must be obeyed, but they do not simply give orders; they also nurture and. protect those under their authority.

Most traditional Amish parents teach obedience by being firm and consistent, rather than by violent, confrontations or single instances of breaking the child's will. The switch is used freely, but not harshly. In their handling of disobedience, the Amish vary considerably as to the age at which and degree to which they require obedience, in the lengths to which parents will go to get obedience, and in the emotional attitude of the parents in handling a disobedient preschooler. None of the Amish condone willfulness, stubbornness, or defiance on the part of the child, but they may have different opinions as, to whether a child's behavior is caused by stubbornness or lack of understanding. The traditional Amish are matter-of-fact rather than moralistic in dealing with their children.

Work is perceived as helping others and fulfilling one's responsibility to them. A child is rarely thanked for doing his chores. Thanks are not expected for carrying out responsibilities. More often the parent may make a simple statement, "Now the floor is clean." The child is rewarded by the task having been accomplished. Work well done is its own reward. Children are trained to help one another rather than to be independent. Thus a four-year-old child will get the boots for the two-year-old and put them on for him, then instead of putting on his own boots he will wait for his older sister to help him. Although the Amish girls always wear dresses and the little boys, after they are toilet-trained, wear trousers, there is little difference in tasks they are taught to perform. Boys are encouraged to like horses and machinery, but children of both sexes accompany their father around the farm and help their mother with simple household tasks.

Young preschool children may scream to get attention or to solicit adult protection from teasing by another child or from the aggression of an age-mate. This is not acceptable for an older child, who is expected to be able to cope with the situation without summoning adult help. Tears are permitted anyone in response to deep emotion, but are discouraged as a response to physical pain or self-pity.

Amish preschool children have great freedom of movement as they accompany their father around the farm, care for a younger sibling, or run simple errands for their mother or grandmother. They are encouraged to be useful but are not pushed to tasks beyond their ability. The environment is neither harsh nor over-protective. Initiative in the physical realm is encouraged, but intellectual initiative or asking questions is severely channeled. Thus, using Erikson's classification (1950:251) of this stage as autonomy-versus-doubt, there is a dichotomy in the development of the Amish child. The Amish child develops the feeling that his physical participation in the world of adults is good, but that his questions are often a nuisance or silly. He acquires a sense of caution about initiating new ideas. Instead of asking how or why, he learns to observe and imitate on a behavioral level.

The presence of the father in and around the home is considered necessary for the proper upbringing of preschool children. As more Amish fathers work in specialized jobs such as carpentry that take them away from the home for part of each day, there is some concern expressed that the children cannot be properly taught.

The community as well as the family has an essential role to play in the socialization of the preschool child. Preschool children attend church with their parents; they sit through the long service—the girls usually with their mothers, the boys often with their fathers—learning to be considerate of others, quiet, and patient. After the service they share in the community meal and perhaps take a nap on a big bed with other Amish babies. The rest of the time they play freely and vigorously about the house and yard, safe in the presence of many adults who care for them and guide them. If a small child suddenly feels lost, someone quickly returns him to a member of his family. To the preschooler the community seems to be composed of many people, all of whom know him and protect him. He is comfortable and secure within the encompassing community.

Preschool Amish children are kept as far away from the outside world as is practical. When shopping with their parents, they stay very close to them. Little Amish children are not introduced to non-Amish and are not taught about the world outside the community. They may know

Amish schoolhouse

the exact location of many farms, but not the road to the nearest city.

The Amish generally do not send their children to kindergarten. A 1937 policy states (Beiler 1961:7): "Kindergarten is not sanctioned by the Amish people. Children of this age should be under parents' care. The nurture and admonition that Moses received while under the care of his mother was implanted so deep, that after being taught the wisdom of the Egyptians, [he] chose rather 'to suffer affliction with the people of God, than to enjoy the pleasure of sin for a season.'" In some communities children who will be first-graders in the Amish school the following autumn will visit school in the spring to become acquainted with the new surroundings.

SCHOLARS

The children in this stage, between the ages of about 6 and 15 years, are called scholars. Throughout the school years the family continues to be the primary locus for the child's socialization. Amish families continue to teach their school-age children the same attitudes and values they taught to their preschoolers, and they maintain much the same relation to them in respect to the community and the world. The parents' role is protective and supportive as well as didactic. The parent has the responsibility to punish transgressions; but also the power to forgive. Punishment is used primarily as necessary for the safety of the child: for his physical safety ("stay away from that nervous horse"), for his cultural safety ("be respectful to older people"), for his legal safety ("don't hunt without a hunting license"), or for his moral safety ("be obedient"). Rewards are used to develop the right attitudes in the child: humility, forgiveness, admission of error, sympathy, responsibility, and appreciation of work. Children are motivated primarily by concern for other people and not by fear of punishment.

The Amish, even those who have their own schools, emphasize that children are the responsibility of their parents; the school and the church are supplemental. The parents must see that their children stay within the discipline of the church. If they do not, the preacher or deacon should talk to the parents, not to the children, about their laxness. The school's task is to cooperate with the parent to preserve the faith taught by the parents, for it is the role of the family, not of the school or even the church, to make Christians of the children.

The parents of school-age children are not only teaching their children Christianity, they are also teaching them the work skills necessary to live an Amish Christianity. By the time the child is eight or nine he begins to have fairly demanding tasks to perform. Boys tend to help their fathers and girls work with their mothers. But everyone helps, regardless of sex, where he is most needed. Formerly the Amish felt secure enough about their children of six or seven, to hand them over to the world for their schooling, During the last 35 years, however, changes in the public schools and in the surrounding rural American culture have created greater problems for the Amish. Modern consolidated schools are not suitable agents of socialization for the Amish child. Two reactions to the disruptive influence of the public school are possible, both of which are currently being tried. The first is to tolerate the public school, attempting to isolate its influence and to counteract the disruption it causes. The second solution is for the Amish to build and conduct their own schools, a new undertaking for the Amish community.

The primary function of the Amish school is to teach Amish children the three R's in an environment where they do not have to learn the assumptions of twentieth-century America, where they can learn discipline, true values, and getting along with each other in life. Participants in a county Amish school meeting reported that "our goal should be that the church, the home, and the school should teach the same things. Let us not confuse our children, but help them to fill their places in the church and community." By contrast the public schools train children to function as individuals, and to find a community of their choosing in the world.

Amish elementary pupils generally have similar experiences within their families and within the community, but their contact with the world differs greatly, depending on whether they attend a public school or an Amish school. Oversimplifying somewhat for purposes of illustration, we will contrast the two types of schools as socializing agents for the Amish child of school age. A primary difference between the public and the Amish school is its relation to the community. The public school is a part of the world and the Amish feel that they have little hope of affecting it. Amish parents, therefore, participate minimally in the public schools. The Amish build their own schools, not only with their own money, but also with their own hands. They make all the decisions, within the limits of the state law, about the school calendar, the subjects to be taught, the teachers to be hired, and the books to be used. Parents, ministers, and travelers from other Amish communities are always welcome visitors at the school. Physically and emotionally the school belongs within the Amish community.

Operating private schools introduces certain problems within the Amish community. Supporting an Amish school is sometimes an economic strain. A certain amount of borrowing of techniques and practices from worldly schools is necessary. Therefore, unless carefully managed, the boundary between the world and the church may become blurred. This is especially true if the community is not "of one mind." Misunderstandings sometimes arise because the roles of the teacher and the school board members are still in the process of becoming institutionalized. Regional and national meetings, attended by teachers, board members, and ministers, are helping to define the teacher's role within both the school and the larger Amish community. Some Amish parents are also concerned that the children learn too little about the world when they attend only Amish schools. They realize that one must understand the world fairly well in order to reject it selectively and in such a way that survival is possible within the twentieth century. They feel that the children should master English and understand the ways of worldly people to the extent that is necessary for business transactions with them.

Both the public schools and the Amish schools teach the three R's, but their methods are quite different and their attitudes toward the ultimate use of the knowledge is very different. The public schools use a greater variety of material and stress speed, sometimes at the expense of accuracy. The Amish schools tend to use a more limited amount of material, but the children learn it thoroughly. They stress accuracy rather than speed, drill rather than variety, proper sequence rather than freedom of choice. The public school tends to teach subject matter as a tool needed by the child to achieve social mobility and to realize his highest individual potential. The Amish schools teach the same material, but they aim to help the child become a part of his community and remain within his community. They emphasize shared knowledge rather than individualized knowledge and the dignity of tradition rather than progress.

In the public school, children are separated from their siblings and placed into narrow age groups. Individual achievement is emphasized. In Amish schools brothers and sisters are in the same room, age grading is not so rigid, and group excellence or group competition is used as a stimulus. A whole school will strive to have a perfect score in spelling;

a chart will be kept of each class's average in the arithmetic test scores. This is similar to the use of competition in the Soviet children's collectives, where competition is used to enhance the group and build group responsibility rather than to bring praise to the individual (Bronfenbrenner 1970:50).

Public schools tend to teach that weakness is bad and should be overcome by the individual; Amish schools assume that all individuals are weak and that they need help from one another and from a higher power as well as individual effort in order to improve. Within the public school the child is regarded as a citizen and an intellect; within the Amish school, as a future Amishman and a soul. In the public schools a teacher's academic training, knowledge of his subject, and teaching techniques are the criteria for hiring. In the Amish schools the teacher's example in daily life and wisdom are more important than training and factual knowledge. Amish teachers have no tenure, for obviously someone who turns out to be a poor teacher is not fulfilling the role God intended for him and should do some other, more suitable kind of work. Public elementary school is conceived as preparing the child for high school, not as sufficient in itself. The Amish school assumes that the child will go on learning for the rest of his life, but that his formal schooling will, end with the eighth grade.

The greatest dangers of public school for the Amish child are not the differences in attitudes between his parents and his teacher, not the specific subject matter taught in the public school, not such frills as visual aids and physical education, but the possibility that he may form close personal friendships with non-Amish children and that he may become too comfortable in the ways of the world. Continuity with faith, family, and community would then be broken.

During his school years the Amish child spends most of his time outside of school with his family at home or visiting as a member of his family at the homes of friends and relatives. The family attends church as a unit, and people of all ages listen to the same service. The Amish schoolchild, unlike the typical suburban schoolchild, is usually in a mixed age group rather than isolated with his peers (Bronfenbrenner 1970:96–102, 115). If he attends an Amish school his classroom is shared with seven other grades. He knows many adults in addition to his parents, and they have a comfortable interest in him and his development.

During the elementary school years Amish children are encouraged in their efforts to make things with their own hands. Girls cook, bake, sew, and make things for their play-houses. Boys often build toys or birdhouses, and they help with the farm work, learning the necessary routine of feeding poultry and livestock. Their sense of industry is enhanced by the work of their hands, by being praised and rewarded with the results, and by being allowed to finish their products. The child in an Amish school is more than a personality in a schoolroom. His world includes his home and family, which play a central role in his development. Whether the child develops a sense of industry or inferiority (Erikson 1950:258) during the school years depends to a great extent on all the adults in his life—not only the schoolteacher. He has many role models and informal teachers.

YOUNG PEOPLE

The young people are those in the age category between 14 or 16 years of age and marriage. In this stage the Amish individual progresses toward adulthood in an orderly, clearly defined manner through a series of accepted stages. Two governmental institutions, schooling and the draft, threaten this order by prolonging childhood in one case and adolescence in the other. Forcing an Amish person to attend school daily places him in the child category, for the hours spent in school prevent him from doing a full day's work, which is the criterion for achieving the status of young adult. The alternative service program of the draft removes the young man from the community and from the opportunity to accept an adult role, thereby extending his adolescence. When the individual is prevented by the state from achieving a status position within his culture believed to be his due, both the individual and the culture suffer.

Compulsory schooling appeared with the growth of the industrialized state and is tied to industry, government, and the military. In the United States, school is a prerequisite for membership in a managerial middle class. The Amish reject membership in a managerial middle class; they reject urbanization, industrialization, and participation in the armed services, and they reject the training that would prepare them for unacceptable occupations. They withdraw their children at the end of elementary school—or in some areas at the end of vocational school—to train them within the home and the community to become skilled in and to enjoy the work they will actually be doing as adults.

The Amish have consistently maintained that further formal education beyond elementary school is not only unnecessary but detrimental to the successful performance of Amish adult work roles. Recent studies seem to bear out these assumptions. Ivar Berg (1970:50) suggests that the over-educated are less productive, whether they are factory workers or elementary school teachers, and that in many kinds of work on-the-job training is more important than educational credentials. Certainly the skills the Amish need are best learned by doing. The enjoyment of physical labor can be learned better by laboring than by studying in a classroom.

For an individual to become Amish he must be kept within the Amish community, physically and emotionally, during his crucial adolescent years. High school removes the Amish child from the community by changing his status, by removing him from it physically for many of his waking hours, by teaching him skills and attitudes that are disruptive to his way of life, and by enabling him to form personal friendships with non-Amish young people. The school is disruptive both in what it teaches the Amish child and in what it prevents him from learning. If he is in school, he cannot attend sales and learn how to buy and sell in the worldly market, and he cannot attend work bees or weddings or church services for visiting preachers and learn adult roles of social integration. Amish children who attend high school experience conflict and anguish that often last well into adulthood.

In this age stage excursions will be made out into the world, but, it is hoped, not until late in adolescence. Nor should these excursions last for long. They should never remove the young person to a great physical distance from an Amish community. Amish young people may work for "English people," in this way learning about the world, but they must return home every weekend. Young people may work in small rural factories, but they return home in the evening and do not join labor unions. Even this amount of contact with the world is not permitted until almost the end of this age stage, and if it appears that the young person is not ready for this degree of contact, his parents may try to make him quit his worldly work.

During adolescence the peer group is of supreme importance, for most of the Amish young person's socialization takes place within this group rather than within the church or the family. If the young person's peer group remains Amish, he has a reference point, a balance, and a support. Even though as an individual or as a member of this Amish peer group he transgresses many rules and crosses most of the boundaries between the Amish community and the world, he will eventually return to the church and become a lifelong Amishman. However, if during this stage he makes English friends and identifies with an alien peer group, even though he is well behaved, he will probably leave the Amish church never to return.

Courting age, called rum springa or "running around," begins at about 16. Attendance at Amish young people's gatherings are important aspects of socialization during this period. The most important gathering is the Sunday evening singing attended by the young people. Aside from hymn singing, it is an evening of informal association, where an hour or more is spent visiting and joking, and where dates are arranged. Other social occasions are at weddings, cornhusking bees, and various kinds of mutual aid parties or "frolics." In addition to taking his girl home on Sunday evenings after the singing, in some communities a young man who is going steady will see his girl friend every other Saturday evening at her home. When Saturday evening comes he dresses in his best, and making a quiet departure from his home, he may leave the impression that he is going to town on business. Secrecy pervades the entire period of courtship regardless of its length. Most boys marry between the ages of 22 and 24. Girls tend on the average to be a year or more younger than boys at marriage.

The choice of a mate is conditioned by the values of Amish culture. A boy must obtain a partner from his own Amish faith, but not necessarily from his own community. Young people intermarry among Amish districts of the same affiliation and among settlements that maintain "fellowship" with one another. Marriage must be endogamous with respect to religious affiliation, for an Amish person who marries a non-Amish person is excommunicated and shunned.

First-cousin marriages are taboo and second-cousin marriages are discouraged, but do occur. The newly married couple receives economic assistance from both of their parents, often consisting of furniture, a cook stove, livestock, and basic farming equipment. Every mother is concerned that each of her children receive a homemade quilt and comforter. These are often made several years in advance so they will be ready when marriage takes place.

Conscription is especially disruptive to the Amish. Throughout their history the Amish have been pacifists, refusing to serve in any army. Today drafted Amish young men spend two years performing alternative service under the Selective Service classification of 1-W. A memo from Selective Service instructs local draft boards that suitable 1-W employment should "constitute a disruption" in the life of a conscientious objector (Local Board Memorandum No. 64, September, 1968). This is in addition to the requirements that (1) the work must contribute to the national health, safety, or interest, (2) the work should be performed outside the community in which the person resides, and (3) the job should be one that cannot be readily filled from the competitive job market. The Selective Service program is more disruptive to the Amish community than is apparent from the number of individuals actually in service. Those who are drafted must live outside the Amish community, often alone, in a city, perhaps wearing non-Amish clothing while at work. These measures separate the young men from community control and to a limited extent make them non-Amish.

Baptism has always been an important rite de passage among the Amish, for it signifies not only total commitment to the believing church-community, physically and spiritually separated from the world, but also admission to adulthood. If the drafted young man is baptized before his 1-W service he cannot live physically separated from the world, as he is pledged to do. If he is not baptized before his service, he has not committed himself to the church-community, and so is more vulnerable to outside influences. Not only does 1-W service make less clear and less meaningful the rite of baptism, it also affects marriage. Is it best for a young man to marry before, during, or after his service? If he goes into the world without a wife he may form friendships with non-Amish girls, and because marriage must be "in the Lord"—that is, with a co-religionist—such friendships are dangerous. If he has a wife, she helps protect him from worldly influences, but they start their married life with modern conveniences, electricity, and telephones that are hard to give up when they return to an Amish way of life. And what about children who are born outside the community? During 1-W service both the Amish men and their wives learn non-Amish work patterns and may receive training they will never use on an Amish farm. They work exclusively in a non-Amish environment with non-Amish people.

Probably the most disruptive influence for the young men is learning to know kind, highly verbal fundamentalists who are not Amish and who challenge the specific rules of the Amish church. The young men in 1-W service often receive higher wages than they would within the Amish community and sometimes they are tempted to work longer than the required two years. Many young men and even couples find the adjustment back to the watchful community difficult after the autonomy and anonymity of city living.

The most traditional Amish refuse alternative or 1-W service. As one member said, "God did not mean for the Amish to take the way of 1-W service. He is not blessing or prospering us for accepting 1-W service. It is better for the Amish to go to prison, though it is hard. God is with them there." In contrast to the men who accept alternative service, those few who go to prison generally return to the Amish community stronger in their faith and more secure in their conviction. They do not go through a period of uncertainty when they return. The rite of baptism retains its significance and is perhaps enhanced, for these Amishmen, for the time they spend outside the community serves to clarify the boundary between the world and the church. It enables them to identify with the martyrs of their heritage and it reinforces their belief in the necessity of separation from an evil world.

A certain degree of adolescent rebellion has become institutionalized among the Amish. The Amish child is raised in a carefully protected environment by relatively authoritarian parents and teachers. However, by the close of this age stage the Amish young person will have made the two greatest commitments of his life: he will have decided to join the church and will have chosen a spouse. He is expected to make these commitments as an individual with the help of God. In order to make such important decisions he must establish a degree of independence from his family and to some extent from his community in order to develop his own identity. This is done in many ways, most of them carefully institutionalized. First, the family relaxes some of its tight control over the young person. He goes to social gatherings of his peers rather than having all of his social life with his family. This is believed to be a time during which the young person learns what it means to be Amish. The community does not officially have control over him. During this period he often tests some of the boundaries of the Amish community, sampling the world by such means as perhaps owning a radio, having his photograph taken, attending a movie, and occasionally wearing clothes that are outside the Ordnung. As long as these forays are discreet, they are ignored by the parents and the community, for it is believed the young person should have some idea of the world he is voluntarily rejecting. One of the reasons courtship is secretive is that this is one of the only means of achieving privacy in a closely knit community and within a large family. The young person is protected by a degree of institutionalized blindness on the part of adults who thereby give him some freedom.

Earlier in his life the Amish child accepted being Amish as part of his identity. During this age stage he strives to determine what it means to him to be Amish. His family and the community help him by overseeing his vocational training. Both the young Amishman and young Amish woman work for a variety of different people during these years, learning various acceptable vocational roles and getting, through their jobs, a knowledge of other Amish families and other Amish communities and a glimpse of the world.

Amish cemetery

During their working hours the young people are respectful of community standards. However, during free time with their peers, there is considerable testing of boundaries and striving for self-knowledge. This period is made much more difficult if the young person attends high school, is removed from the community by the draft, develops close friendships with English young people or becomes interested in a fundamentalist religious group. When any of these things happen, there may be a long and difficult period during which the young person strives towards integration. In the more typical cases, where the Amish young person remains emotionally within the community, there is rarely much role confusion, and in Erikson's terms (1950:261) this age stage could be characterized by ego identity. The typical Amish young person is not an impatient idealist nor is he in search of negative identity. The preparation for this phase of his life began in the cradle, where he was cared for in such a way that he developed trust in himself and his environment. In the stages that followed he developed confidence in his physical participation in the world around him, coupled with some insecurity in the area of manipulating ideas. Amish young people find continuity between what they learned as children and what they experience as adolescents. By the end of this age stage the Amish adolescent is able to bring together his newfound abilities—the things he has learned about himself as a person, a family member, a worker, a member of the Amish peer group—and integrate these images of himself into a whole that makes sense. Within his family and community he arrives at a sense of who he is, where he has come from, and where he is going.

The Inupiac (Eskimo)

By Richard Nelson

J ust below the Arctic Circle in the boreal forest of interior Alaska; an amber afternoon in mid-November; the temperature -20°; the air adrift with frost crystals, presaging the onset of deeper cold.

Five men—Koyukon Indians—lean over the carcass of an exceptionally large black bear. For two days they've traversed the Koyukuk River valley, searching for bears that have recently entered hibernation dens. The animals are in prime condition at this season but extremely hard to find. Den entrances, hidden beneath 18 inches of powdery snow, are betrayed only by the subtlest of clues—patches where no grass protrudes from the surface because it's been clawed away for insulation, faint concavities hinting of footprint depressions in the moss below.

Earlier this morning the hunters took a yearling bear. In accordance with Koyukon tradition, they followed elaborate rules for the proper treatment of killed animals. For example, the bear's feet were removed first, to keep its spirit from wandering. Also, certain parts were to be eaten away from the village, at a kind of funeral feast. All the rest would be eaten either at home or at community events, as people here have done for countless generations.

Koyukon hunters know that an animal's life ebbs slowly, that it remains aware and sensitive to how people treat its body. This is especially true for the potent and demanding spirit of the bear.

The leader of the hunting group is Moses Sam, a man in his 60s who has trapped in this territory since childhood. He is known for his detailed knowledge of the land and for his extraordinary success as a bear hunter. "No one else has that kind of luck with bears," I've been told. "Some people are born with it. He always takes good care of his animals—respects them. That's how he keeps his luck."

Richard Nelson, "The Inupiac (Eskimo)," *Audubon*, September/October 1993, pp. 102–109. Permission to reprint granted by the publisher.

Moses pulls a small knife from his pocket, kneels beside the bear's head, and carefully slits the clear domes of its eyes. "Now," he explains softly, "the bear won't see if one of us makes a mistake or does something wrong."

* * *

Contemporary Americans are likely to find this story exotic, but over the course of time episodes like this have been utterly commonplace, the essence of people's relationship to the natural world. After all, for 99 percent of human history we lived exclusively as hunter-gatherers; by comparison, agriculture has existed only for a moment and urban societies scarcely more than a blink.

From this perspective, much of human experience over the past several million years lies beyond our grasp. Probably no society has been so deeply alienated as ours from the community of nature, has viewed the natural world from a greater distance of mind, has lapsed into a murkier comprehension of its connections with the sustaining environment. Because of this, we have great difficulty understanding our rootedness to earth, our affinities with nonhuman life.

I believe it's essential that we learn from traditional societies, especially those whose livelihood depends on the harvest of a wild environment—hunters, fishers, trappers, and gatherers. These people have accumulated bodies of knowledge much like our own sciences. And they can give us vital insights about responsible membership in the community of life, insights founded on a wisdom we'd long forgotten and now are beginning to rediscover.

Since the mid-1960s I have worked as an ethnographer in Alaska, living intermittently in remote northern communities and recording native traditions centered around the natural world. I spent about two years in Koyukon Indian villages and just over a year with Inupiaq Eskimos on the Arctic coast—traveling by dog team and snowmobile, recording traditional knowledge, and learning the hunter's way.

Eskimos have long inhabited some of the harshest environments on earth, and they are among the most exquisitely adapted of all human groups. Because plant life is so scarce in their northern terrain, Eskimos depend more than any other people on hunting.

Eskimos are famous for the cleverness of their technology—kayaks, harpoons, skin clothing, snow houses, dog teams. But I believe their greatest genius, and the basis of their success, lies in the less tangible realm of the intellect—the nexus of mind and nature. For what repeatedly struck me above all else was their profound knowledge of the environment.

Several times, when my Inupiaq hunting companion did something especially clever, he'd point to his head and declare: "You see—Eskimo scientist!" At first I took it as hyperbole, but as time went by I realized he was speaking the truth. Scientists had often come to his village, and he saw in them a familiar commitment to the empirical method.

Traditional Inupiaq hunters spend a lifetime acquiring knowledge—from others in the community and from their own observations. If they are to survive, they must have absolutely reliable information. When I first went to live with Inupiaq people, I doubted many things they told me. But the longer I stayed, the more I trusted their teachings.

For example, hunters say that ringed seals surfacing in open leads—wide cracks in the sea ice—can reliably forecast the weather. Because an unexpected gale might set people adrift on the pack ice, accurate prediction is a matter of life and death. When seals rise chest-high in the water, snout pointed skyward, not going anywhere in particular, it indicates stable weather, the Inupiaq say. But if they surface briefly, head low, snout parallel to the water, and show themselves only once or twice, watch for a sudden storm. And take special heed if you've also noticed the sled dogs howling incessantly, stars twinkling erratically, or the current running strong from the south. As time passed, my own experiences with seals and winter storms affirmed what the Eskimos said.

Like a young Inupiaq in training, I gradually grew less skeptical and started to apply what I was told. For example, had I ever been rushed by a polar bear, I would have jumped away to the animal's right side. Inupiaq elders say polar bears are left-handed, so you have a slightly better chance to avoid their right paw, which is slower and less accurate. I'm pleased to say I never had the chance for a field test. But in judging assertions like this, remember that Eskimos have had close contact with polar bears for several thousand years.

During winter, ringed and bearded seals maintain tunnel-like breathing holes in ice that is many feet thick. These holes are often capped with an igloo-shaped dome created by water sloshing onto the surface when the animal enters from below. Inupiaq elders told me that polar bears are clever enough to excavate around the base of this dome, leaving it perfectly intact but weak enough that a hard swat will shatter the ice and smash the seal's skull. I couldn't help wondering if this were really true; but then a younger man told me he'd recently followed the tracks of a bear that had excavated one seal hole after another, exactly as the elders had described.

In the village where I lived, the most respected hunter was Igruk, a man in his 70s. He had an extraordinary sense of animals—a gift for understanding and predicting their behavior. Although he was no longer quick and strong, he joined a crew hunting bowhead whales during the spring migration, his main role being that of adviser. Each time Igruk spotted a whale coming from the south, he counted the number of blows, timed how long it stayed down, and noted the distance it traveled along the open lead, until it vanished toward the north. This way he learned to predict, with uncanny accuracy, where hunters could expect the whale to resurface.

* * *

I believe the expert Inupiaq hunter possesses as much knowledge as a highly trained scientist in our own society, although the information may be of a different sort. Volumes could be written on the behavior, ecology, and utilization of Arctic animals—polar bear, walrus, bowhead whale, beluga, bearded seal, ringed seal, caribou, musk ox, and others—based entirely on Eskimo knowledge.

Comparable bodies of knowledge existed in every Native American culture before the time of Columbus. Since then, even in the far north, Western education and cultural change have steadily eroded these traditions. Reflecting on a time before Europeans arrived, we can imagine the whole array of North American animal species—deer, elk, black bear, wolf, mountain lion, beaver, coyote, Canada goose, ruffed grouse, passenger pigeon, northern pike—each known in hundreds of different ways by tribal communities; the entire continent, sheathed in intricate webs of knowledge. Taken as a whole, this composed a vast intellectual legacy, born of intimacy with the natural world. Sadly, not more than a hint of it has ever been recorded.

Like other Native Americans, the Inupiaq acquired their knowledge through gradual accretion of naturalistic observations—year after year, lifetime after lifetime, generation after generation, century after century. Modern science often relies on other techniques—specialized full-time observation, controlled experiments, captive-animal studies, technological devices like radio collars—which can provide similar information much more quickly.

Yet Eskimo people have learned not only about animals but also from them. Polar bears hunt seals not only by waiting at their winter breathing holes, but also by stalking seals that crawl up on the ice to bask in the spring warmth. Both methods depend on being silent, staying downwind, keeping out of sight, and moving only when the seal is asleep or distracted. According to the elders, a stalking bear will even use one paw to cover its conspicuous black nose.

Inupiaq methods for hunting seals, both at breathing holes and atop the spring ice, are nearly identical to those of the polar bear. Is this a case of independent invention? Or did ancestral Eskimos learn the techniques by watching polar bears, who had perfected an adaptation to the sea-ice-environment long before humans arrived in the Arctic?

The hunter's genius centers on knowing an animal's behavior so well he can turn it to his advantage. For instance, Igruk once saw a polar bear far off across flat ice, where he couldn't stalk it without being seen. But he knew an old technique of mimicking a seal. He lay down in plain sight, conspicuous in his dark parka and pants, then lifted and dropped his head like a seal, scratched the ice, and imitated flippers with his hands. The bear mistook his pursuer for prey. Each time Igruk lifted his head the animal kept still; whenever Igruk "slept" the bear crept closer. When it came near enough, a gunshot pierced the snowy silence. That night, polar bear meat was shared among the villagers.

Inupiac family, circa 1917

A traditional hunter like Igruk plumbs the depths of his intellect—his capacity to manipulate complex knowledge. But he also delves into his animal nature, drawing from intuitions of sense and body and heart: feeling the wind's touch, listening for the tick of moving ice, peering from crannies, hiding as if he himself were the hunted. He moves in a world of eyes, where everything watches—the bear, the seal, the wind, the moon and stars, the drifting ice, the silent waters below. He is beholden to powers we have long forgotten or ignored.

In Western society we rest comfortably on our own accepted truths about the nature of nature. We treat the environment as if it were numb to our presence and blind to our behavior. Yet despite our certainty on this matter, accounts of traditional people throughout the world reveal that most of humankind has concluded otherwise. Perhaps our scientific method really does follow the path to a single, absolute truth. But there may be wisdom in accepting other possibilities and opening ourselves to different views of the world.

I remember asking a Koyukon man about the behavior and temperament of the Canada goose. He described it as a gentle and good-natured animal, then added: "Even if [a goose] had the power to knock you over, I don't think it would do it."

For me, his words carried a deep metaphorical wisdom. They exemplified the Koyukon people's own restraint toward the world around them. And they offered a contrast to our culture, in which possessing the power to overwhelm the environment has long been sufficient justification for its use.

We often think of this continent as having been a pristine wilderness when the first Europeans arrived. Yet for at least 12,000 years, and possibly twice that long, Native American people had inhabited and intensively utilized the land; had gathered, hunted, fished, settled, and cultivated; had learned the terrain in all its details, infusing it with meaning and memory; and had shaped every aspect of their life around it. That humans could sustain membership in a natural community for such an enormous span of time without profoundly degrading it fairly staggers the imagination. And it gives strong testimony to the adaptation of mind—the braiding together of knowledge and ideology—that linked North America's indigenous people with their environment.

A Koyukon elder, who took it upon himself to be my teacher, was fond of telling me: "Each animal knows way more than you do." He spoke as if it summarized all that he understood and believed.

This statement epitomizes relationships to the natural world among many Native American people. And it goes far in explaining the diversity and fecundity of life on our continent when the first sailing ship approached these shores.

There's been much discussion in recent years about what biologist E. O. Wilson has termed "biophilia"—a deep, pervasive, ubiquitous, all-embracing affinity for nonhuman life. Evidence for this "instinct" may be elusive in Western cultures, but not among traditional societies. People like the Koyukon manifest biophilia in virtually all dimensions of their existence. Connectedness with non-human life infuses the whole spectrum of their thought, behavior, and belief.

It's often said that a fish might have no concept of water, never having left it. In the same way, traditional peoples might never stand far enough outside themselves to imagine a generalized concept of biophilia. Perhaps it would be impossible for people to intimately bound with the natural world, people who recognize that all nature is our own embracing community. Perhaps, to bring a word like biophilia into their language, they would first need to separate themselves from nature.

* * *

In April 1971 I was in a whaling camp several miles off the Arctic coast with a group of Inupiaq hunters, including Igruk, who understood animals so well he almost seemed to enter their minds.

Onshore winds had closed the lead that migrating whales usually follow, but one large opening remained, and here the Inupiaq men placed their camp. For a couple of days there had been no whales, so everyone stayed inside the warm tent, talking and relaxing. The old man rested on a soft bed of caribou skins with his eyes closed. Then, suddenly, he interrupted the conversation: "I think a whale is coming, and perhaps it will surface very close. ..."

To my amazement everyone jumped into action, although none had seen or heard anything except Igruk's words. Only he stayed behind, while the others rushed for the water's edge. I was last to leave the tent. Seconds after I stepped outside, a broad, shining back cleaved the still water near the opposite side of the opening, accompanied by the burst of a whale's blow.

Later, when I asked how he'd known, Igruk said, "There was a ringing inside my ears." I have no explanation other than his; I can only report what I saw. None of the Inupiaq crew members even commented afterward, as if nothing out of the ordinary had happened.

The Forest People

By Colin Turnbull

I N THE NORTHEAST CORNER of the Belgian Congo, almost exactly in the middle of the map of Africa, ... lies the Ituri Forest, a vast expanse of dense, damp and inhospitable-looking darkness. Here is the heart of Stanley's Dark Continent, the country he loved and hated, the scene of his ill-fated expedition to relieve Emin Pasha, an expedition costing hundreds of lives and imposing almost unbearable hardships on the survivors, who trekked across the great forest not once, but three times, losing more lives each time through fighting, sickness and desertion.

Anyone who has stood in the silent emptiness of a tropical rain forest must know how Stanley and his followers felt, coming as they all did from an open country of rolling plains, of sunlight and warmth. Many people who have visited the Ituri since, and many who have lived there, feel just the same, overpowered by the heaviness of everything—the damp air, the gigantic water-laden trees that are constantly dripping, never quite drying out between the violent storms that come with monotonous regularity, the very earth itself heavy and cloying after the slightest shower. And, above all, such people feel overpowered by the seeming silence and the age-old remoteness and loneliness of it all.

But these are the feelings of outsiders, of those who do not belong to the forest. If you are of the forest it is a very different place. What seems to other people to be eternal and depressing gloom becomes a cool, restful, shady world with light filtering lazily through the tree tops that meet high overhead and shut out the direct sunlight—the sunlight that dries up the non-forest world of the outsiders and makes it hot and dusty and dirty.

Even the silence is a myth. If you have ears for them, the forest is full of sounds—exciting, mysterious, mournful, joyful. The shrill trumpeting of an elephant, the sickening cough of a leopard (or the hundred and one sounds that can be mistaken for it), always makes your heart beat a little unevenly, telling you that you are just the slightest bit scared, or even more. At night, in the honey season, you hear a weird, long-drawn-out, soulful

Turnbull, Colin. "The World of the Forest," *The Forest People*. Simon & Schuster, 1962, pp. 11–26. Permission to reprint granted by the publisher.

cry high up in the trees. It seems to go on and on, and you wonder what kind of creature can cry for so long without taking breath. The people of the forest say it is the chameleon, telling them that there is honey nearby. Scientists will tell you that chameleons are unable to make any such sound. But the forest people of faraway Ceylon also know the song of the chameleon. Then in the early morning comes the pathetic cry of the pigeon, a plaintive cooing that slides from one note down to the next until it dies away in a soft, sad, little moan.

There are a multitude of sounds, but most of them are as joyful as the brightly colored birds that chase one another through the trees, singing as they go, or the chatter of the handsome black-and-white Colobus monkeys as they leap from branch to branch, watching with curiosity everything that goes on down below. And the most joyful sound of all to me is the sound of the voices of the forest people as they sing a lusty chorus of praise to this wonderful world of theirs—a world that gives them everything they want. This cascade of sound echoes among the giant trees until it seems to come at you from all sides in sheer beauty and truth and goodness, full of the joy of living. But if you are an outsider from the non-forest world, I suppose this glorious song would just be another noise to grate on your nerves.

The world of the forest is a closed, possessive world, hostile to, all those who do not understand it. At first sight you might think it hostile to all human beings, because in every village you find the same suspicion and fear of the forest, that blank, impenetrable wall. The villagers are friendly and hospitable to strangers, offering them the best of whatever food and drink they have, and always clearing out a house where the traveler can rest in comfort and safety. But these villages are set among plantations in great clearings cut from the heart of the forest around them. It is from the plantations that the food comes, not from the forest, and for the villagers life is a constant battle to prevent their plantations from being overgrown.

They speak of the world beyond the plantations as being a fearful place, full of malevolent spirits and not fit to be lived in except by animals and BaMbuti, which is what the village people call the Pygmies. The villagers, some Bantu and some Sudanic, keep to their plantations and seldom go into the forest unless it is absolutely necessary. For them it is a place of evil. They are outsiders.

But the BaMbuti are the real people of the forest. Whereas the other tribes are relatively recent arrivals, the Pygmies have been in the forest for many thousands of years. It is their world, and in return for their affection and trust it supplies them with all their needs. They do not have to cut the forest down to build plantations, for they know how to hunt the game of the region and gather the wild fruits that grow in abundance there, though hidden to outsiders. They know how to distinguish the innocent-looking *itaba* vine from the many others it resembles so closely, and they know how to follow it until it leads them to a cache of nutritious, sweet-tasting roots. They know the tiny sounds that tell where the bees have hidden their honey; they recognize the kind of weather that brings a multitude of different kinds of mushrooms springing to the surface; and they know what kinds of wood and leaves often disguise this food. The exact moment when termites swarm, at which they must be caught to provide an important delicacy, is a mystery to any but the people of the forest. They know the secret language that is denied all outsiders and without which life in the forest is an impossibility.

The BaMbuti roam the forest at will, in small isolated bands or hunting groups. They have no fear, because for them there is no danger. For them there is little hardship, so they have no need for belief in evil spirits. For them it is a good world. The fact that they average less than four and a half feet in height is of no concern to them; their taller neighbors, who jeer at them for being so puny, are as clumsy as elephants—another reason why they must always remain outsiders in a world where your life may depend on your ability to run swiftly and silently. And if the Pygmies are small, they are powerful and tough.

How long they have lived in the forest we do not know, though it is a considered opinion that they are among the oldest inhabitants of Africa. They may well be the original inhabitants of the great tropical rain forest which stretches nearly from coast to coast. They were certainly well established there at the very beginning of historic times.

The earliest recorded reference to them is not Homer's famous lines about the battle between the Pygmies and the cranes, as one might think, but a record of an expedition sent from Egypt in the Fourth Dynasty, some twenty-five hundred years before the Christian era, to discover the source of the Nile. In the tomb of the Pharaoh Nefrikare is preserved the report of his commander, Herkouf, who entered a great forest to the west of the Mountains of the Moon and discovered there a people of the trees, a tiny people who sing and dance to their god, a dance such as had never been seen before. Nefrikare sent a reply ordering Herkouf to bring one of these Dancers of God back with him, giving explicit instructions as to how he should be treated and cared for so that no harm would come to him. Unfortunately that is where the story ends, though later records show that the Egyptians had become relatively familiar with the Pygmies, who were evidently living, all those thousands of years back, just where they are living today, and leading much the same kind of life, characterized, as it still is, by dancing and singing to their god.

When Homer refers to the Pygmies, in describing a battle between Greek and Trojan forces in the Iliad, he may well be relying on information from Egyptian sources, but the element of myth is already creeping in.

> *When by their sev'ral chiefs the troops were rang'd,*
> *With noise and clamour, as a flight of birds,*
> *The men of Troy advanc'd; as when the cranes,*

Flying the wintry storms, send forth on high
Their dissonant clamours, while o'er th' ocean stream
They steer their course, and on their pinions bear
Battle and death to the Pygmaean race. *

By Aristotle's time the Western world was evidently still more inclined to treat the pygmies as legend because Aristotle himself has to state categorically that their existence is no fable, as some men believe, but the truth, and that they live in the land "from which flows the Nile."**

Mosaics in Pompeii show that, whether the Pygmies were believed to be fable or not, the makers of the mosaics in fact knew just how they lived, even the kinds of huts they built in the forest. But from then until the turn of the present century, our knowledge of the Pygmies decreased to the point where they were thought of as mythical creatures, semi-human, flying about in tree tops, dangling by their tails, and with the power of making themselves invisible. The cartographer who drew the thirteenth-century Mappa Mundi, preserved in Hereford Cathedral, England, located the Pygmies accurately enough, but his representations show them as subhuman monsters.

Evidently there was still some question as to their reality up to the seventeenth century, because the English anatomist Edward Tyson felt obliged to publish a treatise on "The Anatomy of a Pygmie compared with that of a Monkey, an Ape, and a Man." He had obtained from Africa the necessary skeletons, on which he based his conclusion that the so-called "pygmie" was, quite definitely, not human. The "pygmie" skeleton was preserved until recently in a London museum, and it was easy to see how Tyson arrived at so firm a conclusion. The skeleton was that of a chimpanzee.

Portuguese explorers of the sixteenth and seventeenth centuries were responsible for many of the more extravagant accounts. It may well be that they actually did see Pygmies near the west coast of Africa, or they may have seen chimpanzees and mistaken them for Pygmies. But it is curious that they should have thought of the Pygmies as being able to make themselves invisible, and all so have as having the power, small as they were, to kill elephants. The Pygmies today still kill elephants single-handed, armed only with a short-handled spear. And they blend so well with the forest foliage that you can pass right by without seeing them. As for their having tails, it is easy enough to see how this story came into being, if the Pygmies seen by the Portuguese dressed as they do today, as is more than likely. The loincloth they wear is made of the bark of a tree, softened and hammered out until it is a long slender cloth, tucked between the legs and over a belt, front and back. The

---

* Homer, *Iliad* (tr. Derby), iii, 1–7.
** Aristotle, *Historia Animalium* (tr. D'Arcy Wentworth Thompson), vii, 2.

women particularly like to have a long piece of cloth so that it hangs down behind, almost to the ground. They say it looks well when dancing.

Some of the accounts of nineteenth-century travelers in the Congo are no less fanciful, and it was George Schweinfurth who first made known to the world, in his book *The Heart of Africa,* that Pygmies not only existed but were human. He was following in the path of the Italian explorer Miani, who a few years earlier had reached the Ituri but had died before he could return. One of the most curious of little-known stories about the Pygmies is that Miani actually sent two of them back to Italy, to the Geographic Association, which had sponsored his trip. The president of the association, Count Miniscalchi of Verona, took the two boys and educated them. Contemporary newspaper reports describe them as strolling the boulevards, arm in arm with their Italian friends, chatting in Italian. One of them even learned to play the piano. From the present Count Miniscalchi I learned that both Pygmies eventually returned to Africa, where one died and the other became a saddler in the Ethiopian army. He last heard from the latter, who must then have been an old man, just before the outbreak of World War II.

Stanley describes his meetings with the Pygmies in the Ituri, but without telling us much about them, and indeed little was known beyond the actual fact of their existence until a White Father, the Reverend Paul Schebesta, set out from Vienna in the nineteen-twenties to study them.

Schebesta's first trip was an over-all survey of the forest area, in which he established the fact that this was a stronghold of the pure Pygmy, as opposed to the "Pygmoid" in other parts of the equatorial belt, where there has been intermarriage with Negro tribes. In subsequent trips Schebesta gathered material which showed that these Ituri Pygmies—whose term for themselves, BaMbuti, he adopts—are in fact racially distinct from the Negro people, Bantu and Sudanic, who live around them. This fact has been confirmed by later genetic studies, up to the present. Though we cannot be sure, it seems reasonable to assume that the BaMbuti were the original inhabitants of the great tropical rain forest stretching from the west coast right across to the open savanna country of the east, on the far side of the chain of lakes that divides the Congo from East Africa.

But when I read Schebesta's account of the Pygmies it just did not ring true when compared with my own experiences on my first trip to the Ituri. For instance, in one of his first books he says that the Pygmies are not great musicians, but that they sing only the simplest melodies and beat on drums and dance wild erotic dances. Even much later, after he had come to know the Pygmies better and had spent several years in the region, when he wrote his major work, running to several volumes, he devoted only a few pages to music, attributing little importance to it and dismissing it as simple and undeveloped. This could not have been further from the truth.

In several other ways I felt that all was not well with Schebesta's account, particularly with his description of Pygmies and Negroes. He gave the impression that the Pygmies were dependent on the Negroes both for food and for metal products and that there was an unbreakable hereditary relationship by which a Pygmy and all his progeny were handed down in a Negro family from father to son, and bound to it in a form of serfdom, not only hunting but also working on plantations, cutting wood and drawing water. None of this was true of the Pygmies that I knew. But I did agree with Schebesta about the *molimo* (a religious festival). Although he had not seen it himself, from what he heard about it and about similar practices among other groups of Pygmies, he felt sure that it was essentially different from the practices of neighboring Negroes, however similar they might appear to be on the surface. This certainly tallied with my own experience.

The general picture that emerged from his studies was that there were, living in the Ituri Forest, some 35,000 BaMbuti Pygmies, divided into three linguistic groups, speaking dialects of three major Negro languages. The Pygmies seemed to have lost their own language, due to the process of acculturation, though traces remained, especially in tonal pattern. Only in the easternmost group did Schebesta feel that the language had survived to any recognizable extent. These were the Efe Pygmies who lived among the BaLese, an eastern Sudanic tribe with a not very savory reputation for cannibalism, witchcraft and sorcery.

But in spite of this linguistic difference, and the fact that the Efe also differed in that they did not hunt with nets but with bow and arrow and spear, Schebesta believed that all the BaMbuti were a single cultural unit. They tended to live in small groups of from three families upward moving around the forest from camp to camp, though always attached to some Negro village with which they traded meat for plantation products. There was no form of chieftainship, and no mechanism for maintaining law and order, and it was difficult—from Schebesta's account—to see what prevented these isolated groups from falling into complete chaos. The most powerful unifying factor, it appeared, was the domination of the Pygmies by the Negros. Schebesta cited the *nkumbi* initiation as an example of the way Negroes forced the BaMbuti to accept their authority and that of their tribal lore. Remembering what I had seen living in an initiation camp, I could not accept this point of view at all. Yet it was one shared by others, some of whom had lived in the area for years.

The explanation was simple enough, and it was not that either one of us was right and the other wrong. Whereas Father Schebesta had always had to work through Negroes, and largely in Negro villages, I had been fortunate in being able to make direct contact with the Pygmies, and in fact had spent most of my time with them away from Negro influence. Other Europeans had also only seen the Pygmies either in Negro villages or on Negro plantations. But I had seen enough of them both in the forest and in the village to know that they were completely different people in the two sets of circumstances. All that we knew of them to date had been based on observations made either in the villages or in the presence of Negroes.

Whereas my first visit to the Ituri Forest, in 1951, had been made mainly out of curiosity, I had seen enough to make me want to return to this area for more intensive study. An ideal location was provided by a strange establishment set up on the banks of the Epulu River back in the nineteen-twenties by an American anthropologist, Patrick Putnam.* He had gone there to do his field work but had liked the place and the people so much that he decided to stay. He built himself a huge mud mansion, and gradually a village grew up around him and became known as "Camp Putnam." The Pygmies treated it just as they treated any other Bantu village (the main Negro tribes nearby were the BaBira and BaNdaka, with a few Moslem BaNgwana), and used to visit it to trade their meat for plantation products. This was where I first met them.

But on my second visit, in 1954, I was provided with a real opportunity for studying the relationship between the Pygmies and their village neighbors. The event was the decision of the local Negro chief to hold a tribal nkumbi initiation festival. This is a festival in which all boys between the ages of about nine and twelve are circumcised, then set apart and kept in an initiation camp where they are taught the secrets of tribal lore, to emerge after two or three months with the privileges and responsibilities of adult status.

The nkumbi is a village custom, but in areas where the practice prevails the Pygmies always send their children to be initiated along with the Negro boys. This has been cited as an example of their dependence on the Negroes and of their lack of an indigenous culture. The Negroes take all the leading roles in the festival, and as no Pygmy belongs to the tribe, none can become a ritual specialist, so the Pygmy boys always have to depend on the Negroes for admission to an initiation, and for the subsequent instruction. An uninitiated male, Pygmy or Negro, young or old, is considered as a child—half a man at best.

Only relatives of the boys undergoing initiation are allowed to live in the camp, though any adult initiated male can visit the camp during the daytime.

But it so happened that on this occasion there were no Negro boys of the right age for initiation, so the only men who could live in the camp and stay there all night were Pygmies. To go against the custom of allowing just relatives to live in the camp would have brought death and disaster. Nevertheless the Negroes went ahead with the festival because it has to be held to avoid offending the tribal ancestors. The Negro men would have liked

---

* Patrick Putnam first went to the Belgian Congo in 1927 to do field work for Harvard University. Apart from one or two brief return visits to the United States he remained there until his death at the end of 1953. At Camp Putnam he established a dispensary and a leper colony, turning his home into a guest house to help pay the expenses of his hospital work.

to stay in the camp all night, as normally instruction goes on even then, the boys being allowed to sleep only for short periods. But custom was too strong, and they had to rely on the Pygmy fathers to maintain order in the camp after dark and not allow the children to have too much sleep.

The Pygmies, however, did not feel bound by the custom, as it was not theirs anyway, and they invited me to stay with them, knowing perfectly well that I would bring with me plenty of tobacco, palm wine, and other luxuries. I was, after all, they said, father of all the children, so I was entitled to stay. The Negroes protested, but there was nothing they could do. On the one hand they felt that I would be punished for my offense by their supernatural sanctions; on the other they themselves hoped to profit by my presence. At least I could be expected to share in the expenses, which otherwise they would have to bear, of initiating the eight Pygmy boys.

And so I entered the camp and saw the initiation through from beginning to end. It was not a particularly comfortable time, as we got very little sleep. The Pygmy fathers were not in the least interested in staying awake simply to keep their children awake and teach them nonsensical songs, so the Negroes used to make periodic raids during the night, shouting and yelling and lashing out with whips made of thorny branches, to wake everyone up. Besides that, the camp was not very well built and the heavy rains used to soak the ground we slept on; only the boys, sleeping on their rough bed made of split logs, were dry. In the end we all used to climb up there and sit—there was not room for everyone to lie down—cold and miserable, waiting for the dawn to bring another daily round of exhausting singing and dancing.

But at the end of it all I knew something about the Pygmies, and they knew something about me, and a bond had been made between us by all the discomforts we had shared together as well as by all the fun. And when the initiation was over and we were off in the forest I learned still more. It was then that I knew for sure that much of what had been written about the Pygmies to date gave just about as false a picture as did the thirteenth-century cartographer who painted them as one-legged troglodytes. In the village, or in the presence of even a single Negro or European, the Pygmies behave in one way. They are submissive, almost servile, and appear to have no culture of their own. But at night in the initiation camp when the last Negro had left, or off in the forest, those same Pygmies were different people. They cast off one way of life and took on another, and from the little I saw of their forest life it was as full and satisfactory as village life seemed empty and meaningless.

The Pygmies are no more perfect than any other people, and life, though kind to them, is not without hardships. But there was something about the relationship between these simple, unaffected people and their forest home that was captivating. And when the time came that I had to leave, even though we were camped back near the village, the Pygmies gathered around their fire on the eve of my departure and sang their forest songs for me; and for the first time I heard the voice of the molimo. Then I was sure that I could never rest until I had come out again, free of any obligations to stay in the village, free of any limitations of time, free simply to live and roam the forest with the BaMbuti, its people; and free to let them teach me in their own time what it was that made their life so different from that of other people.

The evening before I left, before the singing started, three of the great hunters took me off into the forest. They said they wanted to be sure that I would come back again, so they thought they would make me "of the forest." There was Njobo, the killer of elephants; his close friend and distant relative, Kolongo; and Moke, an elderly Pygmy who never raised his voice, and to whom everyone listened with respect. Kolongo held my head and Njobo casually took a rusty arrow blade and cut tiny but deep vertical slits in the center of my forehead and above each eye. He then gauged out a little flesh from each slit and asked Kolongo for the medicine to put in. But Kolongo had forgotten to bring it, so while I sat on a log, not feeling very bright, Kolongo ambled off to get the medicine, and Moke wandered around cheerfully humming to himself, looking for something to eat.

It began to rain, and Njobo decided that he was not going to stay and get wet, so he left. Moke was on the point of doing the same when Kolongo returned. Obviously anxious to get the whole thing over with as little ceremony as possible and return to his warm dry hut, he rubbed the black ash-paste hard into the cuts until it filled them and congealed the blood that still flowed. And there it is today, ash made from the plants of the forest, a part of the forest that is a part of the flesh, carried by every self-respecting Pygmy male. And as long as it is with me it will always call me back.

The women thought it a great joke when I finally got back to camp, wet and still rather shaky. They crowded around to have a look and burst into shrieks of laughter. They said that now I was a real man with the marks of a hunter, so I would have to get married and then I would never be able to leave. Moke looked slyly at me. He had not explained that the marks had quite that significance.

It was later that evening when the men were singing that I heard the molimo. By then I had learned to speak the language quite well, and I had heard them discussing whether or not to bring the molimo out; there was some opposition on the grounds that it was "a thing of the forest," and not of the village, but old Moke said it was good for me to hear it before I left, as it would surely not let me stay long away but would bring me safely back.

First I heard it call out of the night from the other side of the Nepussi River, where three years earlier I had helped Pat Putnam build a dam. The dam was still there, though breached by continuous flooding. The hospital where Pat had given his life lay just beyond, now an overgrown jungle, only a few crumbling vine-covered walls left standing, the rest lost in a wilderness of undergrowth. Somewhere over there, in the darkness, the molimo now called; it sounded like someone singing but it was not a human voice. It was a deep, gentle, lowing sound, sometimes breaking off into a quiet falsetto, sometimes growling like a leopard. As the men sang their songs of praise to the forest, the molimo answered them, first on this side, then on that, moving around so swiftly and silently that it seemed to be everywhere at once.

Then, still unseen, it was right beside me, not more than two feet away, on the other side of a small but thick wall of leaves. As it replied to the song of the men, who continued to sing as though nothing were happening, the sound was sad and wistful, and immensely beautiful. Several of the older men were sitting near me, and one of them, without even looking up, asked me if I wanted to see the molimo. He then continued singing as though he didn't particularly care what my reply was, but I knew that he did. I was so overcome by curiosity that I almost said "yes"; I had been fighting hard to stop myself from trying to peer through the leaves to where it was now growling away almost angrily. But I knew that Pygmy youths were not allowed to see it until they had proved themselves as hunters, as adults in Pygmy eyes, and although I now carried the marks on my forehead I still felt unqualified. So I simply said, no, I did not think I was ready to see it.

The molimo gave a great burst of song and with a wild rush swept across the camp, surrounded by a dozen youths packed so tightly together that I could see nothing, and disappeared into the forest. Those left in the camp made no comment; they just kept on with their song, and after a while the voice of the molimo, replying to them, became fainter and fainter and was finally lost in the night and in the depths of the forest from where it had come.

This experience convinced me that here was something that I could do that was really worth while, and that I was not doing it justice by coming armed with cameras and record-ing equipment, as I had on this trip. The Pygmies were more than curiosities to be filmed, and their music was more than a quaint sound to be put on records. They were a people who had found in the forest something that made their life more than just worth living, something that made it, with all its hardships and problems and tragedies, a wonderful thing full of joy and happiness and free of care.

CHAPTER FOUR:
MARRIAGE AND THE FAMILY

READINGS IN THIS SECTION

Introduction

By David Julian Hodges

What is the purpose of marriage and family, and where do the beliefs of a culture place the emphasis? The overriding purpose could be to provide a context to conceiving, giving birth to, rearing, and socializing children. Or it could relate to providing economic advantage and well-being for the family unit or to providing physical, emotional, and psychological security. Or it could be to provide social control, especially regarding sexual behavior and procreation, or to achieve political objectives, or to promote individual satisfaction and happiness. Across diverse cultures, it is common to find some pattern of belief and behavior pertaining to marriage and family. In each culture, shared definitions of marriage and family embrace one or more ideas of essential purpose and shape behavior. These readings bring to light two circumstances. First, depending on overarching purpose, there is more than one viable way for conceiving marriage and family; second, among these diverse conceptions of marriage and family, each has positive and negative attributes.

As reported in the article by Serena Nanda, the practice of arranging marriages by families continues to be widely practiced in India, even among educated and relatively affluent families and individuals. The idea of such marriages is anathema to middle class, fiercely independent Western people. The American author, however, came to appreciate much of the rationale and the practices associated with arranged marriages. On the positive side, understanding the importance of family in all aspects of Indian life, the author realized that a couple who took marriage into their own hands was taking a big risk, particularly if the families were opposed to the match. On the negative side, the family of the male in the potential marriage appears to exert the greatest degree of control and experience most of the benefits of the process. This leaves women and their families in positions of vulnerability and potential loss. The "evils of dowry" and the larger issue of the powerlessness of women define the truly dark side of arranged marriages.

Among the Bari Indians of Venezuela, belief about conception and growth of the fetus leads to the notion that more than one male may share the state of fatherhood. These beliefs shape forms of parental responsibility and ideas of family. It also turns out that claims of secondary fatherhood play a role in the survivability of children because more than one male may provide for the material well-being of the mother during pregnancy.

Introduction ❖ 125

Although the practice is becoming less common, there has been a tradition in Tibet of brothers marrying a single woman. The mechanics of this fraternal polyandry are simple. Two, three, four, or more brothers jointly take a wife, who leaves her home to come and live with them. Tibetans explain the rationale for fraternal polyandry as materialistic. Given a subsistence economy and limited arable land, fraternal polyandry prevents the division of family farms and animals and thus facilitates all of the siblings in achieving a higher standard of living. Women explain that such marriages cause them and their children to be better off economically and produces only one set of heirs per generation. Although Tibetans do not perceive of this as a reason for choosing this form of marriage, a consequence is reduction of population growth and pressure on resources.

In Japan, A tiny fraction of all births is associated with unwed mothers; in the United States the proportion is more than a third. The rate of divorce in Japan is less than half that of the United States. Mutual passion, compatibility, and happiness do not explain the stability of marriages in Japan. Ironically, this relative stability and the durability of Japanese families seem to be because couples are, by international standards, exceptionally incompatible. Rather, given the sanctity of family in Japanese culture, the author argues that the secret to the strength of the family consists of three ingredients: low expectations, patience, and shame.

Ethel J. Alpenfels

Arranging a Marriage in India

By Serena Nanda

I n India, almost all marriages are arranged. Even among the educated middle classes in modern, urban India, marriage is as much a concern of the families as it is of the individuals. So customary is the practice of arranged marriage that there is a special name for a marriage which is not arranged: It is called a "love match."

On my first field trip to India, I met many young men and women whose parents were in the process of "getting them married." In many cases, the bride and groom would not meet each other before the marriage. At most they might meet for a brief conversation, and this meeting would take place only after their parents had decided that the match was suitable. Parents do not compel their children to marry a person who either marriage partner finds objectionable. But only after one match is refused will another be sought.

As a young American woman in India for the first time, I found this custom of arranged marriage oppressive. How could any intelligent young person agree to such a marriage without great reluctance? It was contrary to everything I believed about the importance of romantic love as the only basis of a happy marriage. It also clashed with my strongly held notions that the choice of such an intimate and permanent relationship could be made only by the individuals involved. Had anyone tried to arrange my marriage, I would have been defiant and rebellious!

At the first opportunity, I began, with more curiosity than tact, to question the young people I met on how they felt about this practice. Sita, one of my young informants, was a college graduate with a degree in political science. She had been waiting for over a year while her parents were arranging a match for her. I found it difficult to accept the docile manner in which this well-educated young woman awaited the outcome of a process that would result in her spending the rest of her life with a man she hardly knew, a virtual stranger, picked out by her parents.

"How can you go along with this?" I asked her, in frustration and distress. "Don't you care who you marry?"

Serena Nanda, "Arranging a Marriage in India," *Stumbling Toward Truth: Anthropologists at Work*, ed. Philip R. DeVita. Waveland Press, 2000, pp. 196–204. Permission to reprint granted by the publisher.

"Of course I care," she answered. "This is why I must let my parents choose a boy for me. My marriage is too important to be arranged by such an inexperienced person as myself. In such matters, it is better to have my parents' guidance."

I had learned that young men and women in India do not date and have very little social life involving members of the opposite sex. Although I could not disagree with Sita's reasoning, I continued to pursue the subject.

"But how can you marry the first man you have ever met? Not only have you missed the fun of meeting a lot of different people, but you have not given yourself the chance to know who is the right man for you."

"Meeting with a lot of different people doesn't sound like any fun at all," Sita answered. "One hears that in America the girls are spending all their time worrying about whether they will meet a man and get married. Here we have the chance to enjoy our life and let our parents do this work and worrying for us."

She had-me there. The high anxiety of the competition to "be popular" with the opposite sex certainly was the most prominent feature of life as an American teenager in the late fifties. The endless worrying about the rules that governed our behavior and about our popularity ratings sapped both our self-esteem and our enjoyment of adolescence. I reflected that absence of this competition in India most certainly may have contributed to the self-confidence and natural charm of so many of the young women I met.

And yet, the idea of marrying a perfect stranger, whom one did not know and did not "love," so offended my American ideas of individualism and romanticism, that I persisted with my objections.

"I still can't imagine it," I said. "How can you agree to marry a man you hardly know?"

"But of course he will be known. My parents would never arrange a marriage for me without knowing all about the boy's family background. Naturally we will not rely only on what the family tells us. We will check the particulars out ourselves. No one will want their daughter to marry into a family that is not good. All these things we will know beforehand."

Impatiently, I responded, "Sita, I don't mean know the family, I mean, know the man. How can you marry someone you don't know personally and don't love? How can you think of spending your life with someone you may not even like?"

"If he is a good man, why should I not like him?" she said. "With you people, you know the boy so well before you marry, where will be the fun to get married? There will be no mystery and no romance. Here we have the whole of our married life to get to know and love our husband. This way is better, is it not?"

Her response made further sense, and I began to have second thoughts on the matter. Indeed, during months of meeting many intelligent young Indian people, both male and female, who had the same ideas as Sita, I saw arranged marriages in a different light. I also saw the importance of the family in Indian life and realized that a couple who took their marriage into their own hands was taking a big risk, particularly if their families were ir-reconcilably opposed to the match. In a country where every important resource in life—a job, a house, a social circle—is gained through family connections, it seemed foolhardy to cut oneself off from a supportive social network and depend solely on one person for happiness and success.

* * *

Six years later I returned to India to again do fieldwork, this time among the middle class in Bombay, a modern, sophisticated city. From the experience of my earlier visit, I decided to include a study of arranged marriages in my project. By this time I had met many Indian couples whose marriages had been arranged and who seemed very happy. Particularly in contrast to the fate of many of my married friends in the United States who were already in the process of divorce, the positive aspects of arranged marriages appeared to me to outweigh the negatives. In fact, I thought I might even participate in arranging a marriage myself. I had been fairly successful in the United States in "fixing up" many of my friends, and I was confident that my matchmaking skills could be easily applied to this new situation, once I learned the basic rules. "After all," I thought, "how complicated can it be? People want pretty much the same things in a marriage whether it is in India or America."

An opportunity presented itself almost immediately. A friend from my previous Indian trip was in the process of arranging for the marriage of her eldest son. In "India there is a perceived shortage of "good boys," and since my friend's family was eminently respectable and the boy himself personable, well educated, and nice looking, I was sure that by the end of my year's fieldwork, we would have found a match.

The basic rule seems to be that a family's reputation is most important. It is under-stood that matches would be arranged only within the same caste and general social class, although some crossing of subcastes is permissible if the class positions of the bride's and groom's families are similar. Although dowry is now prohibited by law in India, extensive gift exchanges took place with every marriage. Even when the boy's family do not "make demands," every girl's family nevertheless feels the obligation to give the traditional gifts, to the girl, to the boy, and to the boy's family. Particularly when the couple would be living in the joint family—that is, with the boy's parents and his married brothers and their families, as well as with unmarried siblings—which is still very common even among the urban, upper-middle class in India, the girl's parents are anxious to establish smooth relations between their family and that of the boy. Offering the proper gifts, even when not called "dowry," is often an important factor in influencing the relationship between the bride's and groom's families and perhaps, also, the treatment of the bride in her new home.

In a society where divorce is still a scandal and where, in fact, the divorce rate is exceedingly low, an arranged marriage is the beginning of a lifetime relationship not just between the bride and groom but between their families as well. Thus, while a girl's looks are important, her character is even more so, for she is being judged as a prospective daughter-in-law as much as a prospective bride. Where she would be living in a joint family, as was the case with my friend, the girl's ability to get along harmoniously in a family is perhaps the single most important quality in assessing her suitability.

My friend is a highly esteemed wife, mother, and daughter-in-law. She is religious, soft-spoken, modest, and deferential. She rarely gossips and never quarrels, two qualities highly desirable in a woman. A family that has the reputation for gossip and conflict among its womenfolk will not find it easy to get good wives for their sons. Parents will not want to send their daughter to a house in which there is conflict.

My friend's family were originally from North India. They had lived in Bombay, where her husband owned a business, for forty years. The family had delayed in seeking a match for their eldest son because he had been an Air Force pilot for several years, stationed in such remote places that it had seemed fruitless to try to find a girl who would be willing to accompany him. In their social class, a military career, despite its economic security, has little prestige and is considered a drawback in finding a suitable bride. Many families would not allow their daughters to marry a man in an occupation so potentially dangerous and which requires so much moving around.

The son had recently left the military and joined his father's business. Since he was a college graduate, modern, and well traveled, from such a good family, and, I thought, quite handsome, it seemed to me that he, or rather his family, was in a position to pick and choose. I said as much to my friend.

While she agreed that there were many advantages on their side, she also said, "We must keep in mind that my son is both short and dark; these are drawbacks in finding the right match." While the boy's height had not escaped my notice, "dark" seemed to me inaccurate; I would have called him "wheat" colored perhaps, and in any case, I did not realize that color would be a consideration. I discovered, however, that while a boy's skin color is a less important consideration than a girl's, it is still a factor. An important source of contacts in trying to arrange her son's marriage was my friend's social club in Bombay. Many of the women had daughters of the right age, and some had already expressed an interest in my friend's son. I was most enthusiastic about the possibilities of one particular family who had five daughters, all of whom were pretty, demure, and well educated. Their mother had told my friend, "You can have your pick for your son, whichever one of my daughters appeals to you most."

I saw a match in sight. "Surely," I said to my friend, "we will find one there. Let's go visit and make our choice." But my friend held back; she did not seem to share my enthusiasm, for reasons I could not then fathom.

When I kept pressing for an explanation of her reluctance, she admitted, "See, Serena, here is the problem. The family has so many daughters, how will they be able to provide nicely for any of them? We are not making any demands, but still, with so many daughters to marry off, one wonders whether she will even be able to make a proper wedding. Since this is our eldest son, it's best if we marry him to a girl who is the only daughter, then the wedding will truly be a gala affair." I argued that surely the quality of the girls themselves made up for any deficiency in the elaborateness of the wedding. My friend admitted this point but still seemed reluctant to proceed.

"Is there something else," I asked her, "some factor I have missed?" "Well," she finally said, "there is one other thing. They have one daughter already married and living in Bombay. The mother is always complaining to me that the girl's in-laws don't let her visit her own family often enough. So it makes me wonder, will she be that kind of mother who always wants her daughter at her own home? This will prevent the girl from adjusting to our house. It is not a good thing." And so, this family of five daughters was dropped as a possibility.

Somewhat disappointed, I nevertheless respected my friend's reasoning and geared up for the next prospect. This was also the daughter of a woman in my friend's social club. There was clear interest in this family and I could see why. The family's reputation was excellent; in fact, they came from a subcaste slightly higher than my friend's own. The girl, who was an only daughter, was pretty and well educated and had a brother studying in the United States. Yet, after expressing an interest to me in this family, all talk of them suddenly died down and the search began elsewhere.

"What happened to that girl as a prospect?" I asked one day. "You never mention her any more. She is so pretty and so educated, what did you find wrong?"

"She is too educated. We've decided against it. My husband's father saw the girl on the bus the other day and thought her forward. A girl who 'roams about' the city by herself is not the girl for our family." My disappointment this time was even greater, as I thought the son would have liked the girl very much. But then I thought, my friend is right, a girl who is going to live in a joint family cannot be too independent or she will make life miserable for everyone. I also learned that if the family of the girl has even a slightly higher social status than the family of the boy, the bride may think herself too good for them, and this too will cause problems. Later my friend admitted to me that this had been an important factor in her decision not to pursue the match.

The next candidate was the daughter of a client of my friend's husband. When the client learned that the family was looking for a match for their son, he said, "Look no further, we have a daughter." This man then invited my friends to dinner to see the girl. He had already seen their son at the office and decided that "he liked the boy." We all went together for tea, rather than dinner—it was less of a commitment—and while we were there, the girl's mother showed us around the house. The girl was studying for her exams and was briefly introduced to us.

After we left, I was anxious to hear my friend's opinion. While her husband liked the family very much and was impressed with his client's business accomplishments and reputation, the wife didn't like the girl's looks. "She is short, no doubt, which is an important plus point, but she is also fat and wears glasses." My friend obviously thought she could do better for her son and asked her husband to make his excuses to his client by saying that they had decided to postpone the boy's marriage indefinitely.

By this time almost six months had passed and I was becoming impatient. What I had thought would be an easy matter to arrange was turning out to be quite complicated. I began to believe that between my friend's desire for a girl who was modest enough to fit into her joint family, yet attractive and educated enough to be an acceptable partner for her son, she would not find anyone suitable. My friend laughed at my impatience: "Don't be so much in a hurry," she said. "You Americans want everything done so quickly. You get married quickly and then just as quickly get divorced. Here we take marriage more seriously. We must take all the factors into account. It is not enough for us to learn by our mistakes. This is too serious a business. If a mistake is made we have not only ruined the life of our son or daughter, but we have spoiled the reputation of our family as well. And that will make it much harder for their brothers and sisters to get married. So we must be very careful."

What she said was true and I promised myself to be more patient, though it was not easy. I had really hoped and expected that the match would be made before my year in India was up. But it was not to be. When I left India my friend seemed no further along in finding a suitable match for her son than when I had arrived.

Two years later, I returned to India and still my friend had not found a girl for her son. By this time, he was close to thirty, and I think she was a little worried. Since she knew I had friends all over India, and I was going to be there for a year, she asked me to "help her in this work" and keep an eye out for someone suitable. I was flattered that my judgment was respected, but knowing now how complicated the process was, I had lost my earlier confidence as a matchmaker. Nevertheless, I promised that I would try.

It was almost at the end of my year's stay in India that I met a family with a marriageable daughter whom I felt might be a good possibility for my friend's son. The girl's father was related to a good friend of mine and by coincidence came from the same village as my friend's husband. This new family had a successful business in a medium-sized city in central India and were from the same subcaste as my friend. The daughter was pretty and chic; in fact, she had studied fashion design in college. Her parents would not allow her to go off by herself to any of the major cities in India where she could make a career, but they had compromised with her wish to work by allowing her to run a small dressmaking boutique from their home. In spite of her desire to have a career, the daughter was both modest and home-loving and had had a traditional, sheltered upbringing. She had only one other sister, already married, and a brother who was in his father's business.

I mentioned the possibility of a match with my friend's son. The girl's parents were most interested. Although their daughter was not eager to marry just yet, the idea of living in Bombay—a sophisticated, extremely fashion-conscious city where she could continue her education in clothing design—was a great inducement. I gave the girl's father my friend's address and suggested that when they went to Bombay on some business or whatever, they look up the boy's family.

Returning to Bombay on my way to New York, I told my friend of this newly discovered possibility. She seemed to feel there was potential but, in spite of my urging, would not make any moves herself. She rather preferred to wait for the girl's family to call upon them. I hoped something would come of this introduction, though by now I had learned to rein in my optimism.

A year later I received a letter from my friend. The family had indeed come to visit Bombay, and their daughter and my friend's daughter, who were near in age, had become very good friends. During that year, the two girls had frequently visited each other. I thought things looked promising.

Last, week I received an invitation to a wedding: My friend's son and the girl were getting married. Since I had found the match, my presence was particularly requested at the wedding. I was thrilled. Success at last! As I prepared to leave for India, I began thinking, "Now, my friend's younger son, who do I know who has a nice girl for him …?"

* * *

The previous essay was written from the point of view of a family seeking a daughter-in-law. Arranged marriage looks somewhat different from the point of view of the bride and her family. Arranged marriage continues to be preferred, even among the more educated, Westernized sections of the Indian population. Many young women from these families still go along, more or less willingly, with the practice, and also with the specific choices of their families. Young women do get excited about the prospects of their marriage, but there is also ambivalence and increasing uncertainty, as the bride contemplates leaving the comfort and familiarity of her own home, where as a "temporary guest" she has often been indulged, to live among strangers. Even in the best situation, she will now come under the close scrutiny of her husband's family. How she dresses, how she behaves, how she gets along with others, where she goes, how she spends her time, her domestic abilities—all of this and much more—will be observed and commented on by a whole new set of relations. Her interaction with her family of birth will be monitored and curtailed considerably. Not only will she leave their home, but with increasing geographic mobility, she may also live very far from them, perhaps even on another continent. Too much expression of her fondness for her own family, or her desire to visit them, may be interpreted as an inability to adjust to her new family, and may become a source of conflict. In an arranged marriage, the burden of adjustment is clearly heavier for a woman than for a man. And that is in the best of situations.

In less happy circumstances, the bride may be a target of resentment and hostility from her husband's family, particularly her mother-in-law or her husband's unmarried sisters, for whom she is now a source of competition for the affection, loyalty, and economic resources of their son or brother. If she is psychologically, or even physically abused, her options are limited, as returning to her parent's home, or divorce, are still very stigmatized. For most Indians, marriage and motherhood are still considered the only suitable roles for a woman, even for those who have careers, and few women can comfortably contemplate remaining unmarried. Most families still consider "marrying off" their daughters as a compelling religious duty and social necessity. This increases a bride's sense of obligation to make the marriage a success, at whatever cost to her own personal happiness. The vulnerability of a new bride may also the intensified by the issue of dowry that, although illegal, has become a more pressing issue in the consumer conscious society of contemporary urban India. In many cases, where a groom's family is not satisfied with the amount of dowry a bride brings to her marriage, the young bride will be constantly harassed to get her parents to give more. In extreme cases, the bride may even be murdered, and the murder disguised as an accident or suicide. This also offers the husband's family an opportunity to arrange another match for him, thus bringing in another dowry. This phenomenon, called dowry death, calls attention not just to the "evils of dowry" but also to larger issues of the powerlessness of women as well.

Afterword by Serena Nanda, 2007

How Many Fathers Are Best for a Child?

By Meredith F. Small

nthropologist Stephen Beckerman was well into his forties before he finally understood how babies are made. He had thought, as most people do, that a sperm from one man and an egg from one woman joined to make a child. But one summer day, as he and his colleague Roberto Lizarralde lounged around in hammocks, chatting with Rachel, an elderly woman of the Barí tribe of Venezuela, she pointed out his error. Babies, she explained, can easily have more than one biological father. "My first husband was the father of my first child, my second child, and my third child," Rachel said, recalling her life. "But the fourth child, actually, he has two fathers." It was clear that Rachel didn't mean there was a stepfather hanging around or a friendly uncle who took the kid fishing every weekend. She was simply explaining the Barí version of conception to these ignorant anthropologists: A fetus is built up over time with repeated washes of sperm—which means, of course, that more than one man can contribute to the endeavor. This interview changed not only the way Beckerman and Lizarralde viewed Barí families but also brought into question the very way that anthropologists portray human coupling. If biological fatherhood can be shared—an idea accepted by many indigenous groups across South America and in many other cultures across the globe—then the nuclear family with one mom and one dad might not be the established blueprint for a family that we have been led to expect. If so, the familiar story of traditional human mating behavior, in which man the hunter brings home the bacon to his faithful wife, loses credibility. And if the Barí and other groups work perfectly well with more flexible family styles, the variety of family structures that are increasingly common in Western culture these days—everything from single-parent households to blended families—may not be as dangerous to the social fabric as we are led to believe. People in this culture may simply be exercising the same family options that humans have had for millions of years, options that have been operating in other cultures while the West took a stricter view of what constitutes a family.

Meredith F. Small, "How Many Fathers Are Best for a Child?" *Discover Magazine*, April 2003, pp. 54–61. Permission to reprint granted by the publisher.

* * *

Stephen Beckerman folds his 6-foot-4-inch frame into a chair and turns to the mountain-ous topography of papers on his desk at Pennsylvania State University. Once he manages to locate a map under all the piles, he points to a spot on the border between Venezuela and Colombia where he spent 20 years, off and on, with the indigenous Barí Indians. The traditional Barí culture, Beckerman explains, has come under attack by outside forces, starting with the conquistadors who arrived in the early 16th century. Today Catholic mis-sionaries interact with the Barí, coal and oil companies are trying to seize their land, and drug traffickers and guerrillas are threats. Western influences are apparent: Most families have moved from traditional longhouses to single-family dwellings, and everyone wears modern Western clothes and uses Western goods. However, the Barí continue to practice their traditions of manioc farming, fishing, and hunting, according to Roberto Lizarralde, an anthropologist at the Central University of Venezuela who has been visiting the Barí regularly since 1960. Lizarralde also says that the Barí still have great faith in traditional spirits and ancestral wisdom, including their notion that a child can have multiple biologi-cal fathers. The Barí believe that the first act of sex, which should always be between a husband and wife, plants the seed. Then the fledgling fetus must be nourished by repeated anointings of semen; the woman's body is viewed as a vessel where men do all the work. "One of the reasons women give you for taking lovers is that they don't want to wear out their husbands," Beckerman says. "They claim it's hard work for men to support a pregnancy by having enough sex, and so lovers can help." Just look, the Barí say. Women grow fat during a pregnancy, while men grow thin from all their work.

* * *

Anthropologists study a culture's ideas about conception because those ideas have a pro-found impact on the way people run their lives. In our culture, for example, conceiving children incurs long-term economic responsibility for both the mother and father. We take this obligation so seriously that when a parent fails to provide for a child, it is usually a violation of law. In the Barí system, when a man is named as a secondary biological father he is also placed under an obligation to the mother and the child. In addition, he is expected to give gifts of fish and game. These gifts are a significant burden because the man must also provide for his own wife and primary children. Beckerman and his colleagues have discovered that naming secondary fathers has evolutionary consequences. A team of ethnog-raphers led by Beckerman, Roberto Lizarralde, and his son Manuel, an anthropologist at Connecticut College who has been visiting the Barí since he was 5 years old, interviewed 114 Barí women past childbearing years and asked them about their full reproductive histories.

"These interviews were a lot of fun," Beckerman says, laughing. "Randy old ladies talking about their lovers." In total, the researchers recorded claims of 916 pregnancies, an average of eight pregnancies for each woman. But child mortality was high—about one-third of the children did not survive to age 15. Naming secondary fathers was a critical factor in predicting which babies made it to adulthood. Secondary fathers were involved in 25 percent of pregnancies, and the team determined that two fathers were the ideal number. Children with one father and one secondary father made it to their teens most often; kids with only one father or those with more than two fathers didn't fare as well. The researchers also found that this decrease in mortality occurred not during the child's life but during fetal development: Women were less likely to have a miscarriage or stillbirth if they had a husband and an additional male contributing food. This result was a surprise because researchers had expected that help during childhood would be more important. "The Barí are not hungry; they are not close to the bone. But it must be the extra fat and protein that they get from secondary fathers during gestation that makes the difference," Beckerman explains as he points to photographs of Barí women who look well nourished, even downright plump. Barí women seem to use this more flexible system of paternity when they need it. Within families, some children have secondary fathers, while their siblings belong to the husband alone. The team discovered that mothers are more likely to take on a secondary father when a previous child has died in infancy. Manuel Lizarralde claims the strategy makes perfect sense, given the Barí belief that the best way to cure a sick child is for the father to blow tobacco smoke over the child's body. "It is easy to imagine a bereaved mother thinking to herself that if she had only provided a secondary father and so more smoke for her dead child, she might have saved him—and vowing to provide that benefit for her next child." Beckerman says extra fathers may have always been insurance for uncertain times: "Because the Barí were once hunted as if they were game animals—by other Indians, conquistadors, oilmen, farmers, and ranchers—the odds of a woman being widowed when she still had young children were one in three, according to data we gathered about the years 1930 to 1960. The men as well as the women knew this. None of these guys can go down the street to Mutual of Omaha and buy a life insurance policy. By allowing his wife to take a lover, the husband is doing all he can to ensure the survival of his children." Barí women are also freer to do as they wish because men need their labor—having a wife is an economic "necessity because women do the manioc farming, harvesting, and cooking, while men hunt and fish. "The sexual division of labor is such that you can't make it without a member of the opposite sex," says Beckerman. Initially, the researchers worried that jealousy on the part of husbands would make Barí women reticent about discussing multiple sexual partners. "In our first interviews, we would wait until the husband was out of the house," says Beckerman. "But one day we interviewed an old couple who were enjoying thinking about their lives; they were lying in their hammocks, side by side, and it was obvious he wasn't going anywhere. So we went down the list of her children and asked about other fathers. She said no, no, no for each child, and then the husband interrupted when we got to one and said, 'That's not true, don't you remember, there was that guy ...' And the husband was grinning." Not all women take lovers. Manuel Lizarralde has discovered through interviews that one-third of 122 women were faithful to their husbands during their pregnancies. "These women say they don't need it, or no one asked, or they have enough support from family and don't require another father for their child," Lizarralde says. "Some even admit that their husbands were not that happy about the idea." Or it may be a sign of changing times. Based on his most recent visits to the Barí, Lizarralde thinks that under the influence of Western values, the number of people who engage in multiple fatherhood may be decreasing. But his father, who has worked with the Barí for more than 40 years, disagrees. He says the practice is as frequent but that the Barí discuss it less openly than before, knowing that Westerners object to their views. After all, it took the anthropologists 20 years to hear about other fathers, and today the Barí are probably being even more discreet because they know Westerners disapprove of their beliefs. "What this information adds up to," Beckerman says, "is that the Barí may be doing somewhat less fooling around within marriage these days but that most of them still believe that a child can have multiple fathers." More important, the Barí idea that biological paternity can be shared is not just the quirky custom of one tribe; anthropologists have found that this idea is common across South America. The same belief is shared by indigenous groups in New Guinea and India, suggesting that multiple paternity has been part of human behavior for a long time, undermining all previous descriptions of how human mating behavior evolved.

* * *

Since the 1960s, when anthropologists began to construct scenarios of early human mating, they had always assumed that the model family started with a mom and dad bonded for life to raise the kids, a model that fit well with acceptable Western behavior. In 1981 in an article titled "The Origin of Man," C. Owen Lovejoy, an anthropologist at Kent State University, outlined the standard story of human evolution as it was used in the field—and is still presented in textbooks today: Human infants with their big brains and long periods of growth and learning have always been dependent on adults, a dependence that separates the humans from the apes. Mothers alone couldn't possibly find enough food for these dependent young, so women have always needed to find a mate who would stick close to home and bring in supplies for the family. Unfortunately for women, as evolutionary psychologists suggest, men are compelled by their biology to mate with as many partners as possible to pass along their genes. However, each of these men might be manipulated into staying with one woman who offered him sex and a promise of fidelity. The man, under those conditions, would be assured of paternity, and he might just stay around and make sure his kids survived. This scenario presents humans as naturally monogamous, forming nuclear families as an evolutionary necessity. The only problem is that around the world families don't always operate this way. In fact, as the Barí and other cultures show, there are all sorts of ways to run a successful household. The Na of Yunnan Province in China, for example, have a female-centric society in which husbands are not part of the picture. Women grow up and continue to live with their mothers, sisters, and brothers; they never marry or move away from the family compound. As a result, sisters and brothers rather than married pairs are the economic unit that farms and fishes together. Male lovers in this system are simply visitors. They have no place or power in the household, and children are brought up by their mothers and by the mothers' brothers. A father is identified only if there is a resemblance between him and the child, and even so, the father has no responsibilities toward the child. Often women have sex with so many partners that the biological father is unknown. "I have not found any term that would cover the notion of father in the Na language," writes Chinese anthropologist Cai Hua in his book A Society Without Fathers or Husbands: The Na of China. In this case, women have complete control over their children, property, and sexuality. Across lowland South America, family systems vary because cultures put their beliefs into practice in different ways. Among some native people, such as the Canela, Mehinaku, and Araweté, women control their sex lives and their fertility, and most children have several fathers. Barí women are also sexually liberated from an early age. "Once she has completed her puberty ritual, a Barí girl can have sex with anyone she wants as long as she doesn't violate the incest taboo," Beckerman explains. "It's nobody's business, not even Mom's and Dad's business." Women can also turn down prospective husbands. In other cultures in South America, life is not so free for females, although members of these cultures also believe that babies can have more than one father. The Curripaco of Amazonia, for instance, acknowledge multiple fatherhood as a biological possibility and yet frown on women having affairs. Paul Valentine, a senior lecturer in anthropology at the University of East London who has studied the Curripaco for more than 20 years, says, "Curripaco women are in a difficult situation. The wives come into the village from different areas, and it's a very patrilineal system." If her husband dies, a widow is allowed to turn only to his brothers or to clan members on his side of the family for a new husband. The relative power of women and men over their sex lives has important consequences. "In certain social and economic systems, women are free to make mate choices," says Valentine. In these cultures women are often the foundation of society, while men have less power in the community. Sisters tend to stay in the same household as their mothers. The women, in other words, have power to make choices. "At the other extreme, somehow, it's the men who try to maximize their evolutionary success at the expense of the women," says Valentine. Men and women often have a conflict of interest when it comes to mating, marriage, and who should invest most in children, and the winners have sometimes been the men, sometimes the women. As Beckerman wryly puts it, "Anyone who believes that in a human mating relationship the man's reproductive interests always carry the day has obviously never been married." The Barí and others show that human systems are, in fact, very flexible, ready to accommodate any sort of mating system or type of family. "I think that human beings are capable of making life extremely complicated. That's our way of doing business," says Ian Tattersall, a paleoanthropologist and curator in the division of anthropology at the American Museum of Natural History in New York City. Indeed, such flexibility suggests there's no reason to assume that the nuclear family is the natural, ideal, or even most evolutionarily successful system of human grouping. As Beckerman says, "One of the things this research shows is that human beings are just as clever and creative in assembling their kin relations as they are putting together space shuttles or symphonies."

When Brothers Share a Wife

By Melvyn C. Goldstein

E ager to reach home, Dorje drives his yaks hard over the 17,000-foot mountain pass, stopping only once to rest. He and his two older brothers, Pema and Sonam, are jointly marrying a woman from the next village in a few weeks, and he has to help with the preparations.

Dorje, Pema, and Sonam are Tibetans living in Limi, a 200-square-mile area in the northwest comer of Nepal, across the border from Tibet. The form of marriage they are about to enter—fraternal polyandry in anthropological parlance—is one of the world's rarest forms of marriage but is not uncommon in Tibetan society, where it has been practiced from time immemorial. For many Tibetan social strata, it traditionally represented the ideal form of marriage and family.

The mechanics of fraternal polyandry are simple. Two, three, four, or more brothers jointly take a wife, who leaves her home to come and live with them. Traditionally, marriage was arranged by parents, with children, particularly females, having little or no say. This is changing somewhat nowadays, but it is still unusual for children to marry without their parents' consent. Marriage ceremonies vary by income and region and range from all the brothers sitting together as grooms to only the eldest one formally doing so. The age of the brothers plays an important role in determining this: very young brothers almost never participate in actual marriage ceremonies, although they typically join the marriage when they reach their mid-teens.

The eldest brother is normally dominant in terms of authority, that is, in managing the household, but all the brothers share the work and participate as sexual partners. Tibetan males and females do not find the sexual aspect of sharing a spouse the least bit unusual, repulsive, or scandalous, and the norm is for the wife to treat all the brothers the same.

Offspring are treated similarly. There is no attempt to link children biologically to particular brothers, and a brother shows no favoritism toward his child even if he knows he is the real father because, for example, his other brothers were away at the time the wife

Melvyn C. Goldstein, "When Brothers Share a Wife," *Natural History*, March 1987, pp. 39–48. Permission to reprint granted by the publisher.

became pregnant. The children, in turn, consider all of the brothers as their fathers and treat them equally, even if they also know who is their real father. In some regions children use the term "father" for the eldest brother and "father's brother" for the others, while in other areas they call all the brothers by one term, modifying this by the use of "elder" and "younger."

Unlike our own society, where monogamy is the only form of marriage permitted, Tibetan society allows a variety of marriage types, including monogamy, fraternal polyandry, and polygyny. Fraternal polyandry and monogamy are the most common forms of marriage, while polygyny typically occurs in cases where the first wife is barren. The widespread practice of fraternal polyandry, therefore, is not the outcome of a law requiring brothers to marry jointly. There is choice, and in fact, divorce traditionally was relatively simple in Tibetan society. If a brother in a polyandrous marriage became dissatisfied and wanted to separate, he simply left the main house and set up his own household. In such cases, all the children stayed in the main household with the remaining brother(s), even if the departing brother was known to be the real father of one or more of the children.

The Tibetans' own explanation for choosing fraternal polyandry is materialistic. For example, when I asked Dorje why he decided to marry with his two brothers rather than take his own wife, he thought for a moment, then said it prevented the division of his family's farm. (and animals) and thus facilitated all of them achieving a higher standard of living. And when I later asked Dorje's bride whether it wasn't difficult for her to cope with three brothers as husbands, she laughed and echoed the rationale of avoiding fragmentation of the family and land, adding that she expected to be better off economically, since she would have three husbands working for her and her children.

Exotic as it may seem to Westerners, Tibetan fraternal polyandry is thus in many ways analogous to the way primogeniture functioned in nineteenth-century England. Primogeniture dictated that the eldest son inherited the family estate, while younger sons had to leave home and seek their own employment—for example, in the military or the clergy. Primogeniture maintained family estates intact over generations by permitting only one heir per generation. Fraternal polyandry also accomplishes this but does so by keeping all the brothers together with just one wife so that there is only one set of heirs per generation.

While Tibetans believe that in this way fraternal polyandry reduces the risk of family fission, monogamous marriages among brothers need not necessarily precipitate the division of the family estate: brothers could continue to live together, and the family land could continue to be worked jointly. When I asked Tibetans about this, however, they invariably responded that such joint families are unstable because each wife is primarily oriented to her own children and interested in their success and well-being over that of the children of the other wives. For example, if the youngest brother's wife had three sons while the eldest brother's wife had only one daughter, the wife of the youngest brother might begin to demand more resources for her children since, as males, they represent the future of the family. Thus, the children from different wives in the same generation are competing sets of heirs, and this makes such families inherently unstable. Tibetans perceive that conflict will spread from the wives to their husbands and consider this likely to cause family fission. Consequently, it is almost never done.

Although Tibetans see an economic advantage to fraternal polyandry, they do not value the sharing of a wife as an end in itself. On the contrary, they articulate a number of problems inherent in the practice. For example, because authority is customarily exercised by the eldest brother, his younger male siblings have to subordinate themselves with little hope of changing their status within the family. When these younger brothers are aggressive and individualistic, tensions and difficulties often occur despite there being only one set of heirs.

In addition, tension and conflict may arise in polyandrous families because of sexual favoritism. The bride normally sleeps with the eldest brother, and the two have the responsibility to see to it that the other males have opportunities for sexual access. Since the Tibetan subsistence economy requires males to travel a lot, the temporary absence of one or more brothers facilitates this, but there are also other rotation practices. The cultural ideal unambiguously calls for the wife to show equal affection and sexuality to each of the brothers (and vice versa), but deviations from this ideal occur, especially when there is a sizable difference in age between the partners in the marriage.

Dorje's family represents just such a potential situation. He is fifteen years old and his two older brothers are twenty-five and twenty-two years old. The new bride is twenty-three years old, eight years Dorje's senior. Sometimes such a bride finds the youngest husband immature and adolescent and does not treat him with equal affection; alternatively, she may find his youth attractive and lavish special attention on him. Apart from that consideration, when a younger male like Dorje grows up, he may consider his wife "ancient" and prefer the company of a woman his own age or younger. Consequently, although men and women do not find the idea of sharing a bride or bridegroom repulsive, individual likes and dislikes can cause familial discord.

Two reasons have commonly been offered for the perpetuation of fraternal polyandry in Tibet: that Tibetans practice female infanticide and therefore have to marry polyandrously, owing to a shortage of females; and that Tibet, lying at extremely high altitudes, is so barren and bleak that Tibetans would starve without resort to this mechanism. A Jesuit who lived in Tibet during the eighteenth century articulated this second view: "One reason for this most odious custom is the sterility of the soil, and the small amount of land that can be cultivated owing to the lack of water. The crops may suffice if the brothers all live together, but if they form separate families they would be reduced to beggary."

Both explanations are wrong, however. Not only has there never been institutionalized female infanticide in Tibet, but Tibetan society gives females considerable rights, including inheriting the family estate in the absence of brothers. In such cases, the woman takes a bridegroom who comes to live in her family and adopts her family's name and identity. Moreover, there is no demographic evidence of a shortage of females. In Limi, for example, there were (in 1974) sixty females and fifty-three males in the fifteen- to thirty-five-year age category, and many adult females were unmarried.

The second reason is also incorrect. The climate in Tibet is extremely harsh, and ecological factors do play a major role perpetuating polyandry, but polyandry is not a means of preventing starvation. It is characteristic, not of the poorest segments of the society, but rather of the peasant landowning families.

In the old society, the landless poor could not realistically aspire to prosperity, but they did not fear starvation. There was a persistent labor shortage throughout Tibet, and very poor families with little or no land and few animals could subsist through agricultural labor, tenant farming, craft occupations such as carpentry, or by working as servants. Although the per person family income could increase somewhat if brothers married polyandrously and pooled their wages, in the absence of inheritable land, the advantage of fraternal polyandry was not generally sufficient to prevent them from setting up their own households. A more skilled or energetic younger brother could do as well or better alone, since he would completely control his income and would not have to share it with his siblings. Consequently, while there was and is some polyandry among the poor, it is much less frequent and more prone to result in divorce and family fission.

An alternative reason for the persistence of fraternal polyandry is that it reduces population growth (and thereby reduces the pressure on resources) by relegating some females to lifetime spinsterhood. Fraternal polyandrous marriages in Limi (in 1974) averaged 2.35 men per woman, and not surprisingly, 31 percent of the females of child-bearing age (twenty to forty-nine) were unmarried. These spinsters either continued to live at home, set up their own households, or worked as servants for other families. They could also become Buddhist nuns. Being unmarried is not synonymous with exclusion from the reproductive pool. Discreet extramarital relationships are tolerated, and actually half of the adult unmarried women in Limi had one or more children. They raised these children as single mothers, working for wages or weaving cloth and blankets for sale. As a group, however, the unmarried woman had far fewer offspring than the married women, averaging only 0.7 children per woman, compared with 3.3 for married women, whether polyandrous, monogamous, or polygynous. While polyandry helps regulate population, this function of polyandry is not consciously perceived by Tibetans and is not the reason they consistently choose it.

If neither a shortage of females nor the fear of starvation perpetuates fraternal polyandry, what motivates brothers, particularly younger brothers, to opt for this system of marriage? From the perspective of the younger brother in a land-holding family, the main incentive is the attainment or maintenance of the good life. With polyandry, he can expect a more secure and higher standard of living, with access not only to this family's land and animals but also to its inherited collection of clothes, jewelry, rugs, saddles, and horses. In addition, he will experience less work pressure and much greater security because all responsibility does not fall on one "father." For Tibetan brothers, the question is whether to trade off the greater personal freedom inherent in monogamy for the real or potential economic security, affluence, and social prestige associated with life in a larger, labor-rich polyandrous family.

A brother thinking of separating from his polyandrous marriage and taking his own wife would face various disadvantages. Although in the majority of Tibetan regions all brothers theoretically have rights to their family's estate, in reality Tibetans are reluctant to divide their land into small fragments. Generally, a younger brother who insists on leaving the family will receive only a small plot of land, if that. Because of its power and wealth, the rest of the family usually can block any attempt of the younger brother to increase his share of land through litigation. Moreover, a younger brother may not even get a house and cannot expect to receive much above the minimum in terms of movable possessions, such as furniture, pots, and pans. Thus, a brother contemplating going it on his own must plan on achieving economic security and the good life not through inheritance but through his own work.

The obvious solution for younger brothers—creating new fields from virgin land—is generally not a feasible option. Most Tibetan populations live at high altitudes (above 12,000 feet), where arable land is extremely scarce. For example, in Dorje's village, agriculture ranges only from about 12,900 feet, the lowest point in the area, to 13,300 feet. Above that altitude, early frost and snow destroy the staple barley crop. Furthermore, because of the low rainfall caused by the Himalayan rain shadow, many areas in Tibet and northern Nepal that are within the appropriate altitude range for agriculture have no reliable sources of irrigation. In the end, although there is plenty of unused land in such areas, most of it is either too high or too arid.

Even where unused land capable of being fanned exists, clearing the land and building the substantial terraces necessary for irrigation constitute a great undertaking. Each plot has to be completely dug out to a depth of two to two and half feet so that the large rocks and boulders can be removed. At best, a man might be able to bring a few new fields under cultivation in the first years after separating from his brothers, but he could not expect to acquire substantial amounts of arable land this way.

In addition, because of the limited farmland, the Tibetan subsistence economy characteristically includes a strong emphasis on animal husbandry. Tibetan farmers regularly maintain cattle, yaks, goats, and sheep, grazing them in the areas too high for agriculture. These herds produce wool, milk, cheese, butter, meat, and skins. To obtain these resources, however, shepherds must accompany the animals on a daily basis. When first setting up a monogamous household, a younger brother like Dorje would find it difficult to both farm and manage animals.

In traditional Tibetan society, there was an even more critical factor that operated to perpetuate fraternal polyandry—a form of hereditary servitude somewhat analogous to serfdom in Europe. Peasants were tied to large estates held by aristocrats, monasteries, and the Lhasa government. They were allowed the use of some farmland to produce their own subsistence but were required to provide taxes in kind and corvée (free labor) to their lords. The corvée was a substantial hardship, since a peasant household was in many cases required to furnish the lord with one laborer daily for most of the year and more on specific occasions such as the harvest. This enforced labor, along with the lack of new land and ecological pressure to pursue both agriculture and animal husbandry, made polyandrous families particularly beneficial. The polyandrous family allowed an internal division of adult labor, maximizing economic advantage. For example, while the wife worked the family fields, one brother could perform the lord's corvée, another could look after the animals, and a third could engage in trade.

Although social scientists often discount other people's explanations of why they do things, in the case of Tibetan fraternal polyandry, such explanations are very close to the truth. The custom, however, is very sensitive to changes in its political and economic milieu and, not surprisingly, is in decline in most Tibetan areas. Made less important by the elimination of the traditional serf-based economy, it is disparaged by the dominant non-Tibetan leaders of India, China, and Nepal. New opportunities for economic and social mobility in these countries, such as the tourist trade and government employment, are also eroding the rationale for polyandry, and so it may vanish within the next generation.

Who Needs Love!
In Japan, Many Couples Don't

By Nicholas D. Kristoff

Y uri Uemura sat on the straw tatami mat of her living room and chatted cheerfully about her 40-year marriage to a man whom, she mused, she never particularly liked.

"There was never any love between me and my husband," she said blithely, recalling how he used to beat her. "But, well, we survived."

A 72-year-old midwife, her face as weathered as an old baseball and etched with a thousand seams, Mrs. Uemura said that her husband had never told her that he liked her, never complimented her on a meal, never told her "thank you," never held her hand, never given her a present, never shown her affection in any way. He never calls her by her name, but summons her with the equivalent of a grunt or a "Hey, you."

"Even with animals, the males cooperate to bring the females some food," Mrs. Uemura said sadly, noting the contrast to her own marriage. "When I see that, it brings tears to my eyes."

In short, the Uemuras have a marriage that is as durable as it is unhappy, one couple's tribute to the Japanese sanctity of family.

The divorce rate in Japan is at a record high but still less than half that of the United States, and Japan arguably has one of the strongest family structures in the industrialized world. As the United States and Europe fret about the disintegration of the traditional family, most Japanese families remain as solid as the small red table on which Mrs. Uemura rested her tea.

A study published last year by the Population Council, an international nonprofit group based in New York, suggested that the traditional two-parent household is on the wane not only in America but throughout most of the world. There was one prominent exception: Japan.

Nicholas D. Kristoff, "Who Needs Love! In Japan, Many Couples Don't," *The New York Times*, February 11, 1996. Permission to reprint granted by the publisher.

In Japan, for example, only 1.1 percent of births are to unwed mothers—virtually unchanged from 25 years ago. In the United States, the figure is 30.1 percent and rising rapidly.

Yet if one comes to a little Japanese town like Omiya to learn the secrets of the Japanese family, the people are not as happy as the statistics.

"I haven't lived for myself," Mrs. Uemura said, with a touch of melancholy, "but for my kids, and for my family, and for society."

Mrs. Uemura's marriage does not seem exceptional in Japan, whether in the big cities or here in Omiya. The people of Omiya, a community of 5,700 nestled in the rain-drenched hills of the Kii Peninsula in Mie Prefecture, nearly 200 miles southwest of Tokyo, have spoken periodically to a reporter about various aspects of their daily lives. On this visit they talked about their families.

Survival Secrets Often, the Couples Expect Little

Osamu Torida furrowed his brow and looked perplexed when he was asked if he loved his wife of 33 years.

"Yeah, so-so, I guess," said Mr. Torida, a cattle farmer. "She's like air or water. You couldn't live without it, but most of the time, you're not conscious of its existence."

The secret to the survival of the marriage, Mr. Torida acknowledged, was not mutual passion.

"Sure, we had fights about our work," he explained as he stood beside his barn. "But we were preoccupied by work and our debts, so we had no time to fool around."

That is a common theme in Omiya. It does not seem that Japanese families survive because husbands and wives love each other more than American couples, but rather because they perhaps love each other less.

"I think love marriages are more fragile than arranged marriages," said Tomika Kusukawa, 49, who married her high-school sweetheart and now runs a car repair shop with him. "In love marriages, when something happens or if the couple falls out of love, they split up."

If there is a secret to the strength of the Japanese family it consists of three ingredients: low expectations, patience, and shame.

The advantage of marriages based on low expectations is that they have built-in shock absorbers. If the couple discover that they have nothing in common, that they do not even like each other, then that is not so much a reason for divorce as it is par for the course.

Even the discovery that one's spouse is having an affair is often not as traumatic in a Japanese marriage as it is in the West. A little sexual infidelity on the part of a man (though not on the part of his wife) was traditionally tolerated, so long as he did not become so besotted as to pay his mistress more than he could afford.

Tsuzuya Fukuyama, who runs a convenience store and will mark her 50th wedding anniversary this year, toasted her hands on an electric heater in the front of the store and declared that a woman would be wrong to get angry if her husband had an affair.

"It's never just one side that's at fault," Mrs. Fukuyama said sternly. "Maybe the husband had an affair because his wife wasn't so hot herself. So she should look at her own faults."

Mrs. Fukuyama's daughter came to her a few years ago, suspecting that her husband was having an affair and asking what to do.

"I told her, 'Once you left this house, you can only come back if you divorce; if you're not prepared to get a divorce, then you'd better be patient,' " Mrs. Fukuyama recalled. "And so she was patient. And then she got pregnant and had a kid, and now they're close again."

The word that Mrs. Fukuyama used for patience is "gaman," a term that comes up whenever marriage is discussed in Japan. It means toughing it out, enduring hardship, and many Japanese regard gaman with pride as a national trait.

Many people complain that younger folks divorce because they do not have enough gaman, and the frequency with which the term is used suggests a rather bleak understanding of marriage.

"I didn't know my husband very well when we married, and afterward we used to get into bitter fights," said Yoshiko Hirowaki, 56, a store owner. "But then we had children, and I got very busy with the kids and with this shop. Time passed."

Now Mrs. Hirowaki has been married 34 years, and she complains about young people who do not stick to their vows.

"In the old days, wives had more gaman," she said. "Now kids just don't have enough gaman."

The durability of the Japanese family is particularly wondrous because couples are, by international standards, exceptionally incompatible.

One survey asked married men and their wives in 37 countries how they felt about politics, sex, religion, ethics and social issues. Japanese couples ranked dead last in compatibility of views, by a huge margin. Indeed, another survey found that if they were doing it over again, only about one-third of Japanese would marry the same person.

Incompatibility might not matter so much, however, because Japanese husbands and wives spend very little time talking to each other.

"I kind of feel there's nothing new to say to her," said Masayuki Ogita, an egg farmer, explaining his reticence.

In a small town like Omiya, couples usually have dinner together, but in Japanese cities there are many "7-11 husbands," so called because they leave at 7 A.M. and return after 11 P.M.

Masahiko Kondo now lives in Omiya, working in the chamber of commerce, but he used to be a salesman in several big cities. He would leave for work each morning at 7, and about four nights a week would go out for after-work drinking or mah-jongg sessions with buddies.

"I only saw my baby on Saturdays or Sundays," said Mr. Kondo, a lanky good-natured man of 37. "But in fact, I really enjoyed that life. It didn't bother me that I never spent time with my kid on weekdays."

Mr. Kondo's wife, Keiko, had her own life, spent with her child and the wives of other workaholic husbands.

"We had birthday parties, but they were with the kids and the mothers," she remembers. "No fathers ever came."

A national survey found that 30 percent of fathers spend less than 15 minutes a day on weekdays talking with or playing with their children. Among eighth graders, 51 percent reported that they never spoke with their fathers on weekdays.

As a result, the figures in Japan for single-parent households can be deceptive. The father is often more a theoretical presence than a homework-helping reality.

Still, younger people sometimes want to see the spouses in daylight, and a result is a gradual change in focus of lives from work to family. Two decades ago, nearly half of young people said in surveys that they wanted their fathers to put priority on work rather than family. Now only one-quarter say that.

Social Pressures Shame Is Keeping Bonds in Place

For those who find themselves desperately unhappy, one source of pressure to keep plugging is shame.

"If you divorce, you lose face in society," said Tatsumi Kinoshita, a tea farmer. "People say, 'His wife escaped.' So folks remain married because they hate to be gossiped about."

Shame is a powerful social sanction in Japan, and it is not just a matter of gossip. Traditionally, many companies were reluctant to promote employees who had divorced or who had major problems at home.

"If you divorce, it weakens your position at work," said Akihiko Kanda, 27, who works in a local government office. "Your bosses won't give you such good ratings, and it'll always be a negative factor."

The idea, Mr. Kanda noted, is that if an employee cannot manage his own life properly, he should not be entrusted with important corporate matters.

Financial sanctions are also a major disincentive for divorce. The mother gets the children in three-quarters of divorces, but most mothers in Japan do not have careers and have few financial resources. Fathers pay child support in only 15 percent of all divorces with children, partly because women often hesitate to go to court to demand payments and partly because men often fail to pay even when the court orders it.

"The main reason for lack of divorce is that women can't support themselves," said Mizuko Kanda, a 51-year-old housewife. "My friends complain about their husbands and say that they'd divorce if they could, but they can't afford to."

The result of these social and economic pressures is clear.

Even in Japan, there are about 24 divorces for every 100 marriages, but that compares with 32 in France, 42 in England, and 55 in the United States.

The Outlook Change Creeps In, Imperiling Family

But society is changing in Japan, and it is an open question whether these changes will undermine the traditional family as they have elsewhere around the globe.

The nuclear family has already largely replaced the extended family in Japan, and shame is eroding as a sanction. Haruko Okumura, for example, runs a kindergarten and speaks openly about her divorce.

"My Mom was uneasy about it, but I never had an inferiority complex about being divorced," said Mrs. Okumura, as dozens of children played in the next room. "And people accepted me easily."

Mrs. Okumura sees evidence of the changes in family patterns every day: fathers are playing more of a role in the kindergarten. At Christmas parties and sports contests, fathers have started to show up along with mothers. And Mrs. Okumura believes that divorce is on the upswing.

"If there's a weakening of the economic and social pressures to stay married," she said, "surely divorce rates will soar."

Already divorce rates are rising, approximately doubling over the last 25 years. But couples are very reluctant to divorce when they have children, and so single-parent households account for exactly the same proportion today as in 1965.

Shinsuke Kawaguchi, a young tea farmer, is one of the men for whom life is changing. Americans are not likely to be impressed by Mr. Kawaguchi's open-mindedness, but he is.

"I take good care of my wife," he said. "I may not say 'I love you,' but I do hold her hand. And I might say, after she makes dinner, 'This tastes good.'"

"Of course," Mr. Kawaguchi quickly added, "I wouldn't say that unless I'd just done something really bad."

Even Mrs. Uemura, the elderly women whose husband used to beat her, said that her husband was treating her better.

"The other day, he tried to pour me a cup of tea," Mrs. Uemura recalled excitedly. "It was a big change. I told all my friends."

CHAPTER FIVE:
CONTEMPORARY
PERSPECTIVES AND ISSUES

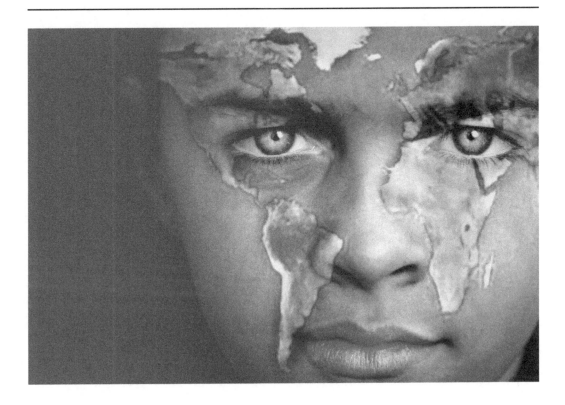

READINGS IN THIS SECTION

Introduction

By David Julian Hodges

The American Proposition and the Challenge of Global Diversity

When it was founded, America offered the world a bright new ray of hope and a new proposition for freedom and democracy. All could come who wanted to—the poor, the rich, the dispossessed, and the disenchanted—all who would leave behind old notions of birthright and adopt new ideals of initiative, hard work, and achievement as measures of social standing. Many came, leaving old homelands of denial and founding new homesteads of personal freedom and higher possibilities.

In framing the historic documents which were to declare the ideals upon which America was begun, a rare coalition of gifted men worked together for long periods of time, and on several different occasions to author the Constitution of the United States, the Declaration of Independence, and other momentous documents. Seldom before or since have men of such extraordinary intellect cooperated as effectively on such monumental undertakings. The resulting documents heralded a new episode in world history and offered greater freedoms to larger numbers than previously afforded by any other country.

But ... the ideals set forth by these "founding fathers" never applied to all Americans. The American promise and dream were exclusive. Clearly, the dream applied to an exclusive set of Americans, who failed to reach even a majority if one considers early gender discrimination. The dream did not apply to all of America.

Native Americans, Blacks, and "others," never fully participated in this great new hope for freedom and opportunity. The glaring facts of injustice and discrimination are a matter of record. The "outsiders" were what the esteemed sociologist Dan W. Dodson termed a "footnote to the dream." Because of this exclusion, a cleavage developed between the integrity of the American dream and the tragedy of a snowballing American reality ... a cleavage which soon erupted into a grave civil war, a cleavage still manifest today in various and sundry forms of oppression.

Cultural anthropology weighs in on this issue in the sense that it explores the fundamental similarities and differences between human beings. This is warp and woof of the cause of discrimination and prejudice. This is what causes the exclusion of "others."

Through the work of cultural anthropology, the "psychic unity of mankind" is introduced, and differences become opportunities to unmask the root of the problem of exclusion.

Three distinctly different articles are presented in this section to illustrate this focus. Through the article by Lauriston Sharp, the reader becomes aware of the malleability of cultural phenomena on the human psyche, and in turn, the effect this may have on whole cultures. Here we see how the introduction of Western technology (European artifacts, ideas, and beliefs) can bring about the virtual dissolution of a traditional culture.

The same principle—but within an entirely different cultural environment and nevertheless just as devastating to the human psyche of the women involved—is the illustration reported by anthropologist Nancy Scheper-Hughes. She describes the ways in which conventional views of motherhood and kinship are altered in situations of high infant and childhood mortality.

Both situations described by Lauriston Sharp and the one described by Nancy Scheper-Hughes illustrate how cultural phenomena can produce a demoralization of the individual and eventually a progressively worsening disintegration of functional aspects of a culture.

The article on female genital mutilation and the article revealing an interesting societal variation on conceptions of beauty underscore still further possibilities for the human psyche to be involved with and affected by social definitions.

Perhaps the most eloquent of contemporary dialogues on race is represented by the Philadelphia speech of U.S. President Barack Obama during his campaign for office. While not a social scientist, the U.S. President demonstrated a remarkable grasp of a pressing societal dilemma that has faced the nation since its inception. For the cultural anthropologist, the pertinent questions are: What are the fundamental similarities and differences between people, and where do these reside? Do they reside in the human psyche? Do they reside in race? Class? Nationality? Is a social contract possible that includes all people? The reader will see that the President has an implicit understanding of these profoundly troubling societal issues.

Relative to the American proposition described above, cultural anthropology helps us to recognize that there was, indeed, a fundamental flaw in the American proposition … and that the dream and the plan were exclusive. The plan did not deal with cultural diversity. It did not deal with race, or with linguistic difference, or with gender difference, or

Dan W. Dodson

with other cultural differences of one sort or another. These flaws are not benign. They affect the human psyche in small and large ways. Nor does this "dilemma" confine itself to America alone. The challenge is global. During the nineteenth century, a full century after the drama of the American proposition was made manifest, modern social science was born. Among the fields of social science that emerged, cultural anthropology was prominent. These questions spawned intense academic and scholarly debate. During the nineteenth century, theories about hierarchical stages of "social evolution" became popular. The idea that human beings could be classified within a framework of stages, ranging from "savage" to "civilized" was the prevailing notion. This notion was soon deposed, but the period represented the birth of a science of society, of which cultural anthropology was significant.

Steel Axes for Stone Age Australians

By Lauriston Sharp

I

Like other Australian aboriginals, the Yir Yoront group which lives at the mouth of the Coleman River on the west coast of Cape York Peninsula originally had no knowledge of metals. Technologically their culture was of the old stone age or paleolithic type. They supported themselves by hunting and fishing, and obtained vegetables and other materials from the bush by simple gathering techniques. Their only domesticated animal was the dog; they had no cultivated plants of any kind. Unlike some other aboriginal groups, however, the Yir Yoront did have polished stone axes hafted in short handles which were most important in their economy.

Towards the end of the 19th century metal tools and other European artifacts began to filter into the Yir Yoront territory. The flow increased with the gradual expansion of the white frontier outward from southern and eastern Queensland. Of all the items of western technology thus made available, the hatchet, or short handled steel axe, was the most acceptable to and the most highly valued by all aboriginals.

In the mid 1930s an American anthropologist lived alone in the bush among the Yir Yoront for 13 months without seeing another white man. The Yir Yoront were thus still relatively isolated and continued to live an essentially independent economic existence, supporting themselves entirely by means of their old stone age techniques. Yet their polished stone axes were disappearing fast and being replaced by steel axes which came to them in considerable numbers, directly or indirectly, from various European sources to the south.

What changes in the life of the Yir Yoront still living under aboriginal conditions in the Australian bush could be expected as a result of their increasing possession and use of the steel axe?

Lauriston Sharp, "Steel Axes for Stone Age Australians," *Human Organization*, ed. Edward H. Spicer, Summer 1952, pp. 17–22. Permission to reprint granted by the publisher.

II: The Course of Events

Events leading up to the introduction of the steel axe among the Yir Yoront begin with the advent of the second known group of Europeans to reach the shores of the Australian continent. In 1623 a Dutch expedition landed on the coast where the Yir Yoront now live.* In 1935 the Yir Yoront were still using the few cultural items recorded in the Dutch log for the aboriginals they encountered. To this cultural inventory the Dutch added beads and pieces of iron which they offered in an effort to attract the frightened "Indians." Among these natives metal and beads have disappeared, together with any memory of this first encounter with whites.

The next recorded contact in this area was in 1864. Here there is more positive assurance that the natives concerned were the immediate ancestors of the Yir Yoront community. These aboriginals had the temerity to attack a party of cattle men who were driving a small herd from southern Queensland through the length of the then unknown Cape York Peninsula to a newly established government station at the northern tip.** Known as the "Battle of the Mitchell River," this was one of the rare instances in which Australian aboriginals stood up to European gunfire for any length of time. A diary kept by the cattle men records that: "… 10 carbines poured volley after volley into them from all directions, killing and wounding with every shot with very little return, nearly all their spears having already been expended. … About 30 being killed, the leader thought it prudent to hold his hand, and let the rest escape. Many more must have been wounded and probably drowned, for 59 rounds were counted as discharged." The European party was in the Yir Yoront area for three days; they then disappeared over the horizon to the north and never returned. In the almost three-year long anthropological investigation conducted some 70 years later—in all the material of hundreds of free association interviews, in texts of hundreds of dreams and myths, in genealogies, and eventually in hundreds of answers to direct and indirect questioning on just this particular matter—there was nothing that could be interpreted as a reference to this shocking contact with Europeans.

The aboriginal accounts of their first remembered contact with whites begin in about 1900 with references to persons known to have had sporadic but lethal encounters with them. From that time on whites continued to remain on the southern periphery of Yir Yoront territory. With the establishment of cattle stations (ranches) to the south, cattle men made occasional excursions among the "wild black-fellows" in order to inspect the country and abduct natives to be trained as cattle boys and "house girls." At least one such

---

* An account of this expedition from Amboina is given in R. Logan Jack, *Northmost Australia* (2 vols.), London, 1921, Vol. 1, pp. 18–57.

** R. Logan Jack, op. cit., pp. 298–335.

expedition reached the Coleman River where a number of Yir Yoront men and women were shot for no apparent reason.

About this time the government was persuaded to sponsor the establishment of three mission stations along the 700-mile western coast of the Peninsula in an attempt to help regulate the treatment of natives. To further this purpose a strip of coastal territory was set aside as an aboriginal reserve and closed to further white settlement.

In 1915, an Anglican mission station was established near the mouth of the Mitchell River, about a three-day march from the heart of the Yir Yoront country. Some Yir Yoront refused to have anything to do with the mission, others visited it occasionally, while only a few eventually settled more or less permanently in one of the three "villages" established at the mission.

Thus the majority of the Yir Yoront continued to live their old self-supporting life in the bush, protected until 1942 by the government reserve and the intervening mission from the cruder realities of the encroaching new order from the south. To the east was poor, uninhabited country. To the north were other bush tribes extending on along the coast to the distant Archer River Presbyterian mission with which the Yir Yoront had no contact. Westward was the shallow Gulf of Carpentaria on which the natives saw only a mission lugger making its infrequent dry season trips to the Mitchell River. In this protected environment for over a generation the Yir Yoront were able to recuperate from shocks received at the hands of civilized society. During the 1930s their raiding and fighting, their trading and stealing of women, their evisceration and two- or three-year care of their dead, and their totemic ceremonies continued, apparently uninhibited by western influence. In 1931 they killed a European who wandered into their territory from the east, but the investigating police never approached the group whose members were responsible for the act.

As a direct result of the work of the Mitchell River mission, all Yir Yoront received a great many more western artifacts of all kinds than ever before. As part of their plan for raising native living standards, the missionaries made it possible for aboriginals living at the mission to earn some western goods, many of which were then given or traded to natives still living under bush conditions; they also handed out certain useful articles gratis to both mission and bush aboriginals. They prevented guns, liquor, and damaging narcotics, as well as decimating diseases, from reaching the tribes of this area, while encouraging the introduction of goods they considered "improving." As has been noted, no item of western technology available, with the possible exception of trade tobacco, was in greater demand among all groups of aboriginals than the short handled steel axe. The mission always kept a good supply of these axes in stock; at Christmas parties or other mission festivals they were given away to mission or visiting aboriginals indiscriminately and in considerable numbers. In addition, some steel axes as well as other European goods were still traded in to the Yir Yoront by natives in contact with cattle stations in the south. Indeed, steel axes had probably come to the Yir Yoront through established lines of aboriginal trade long before any regular contact with whites had occurred.

III: Relevant Factors

If we concentrate our attention on Yir Yoront behavior centering about the original stone axe (rather than on the axe—the object—itself) as a cultural trait or item of cultural equipment, we should get some conception of the role this implement played in aboriginal culture. This, in turn, should enable us to foresee with considerable accuracy some of the results stemming from the displacement of the stone axe by the steel axe.

The production of a stone axe required a number of simple technological skills. With the various details of the axe well in mind, adult men could set about producing it (a task not considered appropriate for women or children). First of all a man had to know the location and properties of several natural resources found in his immediate environment: pliable wood for a handle, which could be doubled or bent over the axe head and bound tightly; bark, which could be rolled into cord for the binding; and gum, to fix the stone head in the haft. These materials had to be correctly gathered, stored, prepared, cut to size and applied or manipulated. They were in plentiful supply, and could be taken from anyone's property without special permission. Postponing consideration of the stone head, the axe could be made by any normal man who had a simple knowledge of nature and of the technological skills involved, together with fire (for heating the gum), and a few simple cutting tools—perhaps the sharp shells of plentiful bivalves.

The use of the stone axe as a piece of capital equipment used in producing other goods indicates its very great importance to the subsistence economy of the aboriginal. Anyone—man, woman, or child—could use the axe; indeed, it was used primarily by women, for theirs was the task of obtaining sufficient wood to keep the family campfire burning all day, for cooking or other purposes, and all night against mosquitoes and cold (for in July, winter temperature might drop below 40 degrees). In a normal lifetime a woman would use the axe to cut or knock down literally tons of firewood. The axe was also used to make other tools or weapons, and a variety of material equipment required by the aboriginal in his daily life. The stone axe was essential in the construction of the wet season domed huts which keep out some rain and some insects; of platforms which provide dry storage; of shelters which give shade in the dry summer when days are bright and hot. In hunting and fishing and in gathering vegetable or animal food the axe was also a necessary tool, and in this tropical culture, where preservatives or other means of storage are lacking, the natives spend more time obtaining food than in any other occupation—except sleeping. In only two instances was the use of the stone axe strictly limited to adult men: for gathering wild honey, the most prized food known to the Yir

Yoront; and for making the secret paraphernalia for ceremonies. From this brief listing of some of the activities involving the use of the axe, it is easy to understand why there was at least one stone axe in every camp, in every hunting or fighting party, and in every group out on a "walkabout" in the bush.

The stone axe was also prominent in interpersonal relations. Yir Yoront men were dependent upon interpersonal relations for their stone axe heads, since the flat, geologically-recent, alluvial country over which they range provides no suitable stone for this purpose. The stone they used came from quarries 400 miles to the south, reaching the Yir Yoront through long lines of male trading partners. Some of these chains terminated with the Yir Yoront men, others extended on farther north to other groups, using Yir Yoront men as links. Almost every older adult man had one or more regular trading partners, some to the north and some to the south. He provided his partner or partners in the south with surplus spears, particularly fighting spears tipped with the barbed spines of sting ray which snap into vicious fragments when they penetrate human flesh. For a dozen such spears, some of which he may have obtained from a partner to the north, he would receive one stone axe head. Studies have shown that the sting ray barb spears increased in value as they move south and farther from the sea. One hundred and fifty miles south of Yir Yoront one such spear may be exchanged for one stone axe head. Although actual investigations could not be made, it was presumed that farther south, nearer the quarries, one sting ray barb spear would bring several stone axe heads. Apparently people who acted as links in the middle of the chain and who made neither spears nor axe heads would receive a certain number of each as a middleman's profit.

Thus trading relations, which may extend the individual's personal relationships beyond that of his own group, were associated with spears and axes, two of the most important items in a man's equipment. Finally, most of the exchanges took place during the dry season, at the time of the great aboriginal celebrations centering about initiation rites or other totemic ceremonials which attracted hundreds and were the occasion for much exciting activity in addition to trading.

Returning to the Yir Yoront, we find that adult men kept their axes in camp with their other equipment, or carried them when travelling. Thus a woman or child who wanted to use an axe—as might frequently happen during the day—had to get one from a man, use it promptly, and return it in good condition. While a man might speak of "my axe," a woman or child could not.

This necessary and constant borrowing of axes from older men by women and children was in accordance with regular patterns of kinship behavior. A woman would expect to use her husband's axe unless he himself was using it; if unmarried, or if her husband was absent, a woman would go first to her older brother or to her father. Only in extraordinary circumstances would she seek a stone axe from other male kin. A girl, a boy, or a young man would look to a father or an older brother to provide an axe for their use. Older men, too, would follow similar rules if they had to borrow an axe.

It will be noted that all of these social relationships in which the stone axe had a place are pair relationships and that the use of the axe helped to define and maintain their character and the roles of the two individual participants. Every active relationship among the Yir Yoront involved a definite and accepted status of superordination or subordination. A person could have no dealings with another on exactly equal terms. The nearest approach to equality was between brothers, although the older was always superordinate to the younger. Since the exchange of goods in a trading relationship involved a mutual reciprocity, trading partners usually stood in a brotherly type of relationship, although one was always classified as older than the other and would have some advantage in case of dispute. It can be seen that repeated and widespread conduct centering around the use of the axe helped to generalize and standardize these sex, age, and kinship roles both in their normal benevolent and exceptional malevolent aspects.

The status of any individual Yir Yoront was determined not only by sex, age, and extended kin relationships, but also by membership in one of two dozen patrilineal totemic clans into which the entire community was divided.* Each clan had literally hundreds of totems, from one or two of which the clan derived its name, and the clan members their personal names. These totems included natural species or phenomena such as the sun, stars, and daybreak, as well as cultural "species": imagined ghosts, rainbow serpents, heroic ancestors; such eternal cultural verities as fires, spears, huts; and such human activities, conditions, or attributes as eating, vomiting, swimming, fighting, babies and corpses, milk and blood, lips and loins. While individual members of such totemic classes or species might disappear or be destroyed, the class itself was obviously ever-present and indestructible. The totems, therefore, lent permanence and stability to the clans, to the groupings of human individuals who generation after generation were each associated with a set of totems which distinguished one clan from another.

The stone axe was one of the most important of the many totems of the Sunlit Cloud Iguana clan. The names of many members of this clan referred to the axe itself to activities in which the axe played a vital part, or to the clan's mythical ancestors with whom the axe was prominently associated. When it was necessary to represent the stone axe in totemic ceremonies, only men of this clan exhibited it or pantomimed its use. In secular life, the

---

* The best, although highly concentrated, summaries of totemism among the Yir Yoront and the other tribes of north Queensland will be found in R. Lauriston Sharp, "Tribes and Totemism in Northeast Australia," Oceania, Vol. 8, 1939, pp. 254–275 and 439–461 (especially pp. 268–275); also "Notes on Northeast Australian Totemism," in Papers of the Peabody Museum of American/Archaeology and Ethnology, Vol. 20, Studies in the Anthropology of Oceania and Asia, Cambridge, 1943, pp. 66–71.

axe could be made by any man and used by all; but in the sacred realm of the totems it belonged exclusively to the Sunlit Cloud Iguana people.

Supporting those aspects of cultural behavior which we have called technology and conduct, is a third area of culture which includes ideas, sentiments, and values. These are most difficult to deal with, for they are latent and covert, and even unconscious, and must be deduced from overt actions and language or other communicating behavior. In this aspect of the culture lies the significance of the stone axe to the Yir Yoront and to their cultural way of life.

The stone axe was an important symbol of masculinity among the Yir Yoront (just as pants or pipes are to us). By a complicated set of ideas the axe was defined as "belonging" to males, and everyone in the society (except untrained infants) accepted these ideas. Similarly spears, spear throwers, and fire-making sticks were owned only by men and were also symbols of masculinity. But the masculine values represented by the stone axe were constantly being impressed on all members of society by the fact that females borrowed axes but not other masculine artifacts. Thus the axe stood for an important theme of Yir Yoront culture: the superiority and rightful dominance of the male, and the greater value of his concerns and of all things associated with him. As the axe also had to be borrowed by the younger people it represented the prestige of age, another important theme running through Yir Yoront behavior.

To understand the Yir Yoront culture it is necessary to be aware of a system of ideas which may be called their totemic ideology. A fundamental belief of the aboriginal divided time into two great epochs: (1) a distant and sacred period at the beginning of the world when the earth was peopled by mildly marvelous ancestral beings or culture heroes who are in a special sense the forebears of the clans; and (2) a period when the old was succeeded by a new order which includes the present. Originally there was no anticipation of another era supplanting the present. The future would simply be an eternal continuation and reproduction of the present which itself had remained unchanged since the epochal revolution of ancestral times.

The important thing to note is that the aboriginal believed that the present world, as a natural and cultural environment, was and should be simply a detailed reproduction of the world of the ancestors. He believed that the entire universe "is now as it was in the beginning" when it was established and left by the ancestors. The ordinary cultural life of the ancestors became the daily life of the Yir Yoront camps, and the extraordinary life of the ancestors remained extant in the recurring symbolic pantomimes and paraphernalia found only in the most sacred atmosphere of the totemic rites.

Such beliefs, accordingly, opened the way for ideas of what should be (because it supposedly was) to influence or help determine what actually is. A man called Dog-chases-iguana-up-a-tree-and-barks-at-him-all-night had that and other names because he believed his ancestral alter ego had also had them; he was a member of the Sunlit Cloud Iguana clan because his ancestor was; he was associated with particular countries and totems of this same ancestor; during an initiation he played the role of a dog and symbolically attacked and killed certain members of other clans because his ancestor (conveniently either anthropomorphic or kynomorphic) really did the same to the ancestral alter egos of these men; and he would avoid his mother-in-law, joke with a mother's distant brother, and make spears in a certain way because his and other people's ancestors did these things. His behavior in these specific ways was outlined, and to that extent determined for him, by a set of ideas concerning the past and the relation of the present to the past.

But when we are informed that Dog-chases-etc. had two wives from the Spear Black Duck clan and one from the Native Companion clan, one of them being blind, that he had four children with such and such names, that he had a broken wrist and was left handed, all because his ancestor had exactly these same attributes, then we know (though he apparently didn't) that the present has influenced the past, that the mythical world has been somewhat adjusted to meet the exigencies and accidents of the inescapably real present.

There was thus in Yir Yoront ideology a nice balance in which the mythical was adjusted in part to the real world, the real world in part to the ideal pre-existing mythical world, the adjustments occurring to maintain a fundamental tenet of native faith that the present must be a mirror of the past. Thus the stone axe in all its aspects, uses, and associations was integrated into the context of Yir Yoront technology and conduct because a myth, a set of ideas, had put it there.

IV: The Outcome

The introduction of the steel axe indiscriminately and in large numbers into the Yir Yoront technology occurred simultaneously with many other changes. It is therefore impossible to separate all the results of this single innovation: Nevertheless, a number of specific effects of the change from stone to steel axes may be noted, and the steel axe may be used as an epitome of the increasing quantity of European goods and implements received by the aboriginals and of their general influence on the native culture. The use of the steel axe to illustrate such influences would seem to be justified. It was one of the first Europe artifacts to be adopted for regular use by the Yir Yoront, and whether made of stone or steel, the axe was clearly one of the most important items of cultural equipment they possessed.

The shift from stone to steel axes provided no major technological difficulties. While the aboriginals themselves could not manufacture steel axe heads, a steady supply from outside continued; broken wooden handles could easily be replaced from bush timbers with aboriginal tools. Among the Yir Yoront the new axe was never used to the extent it was on mission or cattle stations (for carpentry work, pounding tent pegs, as a hammer, and so on); indeed, it had so few more uses than the stone axe that its practical effect on the native standard of living was negligible. It did some jobs better, and could be used longer without breakage. These factors were sufficient to make it of value to the native. The white man believed that a shift from steel to stone axe on his part would be a definite regression. He was convinced that his axe was much more efficient, that its use would save time, and that it therefore represented technical "progress" towards goals which he had set up for the native. But this assumption was hardly born out in aboriginal practice. Any leisure time the Yir Yoront might gain by using steel axes or other western tools was not invested in "improving the conditions of life," nor, certainly, in developing aesthetic activities, but in sleep—an art they had mastered thoroughly.

Previously, a man in need of an axe would acquire a stone axe head through regular trading partners from whom he knew what to expect, and was then dependent solely upon a known and adequate natural environment, and his own skills or easily acquired techniques. A man wanting a steel axe, however, was in no such self-reliant position. If he attended a mission festival when steel axes were handed out as gifts, he might receive one either by chance or by happening to impress upon the mission staff that he was one of the "better" bush aboriginals (the missionaries' definition of "better" being quite different from that of his bush fellows). Or, again almost by pure chance, he might get some brief job in connection with the mission which would enable him to earn a steel axe. In either case, for older men a preference for the steel axe helped change the situation from one of self-reliance to one of dependence, and a shift in behavior from well-structured or defined situations in technology or conduct to ill-defined situations in conduct alone. Among the men, the older ones whose earlier experience or knowledge of the white man's harshness made them suspicious were particularly careful to avoid having relations with the mission, and thus excluded themselves from acquiring steel axes from that source.

In other aspects of conduct or social relations, the steel axe was even more significantly at the root of psychological stress among the Yir Yoront. This was the result of new factors which the missionary considered beneficial: the simple numerical increase in axes per capita as a result of mission distribution, and distribution directly to younger men, women, and even children. By winning the favor of the mission staff, a woman might be given a steel axe which was clearly intended to be hers, thus creating a situation quite different from the previous custom which necessitated her borrowing an axe from a male relative. As a result a woman would refer to the axe as "mine," a possessive form she was never able to use of the stone axe. In the same fashion, young men or even boys also obtained steel axes directly from the mission, with the result that older men no longer had a complete monopoly of all the axes in the bush community. All this led to a revolutionary confusion of sex, age, and kinship roles, with a major gain in independence and loss of subordination on the part of those who now owned steel axes when they had previously been unable to possess stone axes.

The trading partner relationship was also affected by the new situation. A Yir Yoront might have a trading partner in a tribe to the south whom he defined as a younger brother and over whom he would therefore have some authority. But if the partner were in contact with the mission or had other access to steel axes, his subordination obviously decreased. Among other things, this took some of the excitement away from the dry season fiesta-like tribal gatherings centering around initiations. These had traditionally been the climactic annual occasions for exchanges between trading partners, when a man might seek to acquire a whole year's supply of stone axe heads. Now he might find himself prostituting his wife to almost total strangers in return for steel axes or other white man's goods. With trading partnerships weakened, there was less reason to attend the ceremonies, and less fun for those who did.

Not only did an increase in steel axes and their distribution to women change the character of the relations between individuals (the paired relationships that have been noted), but a previously rare type of relationship was created in the Yir Yoront's conduct towards whites. In the aboriginal society there were few occasions outside of the immediate family when an individual would initiate action to several other people at once. In any average group, in accordance with the kipship system, while a person might be superordinate to several people to whom he could suggest or command action, he was also subordinate to several others with whom such behavior would be tabu. There was thus no overall chieftainship or authoritarian leadership of any kind. Such complicated operations as grass-burning animal drives or totemic ceremonies could be carried out smoothly because each person was aware of his role.

On both mission and cattle stations, however, the whites imposed their conception of leadership roles upon the aboriginals, consisting of one person in a controlling relationship with a subordinate group. Aboriginals called together to receive gifts, including axes, at a mission Christmas party found themselves facing one or two whites who sought to control their behavior for the occasion, who disregarded the age, sex, and kinship variables of which the aboriginals were so conscious, and who considered them all at one subordinate level. The white also sought to impose similar patterns on work parties. (However, if he placed an aboriginal in charge of a mixed group of post-hole diggers, for example, half of the group, those subordinate to the "boss," would work while the other half who were superordinate to him, would sleep.) For the aboriginal, the steel axe and other European goods came to symbolize this new and uncomfortable from of social organization, the leader-group relationship.

The most disturbing effects of the steel axe, operating in conjunction with other elements also being introduced from the white man's several subcultures, developed in the realm of traditional ideas, sentiments and values. These were undermined at a rapidly mounting rate, with no new conceptions being defined to replace them. The result was the erection of a mental and moral void which foreshadowed the collapse and destruction of all Yir Yoront culture, if not, indeed, the extinction of the biological group itself.

From what has been said it should be clear how changes in overt behavior, in technology and conduct, weakened the values inherent in a reliance on nature, in the prestige of masculinity and of age, and in the various kinship relations. A scene was set in which a wife, or a young son whose initiation may not yet have been completed, need no longer defer to the husband or father who, in turn, became confused and insecure as he was forced to borrow a steel axe from them. For the woman and boy the steel axe helped establish a new degree of freedom which they accepted readily as an escape from the unconscious stress of the old patterns—but they too, were left confused and insecure. Ownership became less well defined with the result that stealing and trespassing were introduced into technology and conduct. Some of the excitement surrounding the great ceremonies evaporated and they lost their previous gaiety and interest. Indeed, life itself became less interesting, although this did not lead the Yir Yoront to discover suicide, a concept foreign to them.

The whole process may be most specifically illustrated in terms of totemic system, which also illustrates the significant role played by a system of ideas, in this case a totemic ideology in the breakdown of a culture.

In the first place, under pre-European aboriginal conditions where the native culture has become adjusted to a relatively stable environment, few, if any, unheard of or catastrophic crises can occur. It is clear, therefore, that the totemic system serves very effectively in inhibiting radical cultural changes. The closed system of totemic ideas, explaining, and categorizing a well-known universe as it was fixed at the beginning of time, presents a considerable obstacle to the adoption of new or the dropping of old culture traits. The obstacle is not insurmountable and the system allows for the minor variations which occur in the norms of daily life. But the inception of major changes cannot easily take place.

Among the bush Yir Yoront the only means of water transport is a light wood log to which they cling in their constant swimming of rivers, salt creeks, and tidal inlets. These natives know that tribes 45 miles further north have a bark canoe. They know these northern tribes can thus fish from midstream or out at sea, instead of clinging to the river banks and beaches, that they can cross coastal waters infested with crocodiles, sharks, sting rays, and Portuguese men-of-war without danger. They know the materials of which the canoe is made exist in their own environment. But they also know, as they say, that they do not have canoes because their own mythical ancestors did not have them. They assume that the canoe was part of the ancestral universe of the northern tribes. For them, then, the adoption of the canoe would not be simply a matter of learning a number of new behavioral skills for its manufacture and use. The adoption would require a much more difficult procedure; the acceptance by the entire society of a myth, either locally developed or borrowed, to explain the presence of the canoe, to associate it with some one or more of the several hundred mythical ancestors (and how to decide which?), and thus establish it as an accepted totem of one of the clans ready to be used by the whole community. The Yir Yoront have not made this adjustment, and in this case we can only say that for the time being at least, ideas have won out over very real pressures for technological change. In the elaborateness and explicitness of the totemic ideologies we seem to have one explanation for the notorious stability of Australian cultures under aboriginal conditions, an explanation which gives due weight to the importance of ideas in determining human behavior.

At a later stage of the contact situation, as has been indicated, phenomena unaccounted for by the totemic ideological system begin to appear with regularity and frequency and remain within the range of native experience. Accordingly, they cannot be ignored (as the "Battle of the Mitchell" was apparently ignored), and there is an attempt to assimilate them and account for them along the lines of principles inherent in the ideology. The bush Yir Yoront of the mid-thirties represent this stage of the acculturation process. Still trying to maintain their aboriginal definition of the situation, they accept European artifacts and behavior patterns, but fit them into their totemic system, assigning them to various clans on a par with original totems. There is an attempt to have the myth-making process keep up with these cultural changes so that the idea system can continue to support the rest of the culture. But analysis of overt behavior, of dreams, and of some of the new myths indicates that this arrangement is not entirely satisfactory, that the native clings to his totemic system with intellectual loyalty lacking any substitute ideology), but that associated sentiments and values are weakened. His attitudes towards his own and towards European culture are found to be highly ambivalent.

All ghosts are totems of the Head-to-the-East Corpse clan, are thought of as white, and are of course closely associated with death. The white man, too, is closely associated with death, and he and all things pertaining to him are naturally assigned to the Corpse clan as totems. The steel axe, as a totem, was thus associated with the Corpse clan. But as an "axe," clearly linked with the stone axe, it is a totem of the Sunlit Cloud Iguana clan. Moreover, the steel axe, like most European goods, has no distinctive origin myth, nor are mythical ancestors associated with it. Can anyone, sitting in the shade of a ti tree one afternoon, create a myth to resolve this confusion? No one has, and the horrid suspicion arises as to the authenticity of the origin myths, which failed to take into account this vast new universe of the white man. The steel axe, shifting hopelessly between one clan and the other, is not only replacing the stone axe physically, but is hacking at the supports of the entire cultural system.

The aboriginals to the south of the Yir Yoront have clearly passed beyond this stage. They are engulfed by European culture, either by the mission or cattle station sub-cultures or, for some natives, by a baffling, paradoxical combination of both incongruent varieties. The totemic ideology can no longer support the inrushing mass of foreign culture traits, and the myth-making process in its native form breaks down completely. Both intellectually and emotionally a saturation point is reached so that the myriad new traits which can neither be ignored nor any longer assimilated simply force the aboriginal to abandon his totemic system. With the collapse of this system of ideas, which is so closely related to so many other aspects of the native culture, there follows an appallingly sudden and complete cultural disintegration, and a demoralization of the individual such as has seldom been recorded elsewhere. Without the support of a system of ideas well devised to provide cultural stability in a stable environment, but admittedly too rigid for the new realities pressing in from outside, native behavior and native sentiments and values are simply dead. Apathy reigns. The aboriginal has passed beyond the realm of any outsider who might wish to do him well or ill.

Returning from the broken natives huddled on cattle stations or on the fringes of frontier towns to the ambivalent but still lively aboriginals settled on the Mitchell River mission, we note one further devious result of the introduction of European artifacts. During a wet season stay at the mission, the anthropologist discovered that his supply of tooth paste was being depleted at an alarming rate. Investigation showed that it was being taken by old men for use in a new tooth paste cult. Old materials of magic having failed, new materials were being tried out in a malevolent magic directed towards the mission staff and some of the younger aboriginal men. Old males, largely ignored by the missionaries; were seeking to regain some of their lost power and prestige. This mild aggression proved hardly effective, but perhaps only because confidence in any kind of magic on the mission was by this time at a low ebb.

For the Yir Yoront still in the bush, a time could be predicted when personal deprivation and frustration in a confused culture would produce an overload of anxiety. The mythical past of the totemic ancestors would disappear as a guarantee of a present of which the future was supposed to be a stable continuation. Without the past, the present could be meaningless and the future unstructured and uncertain. Insecurities would be inevitable. Reaction to this stress might be some form of symbolic aggression, or withdrawal and apathy, or some more realistic approach. In such a situation the missionary with understanding of the processes going on about him would find his opportunity to introduce his forms of religion and to help create a new cultural universe.

Death Without Weeping

By Nancy Scheper-Hughes

I have seen death without weeping
The destiny of the Northeast is death
Cattle they kill
To the people they do something worse
—Anonymous Brazilian singer (1965)

W hy do the church bells ring so often?" I asked Nailza de Arruda soon after I moved into a corner of her tiny mud-walled hut near the top of the shantytown called the Alto do Cruzeiro (Crucifix Hill). I was then a Peace Corps volunteer and a community development/health worker. It was the dry and blazing hot summer of 1965, the months following the military coup in Brazil, and save for the rusty, clanging bells of N.S. das Dores Church, an eerie quiet had settled over the market town that I call Bom Jesus da Mata. Beneath the quiet, however, there was chaos and panic. "It's nothing," replied Nailza, "just another little angel gone to heaven."

Nailza had sent more than her share of little angels to heaven, and sometimes at night I could hear her engaged in a muffled but passionate discourse with one of them, two-year-old Joana. Joana's photograph, taken as she lay propped up in her tiny cardboard coffin, her eyes open, hung on a wall next to one of Nailza and Ze Antonio taken on the day they eloped.

Nailza could barely remember the other infants and babies who came and went in close succession. Most had died unnamed and were hastily baptized in their coffins. Few lived more than a month or two. Only Joana, properly baptized in church at the close of her first year and placed under the protection of a powerful saint, Joan of Arc, had been expected to live. And Nailza had dangerously allowed herself to love the little girl.

Nancy Scheper-Hughes, "Death Without Weeping," *Natural History*, October 1989. Permission to reprint granted by the author.

In addressing the dead child, Nailza's voice would range from tearful imploring to angry recrimination: "Why did you leave me? Was your patron saint so greedy that she could not allow me one child on this earth?" Ze Antonio advised me to ignore Nailza's odd behavior, which he understood as a kind of madness that, like the birth and death of children, came and went. Indeed, the premature birth of a stillborn son some months later "cured" Nailza of her "inappropriate" grief, and the day came when she removed Joana's photo and carefully packed it away.

More than fifteen years elapsed before I returned to the Alto do Cruzeiro, and it was anthropology that provided the vehicle of my return. Since 1982 I have returned several times in order to pursue a problem that first attracted my attention in the 1960s. My involvement with the people of the Alto do Cruzeiro now spans a quarter of a century and three generations of parenting in a community where mothers and daughters are often simultaneously pregnant.

The Alto do Cruzeiro is one of three shantytowns surrounding the large market town of Bom Jesus in the sugar plantation zone of Pernambuco in Northeast Brazil, one of the many zones of neglect that have emerged in the shadow of the now tarnished economic miracle of Brazil. For the women and children of the Alto do Cruzeiro the only miracle is that some of them have managed to stay alive at all.

The Northeast is a region of vast proportions (approximately twice the size of Texas) and of equally vast social and developmental problems. The nine states that make up the region are the poorest in the country and are representative of the Third World within a dynamic and rapidly industrializing nation. Despite waves of migrations from the interior to the teeming shantytowns of coastal cities, the majority still live in rural areas on farms and ranches, sugar plantations and mills.

Life expectancy in the Northeast is only forty years, largely because of the appallingly high rate of infant and child mortality. Approximately one million children in Brazil under the age of five die each year. The children of the Northeast, especially those born in shantytowns on the periphery of urban life, are at a very high risk of death. In these areas, children are born without the traditional protection of breast-feeding, subsistence gardens, stable marriages, and multiple adult caretakers that exists in the interior. In the hillside shantytowns that spring up around cities or in this case, interior market towns, marriages are brittle, single parenting is the norm, and women are frequently forced into the shadow economy of domestic work in the homes of the rich or into unprotected and oftentimes "scab" wage labor on the surrounding sugar plantations, where they clear land for planting and weed for a pittance, sometimes less than a dollar a day. The women of the Alto may not bring their babies with them into the homes of the wealthy, where the often-sick infants are considered sources of contamination, and they cannot carry the little ones to the riverbanks where they wash clothes because the river is heavily infested with schistosomes and other deadly parasites. Nor can they carry their young children to the plantations, which are often several miles away. At wages of a dollar a day the women of the Alto cannot hire baby sitters. Older children who are not in school will sometimes serve as somewhat indifferent caretakers. But any child not in school is also expected to find wage work. In most cases, babies are simply left at home alone, the door securely fastened. And so many also die alone and unattended.

Bom Jesus da Mata, centrally located in the plantation zone of Pernam-buco, is within commuting distance of several sugar plantations and mills. Consequently, Bom Jesus has been a magnet for rural workers forced off their small subsistence plots by large landowners wanting to use every available piece of land for sugar cultivation. Initially, the rural mi-grants to Bom Jesus were squatters who were given tacit approval by the mayor to put up temporary straw huts on each of the three hills overlooking the town. The Alto do Cruzeiro is the oldest, the largest, and the poorest of the shantytowns. Over the past three decades many of the original migrants have become permanent residents, and the primitive and temporary straw huts have been replaced by small homes (usually of two rooms) made of wattle and daub, sometimes covered with plaster. The more affluent residents use bricks and tiles. In most Alto homes, dangerous kerosene lamps have been replaced by light bulbs. The once tattered rural garb, often fashioned from used sugar sacking, has likewise been replaced by store-bought clothes, often castoffs from a wealthy *patrão* (boss). The trappings are modern, but the hunger, sickness, and death that they conceal are traditional, deeply rooted in a history of feudalism, exploitation, and institutionalized dependency.

My research agenda never wavered. The questions I addressed first crystallized during a veritable "die-off" of Alto babies during a severe drought in 1965. The food and water shortages and the political and economic chaos occasioned by the military coup were reflected in the handwritten entries of births and deaths in the dusty, yellowed pages of the ledger books kept at the public registry office in Bom Jesus. More than 350 babies died in the Alto during 1965 alone—this from a shantytown population of little more than 5,000. But that wasn't what surprised me. There were reasons enough for the deaths in the miserable conditions of shantytown life. What puzzled me was the seeming indifference of Alto women to the death of their infants, and their willingness to attribute to their own tiny offspring an aversion to life that made their death seem wholly natural, indeed all but anticipated.

Although I found that it was possible, and hardly difficult, to rescue infants and tod-dlers from death by diarrhea and dehydration with a simple sugar, salt, and water solution (even bottled Coca-Cola worked fine), it was more difficult to enlist a mother herself in the rescue of a child she perceived as ill-fated for life or better off dead, or to convince her to take back into her threatened and besieged home a baby she had already come to think of as an angel rather than as a son or daughter.

I learned that the high expectancy of death, and the ability to face child death with stoicism and equanimity, produced patterns of nurturing that differentiated between those infants thought of as thrivers and survivors and those thought of as born already "wanting to die." The survivors were nurtured, while stigmatized, doomed infants were left to die, as mothers say, a mingua, "of neglect." Mothers stepped back and allowed nature to take its course. This pattern, which I call mortal selective neglect, is called passive infanticide by anthropologist Marvin Harris. The Alto situation, although culturally specific in the form that it takes, is not unique to Third World shantytown communities and may have its correlates in our own impoverished urban communities in some cases of "failure to thrive" infants.

I use as an example the story of Zezinho, the thirteen-month-old toddler of one of my neighbors, Lourdes. I became involved with Zezinho when I was called in to help Lourdes in the delivery of another child, this one a fair and robust little tyke with a lusty cry. I noted that while Lourdes showed great interest in the newborn, she totally ignored Zezinho who, wasted and severely malnourished, was curled up in a fetal position on a piece of urine- and feces-soaked cardboard placed under his mother's hammock. Eyes open and vacant, mouth slack, the little boy seemed doomed.

When I carried Zezinho up to the community day-care center at the top of the hill, the Alto women who took turns caring for one another's children (in order to free themselves for part-time work in the cane fields or washing clothes) laughed at my efforts to save Ze, agreeing with Lourdes that here was a baby without a ghost of a chance. Leave him alone, they cautioned. It makes no sense to fight with death. But I did do battle with Ze, and after several weeks of force-feeding (malnourished babies lose their interest in food), Ze began to succumb to my ministrations. He acquired some flesh across his taut chest bones, learned to sit up, and even tried to smile. When he seemed well enough, I returned him to Lourdes in her miserable scrap-material lean-to, but not without guilt about what I had done. I wondered whether returning Ze was at all fair to Lourdes and to his little brother. But I was busy and washed my hands of the matter. And Lourdes did seem more interested in Ze now that he was looking more human.

When I returned in 1982, there was Lourdes among the women who formed my sample of Alto mothers—still struggling to put together some semblance of life for a now grown Ze and her five other surviving children. Much was made of my reunion with Ze in 1982, and everyone enjoyed retelling the story of Ze's rescue and of how his mother had given him up for dead. Ze would laugh the loudest when told how I had had to force-feed him like a fiesta turkey. There was no hint of guilt on the part of Lourdes and no resentment on the part of Ze. In fact, when questioned in private as to who was the best friend he ever had in life, Ze took a long drag on his cigarette and answered without a trace of irony, "Why my mother, of course!" "But of course," I replied.

Part of learning how to mother in the Alto do Cruzeiro is learning when to let go of a child who shows that it "wants" to die or that it has no "knack" or no "taste" for life. Another part is learning when it is safe to let oneself love a child. Frequent child death remains a powerful shaper of maternal thinking and practice. In the absence of firm expectation that a child will survive, mother love as we conceptualize it (whether in popular terms or in the psychobiological notion of maternal bonding) is attenuated and delayed with consequences for infant survival. In an environment already precarious to young life, the emotional detachment of mothers toward some of their babies contributes even further to the spiral of high mortality-high fertility in a kind of macabre lock-step dance of death.

The average woman of the Alto experiences 9.5 pregnancies, 3.5 child deaths, and 1.5 stillbirths. Seventy percent of all child deaths in the Alto occur in the first six months of life, and 82 percent by the end of the first year. Of all deaths in the community each year about 45 percent are of children under the age of five.

Women of the Alto distinguish between child deaths understood as natural (caused by diarrhea and communicable diseases) and those resulting from sorcery, the evil eye, or other magical or supernatural afflictions. They also recognize a large category of infant deaths seen as fated and inevitable. These hopeless cases are classified by mothers under the folk terminology "child sickness" or "child attack." Women say that there are at least fourteen different types of hopeless child sickness, but most can be subsumed under two categories—chronic and acute. The chronic cases refer to infants who are born small and wasted. They are deathly pale, mothers say, as well as weak and passive. They demonstrate no vital force, no liveliness. They do not suck vigorously; they hardly cry. Such babies can be this way at birth or they can be born sound but soon show no resistance, no "fight" against the common crises of infancy: diarrhea, respiratory infections, tropical fevers.

The acute cases are those doomed infants who die suddenly and violently. They are taken by stealth overnight, often following convulsions that bring on head banging, shaking, grimacing, and shrieking. Women say it is horrible to look at such a baby. If the infant begins to foam at the mouth or gnash its teeth or go rigid with its eyes turned back inside its head, there is absolutely no hope. The infant is "put aside"—left alone—often on the floor in a back room, and allowed to die. These symptoms (which accompany high fevers, dehydration, third-stage malnutrition, and encephalitis) are equated by Alto women with madness, epilepsy, and worst of all, rabies, which is greatly feared and highly stigmatized.

Most of the infants presented to me as suffering from chronic child sickness were tiny, wasted famine victims, while those labeled as victims of acute child attack seemed to be infants suffering from the deliriums of high fever or the convulsions that can accompany electrolyte imbalance in dehydrated babies.

Local midwives and traditional healers, praying women, as they are called, advise Alto women on when to allow a baby to die. One midwife explained: "If I can see that a baby was born unfortuitously, I tell the mother that she need not wash the infant or give it a cleansing tea. I tell her just to dust the infant with baby powder and wait for it to die." Allowing nature to take its course is not seen as sinful by these often very devout Catholic women. Rather it is understood as cooperating with God's plan.

Often I have been asked how consciously women of the Alto behave in this regard. I would have to say that consciousness is always shifting between allowed and disallowed levels of awareness. For example, I was awakened early one morning in 1987 by two neighborhood children who had been sent to fetch me to a hastily organized wake for a two-month-old infant whose mother I had unsuccessfully urged to breast-feed. The infant was being sustained on sugar water, which the mother referred to as *soro* (serum), using a medical term for the infant's starvation regime in light of his chronic diarrhea. I had cautioned the mother that an infant could not live on *soro* forever.

The two girls urged me to console the young mother by telling her that it was "too bad" that her infant was so weak that Jesus had to take him. They were coaching me in proper Alto etiquette. I agreed, of course, but asked, "And what do you think?" Xoxa, the eleven-year-old, looked down at her dusty flip-flops and blurted out, "Oh, Dona Nanci, that baby never got enough to eat, but you must never say that!" And so the death of hungry babies remains one of the best kept secrets of life in Bom Jesus da Mata.

Most victims are waked quickly and with a minimum of ceremony. No tears are shed, and the neighborhood children form a tiny procession, carrying the baby to the town graveyard where it will join a multitude of others. Although a few fresh flowers may be scattered over the tiny grave, no stone or wooden cross will mark the place, and the same spot will be reused within a few months' time. The mother will never visit the grave, which soon becomes an anonymous one.

What, then, can be said of these women? What emotions, what sentiments motivate them? How are they able to do what, in fact, must be done? What does mother love mean in this inhospitable context? Are grief, mourning, and melancholia present, although deeply repressed? If so, where shall we look for them? And if not, how are we to understand the moral visions and moral sensibilities that guide their actions?

I have been criticized more than once for presenting an unflattering portrait of poor Brazilian women, women who are, after all, themselves the victims of severe social and institutional neglect. I have described these women as allowing some of their children to die, as if this were an unnatural and inhuman act rather than, as I would assert, the way any one of us might act, reasonably and rationally, under similarly desperate conditions. Perhaps I have not emphasized enough the real pathogens in this environment of high risk: poverty, deprivation, sexism, chronic hunger, and economic exploitation. If mother love is, as many psychologists and some feminists believe, a seemingly natural and universal maternal script, what does it mean to women for whom scarcity, loss, sickness, and deprivation have made that love frantic and robbed them of their grief, seeming to turn their hearts to stone?

Throughout much of human history—as in a great deal of the impoverished Third World today—women have had to give birth and to nurture children under ecological conditions and social arrangements hostile to child survival, as well as to their own well-being. Under circumstances of high childhood mortality, patterns of selective neglect and passive infanticide may be seen as active survival strategies.

They also seem to be fairly common practices historically and across cultures. In societies characterized by high childhood mortality and by a correspondingly high (replacement) fertility, cultural practices of infant and child care tend to be organized primarily around survival goals. But what this means is a pragmatic recognition that not all of one's children can be expected to live. The nervousness about child survival in areas of northeast Brazil, northern India, or Bangladesh, where a 30 percent or 40 percent mortality rate in the first years of life is common, can lead to forms of delayed attachment and a casual or benign neglect that serves to weed out the worst bets so as to enhance the life chances of healthier siblings, including those yet to be born. Practices similar to those that I am describing have been recorded for parts of Africa, India, and Central America.

Life in the Alto do Cruzeiro resembles nothing so much as a battlefield or an emergency room in an overcrowded inner-city public hospital. Consequently, morality is guided by a kind of "lifeboat ethics," the morality of triage. The seemingly studied indifference toward the suffering of some of their infants, conveyed in such sayings as "little critters have no feelings," is understandable in light of these women's obligation to carry on with their reproductive and nurturing lives.

In their slowness to anthropomorphize and personalize their infants, everything is mobilized so as to prevent maternal overattachment and, therefore, grief at death. The bereaved mother is told not to cry, that her tears will dampen the wings of her little angel so that she cannot fly up to her heavenly home. Grief at the death of an angel is not only inappropriate, it is a symptom of madness and of a profound lack of faith.

Infant death becomes routine in an environment in which death is anticipated and bets are hedged. While the routinization of death in the context of shantytown life is not hard to understand, and quite possible to empathize with, its routinization in the formal institutions of public life in Bom Jesus is not as easy to accept uncritically. Here the social production of indifference takes on a different, even a malevolent, cast.

In a society where triplicates of every form are required for the most banal events (registering a car, for example), the registration of infant and child death is informal, incomplete, and rapid. It requires no documentation, takes less than five minutes, and demands no witnesses other than office clerks. No questions are asked concerning the circumstances of the death, and the cause of death is left blank, unquestioned and unexamined. A neighbor, grandmother, older sibling, or common-law husband may register the death. Since most infants die at home, there is no question of a medical record.

From the registry office, the parent proceeds to the town hall, where the mayor will give him or her a voucher for a free baby coffin. The full-time municipal coffinmaker cannot tell you exactly how many baby coffins are dispatched each week. It varies, he says, with the seasons. There are more needed during the drought months and during the big festivals of Carnaval and Christmas and São Joao's Day because people are too busy, he supposes, to take their babies to the clinic. Record keeping is sloppy.

Similarly, there is a failure on the part of city-employed doctors working at two free clinics to recognize the malnutrition of babies who are weighed, measured, and immunized without comment and as if they were not, in fact, anemic, stunted, fussy, and irritated starvation babies. At best the mothers are told to pick up free vitamins or a health "tonic" at the municipal chambers. At worst, clinic personnel will give tranquilizers and sleeping pills to quite the hungry cries of "sick-to-death" Alto babies.

The church, too, contributes to the routinization of, and indifference toward, child death. Traditionally, the local Catholic church taught patience and resignation to domestic tragedies that were said to reveal the imponderable workings of God's will. If an infant died suddenly, it was because a particular saint had claimed the child. The infant would be an angel in the service of his or her heavenly patron. It would be wrong, a sign of a lack of faith, to weep for a child with such good fortune. The infant funeral was, in the past, an event celebrated with joy. Today, however, under the new regime of "liberation theology," the bells of N.S. das Dores parish church no longer peal for the death of Alto babies, and no priest accompanies the procession of angels to the cemetery where their bodies are disposed of casually and without ceremony. Children bury children in Bom Jesus da Mata. In this most Catholic of communities, the coffin is handed to the disabled and irritable municipal gravedigger who often chides the children for one reason or another. It may be that the coffin is larger than expected and the gravedigger can find no appropriate space. The children do not wait for the gravedigger to complete his task. No prayers are recited and no sign of the cross made as the tiny coffin goes into its shallow grave.

When I asked the local priest, Padre Marcos, about the lack of church ceremony surrounding infant and childhood death today in Bom Jesus, he replied: "In the old days, child death was richly celebrated. But those were the baroque customs of a conservative church that wallowed in death and misery. The new church is a church of hope and joy. We no longer celebrate the death of child angels. We try to tell mothers that Jesus doesn't want all the dead babies they send him." Similarly, the new church has changed its baptismal customs, now often refusing to baptize dying babies brought to the back door of a church or rectory. The mothers are scolded by the church attendants and told to go home and take care of their sick babies. Baptism, they are told, is for the living; it is not to be confused with the sacrament of extreme unction, which is the anointing of the dying. And so it appears to the women of the Alto that even the church has turned away from them, denying the traditional comfort of folk Catholicism.

The contemporary Catholic church is caught in the clutches of a double bind. The new theology of liberation imagines a kingdom of God on earth based on justice and equality, a world without hunger, sickness, or childhood mortality. At the same time, the church has not changed its official position on sexuality and reproduction, including its sanctions against birth control, abortion, and sterilization. The padre of Bom Jesus da Mata recognizes this contradiction intuitively, although he shies away from discussions on the topic, saying that he prefers to leave questions of family planning to the discretion and the "good consciences" of his impoverished parishioners. But this, of course, sidesteps the extent to which those good consciences have been shaped by traditional church teachings in Bom Jesus, especially by his recent predecessors. Hence, we can begin to see that the seeming indifference of Alto mothers toward the death of some of their infants is but a pale reflection of the official indifference of church and state to the plight of poor women and children.

Nonetheless, the women of Bom Jesus are survivors. One woman, Biu, told me her life history, returning again and again to the themes of child death, her first husband's suicide, abandonment by her father and later by her second husband, and all the other losses and disappointments she had suffered in her long forty-five years. She concluded with great force, reflecting on the days of Carnaval '88 that were fast approaching:

> No, Dona Nanci, I won't cry and I won't waste my life thinking about it from morning to night. ... Can I argue with God for the state that I'm in? No! And so I'll dance and I'll jump and I'll play Carnaval! And yes, I'll laugh and people will wonder at a pobre like me who can have such a good time.

And no one did blame Biu for dancing in the streets during the four days of Carnaval— not even on Ash Wednesday, the day following Carnaval '88 when we all assembled hurriedly to assist in the burial of Mercea, Biu's beloved casula, her last-born daughter who had died at home of pneumonia during the festivities. The rest of the family barely had time to change out of their costumes. Severino, the child's uncle and godfather, sprinkled holy water over the little angel while he prayed: "Mercea, I don't know whether you were called, taken, or thrown out of this world. But look down at us from your heavenly home with tenderness, with pity, and with mercy." So be it.

Brief Epilogue

After reading this article many students write me to ask whether the situation has changed in the Alto do Cruzeiro. Is life better or worse for mothers and newborn babies? One of the advantages of traditional, long-term ethnographic research is that one gets to see history in the making. I began my engagements with the people of the Alto in 1964 at the start of twenty years of military rule, a ruthless political economic regime that produced widespread impoverishment among those excluded populations living in deep urban slums (favelas) and in peripheral rural communities. The scarcities and insecurities of that era contributed to the death of infants and small babies. By the time I completed my study of mother love and child death in the early 1990s Brazil was well on its way to democratization which ushered in many important changes, most notably a free, public, national health care system (SUS) which guaranteed poor women adequate pre-natal care, hospital delivery and basic maternal-infant care during the first years of life. The decade of the 1990s witnessed in Brazil what population experts call the demographic or epidemiologic transition. Both births and infant deaths declined which radically transformed the way newborns were perceived and received by Alto mothers. The old stance of maternal "watchful waiting" that was accompanied by maternal "de-selections" of those infants viewed as having no 'taste' or 'talent' for life, was replaced by a maternal ethos of 'holding on' and 'holding dear' each infant now seen as potentially capable of survival. Today, young women of the Alto can expect to give birth to three or fewer infants and to see all of them live to adolescence.

Many factors came together in producing this reproductive transition. The new teachings of liberation theology did eventually dislodge a baroque folk Catholicism that saw God and the saints as 'authorizing' infant death by 'calling' the infants to themselves. Women began to think of themselves as capable of deciding how many pregnancies they would have. The availability of over or 'under' the counter drug, Cytotec, as a risky "morning after" pill provided an easy means of birth spacing that had not existed before. President Fernando Henrique Cardoso (1995–2003) and his wife, the late Brazilian anthropologist Ruth Cardosa, fortified the national health care system (Serviço Único de Saúde) with a program of local 'health agents', 'barefoot doctors', who visit poor households door to door, identifying those at risk and rescuing a great many vulnerable infants, toddlers and old people from premature death. The primary cause of the decline in infant mortality on the Alto do Cruzeiro, however, was the result of a 'simple' municipal program, the installation of water pipes reaching almost all the homes in the shantytown with sufficient and clean water. Water=life!

It is essential to understand how 'culture', 'belief' and maternal sentiments, like 'mother love' and infant care follow basic changes in the material conditions—and therefore the possibilities—of everyday life. Motherhood is not only a social and a cultural construction but a constellation of embodied practices responding to the requirements and limitations of the political economy that determines the food people eat or don't eat, the water they drink or don't drink, the shoes they wear or don't wear, the books they read or cannot read, the homes made of mud and sticks or of brick and tiles.

There are many other new problems faced by the people of the Alto do Cruzeiro today. Since the publication of "Death without Weeping" drugs and gangs have made their ugly mark on the community as have new disease epidemics. Death squads and 'extermination groups' have sprung up to minister a kind of vigilante justice. These new features of anti-social life in "Bom Jesus da Mata" take some of the pleasure away, as one now sees the young boys of the Alto do Cruzeiro who survived that dangerous first year of life only to be cut down by bullets and knives at the age of 15 or 17 by local gangs, 'strong men', bandidos, and local police in almost equal measure. But that story awaits another and much longer telling.

—Nancy Scheper-Hughes

Where Fat Is a Mark of Beauty

By Ann M. Simmons

In a rite of passage, some Nigerian girls spend months gaining weight and learning customs in a special room. "To be called a 'slim princess' is an abuse," says a defender of the practice.

Akpabuyo, Nigeria—Margaret Bassey Ene currently has one mission in life: gaining weight.

The Nigerian teenager has spent every day since early June in a "fattening room" specially set aside in her father's mudand-thatch house. Most of her waking hours are spent eating bowl after bowl of rice, yams, plantains, beans and gari, a porridge-like mixture of dried cassava and water.

After three more months of starchy diet and forced inactivity, Margaret will be ready to reenter society bearing the traditional mark of female beauty among her Efik people: fat.

In contrast to many Western cultures where thin is in, many culture-conscious people in the Efik and other communities in Nigeria's southeastern Cross River state hail a woman's rotundity as a sign of good health, prosperity and allure.

The fattening room is at the center of a centuries-old rite of passage from maidenhood to womanhood. The months spent in pursuit of poundage are supplemented by daily visits from elderly matrons who impart tips on how to be a successful wife and mother. Nowadays, though, girls who are not yet marriage-bound do a tour in the rooms purely as a coming-of-age ceremony. And sometimes, nursing mothers return to the rooms to put on more weight.

"The fattening room is like a kind of school where the girl is taught about motherhood," said Sylvester Odey, director of the Cultural Center Board in Calabar, capital of Cross River state. "Your daily routine is to sleep, eat and grow fat."

Like many traditional African customs, the fattening room is facing relentless pressure from Western influences. Health campaigns linking excess fat to heart disease and other illnesses are changing the eating habits of many Nigerians, and urban dwellers are opting out of the time-consuming process.

Effiong Okon Etim, an Efik village chief in the district of Akpabuyo, said some families cannot afford to constantly feed a daughter for more than a few months. That compares with a stay of up to two years, as was common earlier this century, he said.

But the practice continues partly because "people might laugh at you because you didn't have money toallow your child to pass through the rite of passage," Etim said. What's more, many believe an unfattened girl will be sickly or unable to bear children.

Etim, 65, put his two daughters in a fattening room together when they were 12 and 15 years old, but some girls undergo the process as early as age 7, after undergoing the controversial practice of genital excision.

BIGGER IS BETTER, ACCORDING TO CUSTOM

As for how fat is fat enough, there is no set standard. But the unwritten rule is the bigger the better, said Mkoyo Edet, Etim's sister.

"Beauty is in the weight," said Edet, a woman in her 50s who spent three months in a fattening room when she was 7. "To be called a 'slim princess' is an abuse. The girl is fed constantly whether she likes it or not."

In Margaret's family, there was never any question that she would enter the fattening room.

"We inherited it from our forefathers; it is one of the heritages we must continue," said Edet Essien Okon, 25, Margaret's stepfather and a language and linguistics graduate of the University of Calabar. "It's a good thing to do; it's an initiation rite."

His wife, Nkoyo Effiong, 27, agreed: "As a woman, I feel it is proper for me to put my daughter in there, so she can be educated."

Effiong, a mother of five, spent four months in a fattening room at the age of 10. Margaret, an attractive girl with a cheerful smile and hair plaited in fluffy bumps, needs only six months in the fattening room because she was already naturally plump, her step-father said.

During the process, she is treated as a goddess, but the days are monotonous. To amuse herself, Margaret has only an instrument made out of a soda bottle with a hole in it, which she taps on her hand to play traditional tunes.

Still, the 16-year-old says she is enjoying the highly ritualized fattening practice.

"I'm very happy about this," she said, her belly already distended over the waist of her loincloth. "I enjoy the food, except for gari."

Day in, day out, Margaret must sit cross-legged on a special stool inside the secluded fattening room. When it is time to eat, she sits on the floor on a large, dried plantain leaf, which also serves as her bed. She washes down the mounds of food with huge pots of water and takes traditional medicine made from leaves and herbs to ensure proper digestion.

As part of the rite, Margaret's face is decorated with a white, claylike chalk.

"You have to prepare the child so that if a man sees her, she will be attractive," Chief Etim said.

Tufts of palm leaf fiber, braided and dyed red, are hung around Margaret's neck and tied like bangles around her wrists and ankles. They are adjusted as she grows.

Typically, Margaret would receive body massages using the white chalk powder mixed with heavy red palm oil. But the teen said her parents believe the skin-softening, blood-stimulating massages might cause her to expand further than necessary.

Margaret is barred from doing her usual chores or any other strenuous physical activities. And she is forbidden to receive visitors, save for the half a dozen matrons who school Margaret in the etiquette of the Efik clan.

They teach her such basics as how to sit, walk and talk in front of her husband. And they impart wisdom about cleaning, sewing, child care and cooking—Efik women are known throughout Nigeria for their chicken pepper soup, pounded yams and other culinary creations.

"They advise me to keep calm and quiet, to eat the gari, and not to have many boyfriends so that I avoid unwanted pregnancy," Margaret said of her matron teachers. "They say that unless you have passed through this, you will not be a full-grown woman."

What little exercise Margaret gets comes in dance lessons. The matrons teach her the traditional ekombi, which she will be expected to perform before an audience on the day she emerges from seclusion—usually on the girl's wedding day, Etim said.

But Okon said his aim is to prepare his stepdaughter for the future, not to marry her off immediately. Efik girls receive more education than girls in most parts of Nigeria, and Okon hopes Margaret will return to school and embark on a career as a seamstress before getting married.

WEDDINGS ALSO STEEPED IN TRADITION

Once she does wed, Margaret will probably honor southeastern Nigeria's rich marriage tradition. It begins with a letter from the family of the groom to the family of the bride, explaining that "our son has seen a flower, a jewel, or something beautiful in your family, that we are interested in," said Josephine Effah-Chukwuma, program officer for women and children at the Constitutional Rights Project, a law-oriented nongovernmental organization based in the Nigerian commercial capital of Lagos.

If the girl and her family consent, a meeting is arranged. The groom and his relatives arrive with alcoholic beverages, soft drinks and native brews, and the bride's parents provide the food. The would-be bride's name is never uttered, and the couple are not allowed to speak, but if all goes well, a date is set for handing over the dowry. On that occasion, the bride's parents receive about $30 as a token of appreciation for their care of the young woman. "If you make the groom pay too much, it is like selling your daughter," Effah-Chukwuma said. Then, more drinks are served, and the engagement is official.

On the day of the wedding, the bride sits on a specially built wooden throne, covered by an extravagantly decorated canopy. Maidens surround her as relatives bestow gifts such as pots, pans, brooms, plates, glasses, table covers—everything she will need to start her new home. During the festivities, the bride changes clothes three times.

The high point is the performance of the ekombi, in which the bride twists and twirls, shielded by maidens and resisting the advances of her husband. It is his task to break through the ring and claim his bride.

Traditionalists are glad that some wedding customs are thriving despite the onslaught of modernity.

Traditional weddings are much more prevalent in southeastern Nigeria than so-called white weddings, introduced by colonialists and conducted in a church or registry office.

"In order to be considered married, you have to be married in the traditional way," said Maureen Okon, a woman of the Qua ethnic group who wed seven years ago but skipped the fattening room because she did not want to sacrifice the time. "Tradition identifies a people. It is important to keep up a culture. There is quite a bit of beauty in Efik and Qua marriages."

FGM: Maasai Women Speak Out

By Ledama Olekina

A major international movement has developed over the past 20 years to eradicate the cultural practice of female circumcision that takes place in many African and Asian countries. At the Nairobi International Conference on Female Genital Mutilation in September, attendees from nations where female circumcision is practiced urged states to adopt political, legal, and social measures to eliminate the tradition. But the activists leading this movement have failed to understand the cultures behind the practice, and their ignorance is dangerous. Legislation, particularly the criminalization of FGM, and other external pressures that do not take local culture into account can have deadly consequences.

Before Maasai girls in Kenya and Tanzania are married, they must undergo circumcision in a ceremony that 99 percent of the time is sponsored by their prospective suitors. Aside from the actual surgical procedure, the rite includes a ceremony in which the entire community comes together to celebrate the girl's passage to adulthood.

Many Maasai families cannot afford to give their children formal schooling, so to protect their daughters from lives of poverty they choose to marry them off at a young age. Because Maasai girls are traditionally considered children until they are circumcised, it is seen as imperative for a Maasai girl to undergo the circumcision rite before she is married. This strongly ingrained cultural belief propels families to go to great lengths to complete the circumcision. Over the past 10 years, I have witnessed people in my Kenyan Maasai community being arrested for practicing female circumcision. I have seen young Maasai children nearly starve to death because their parents were sent to jail. Most painfully, I have heard of girls from my community as young as 10 years old undergoing circumcision and being married.

Representatives of many non-Maasai organizations come to my village and talk about how young girls are mutilated. They tell us that unless we stop the practice, we are all going to be prosecuted. In most cases, these forceful approaches have not succeeded. Many

Ledama Olekina, "FGM: Maasai Women Speak Out," *Cultural Survival Quarterly*, (28:4), December 15, 2005, pp. 21–23. Permission to reprint granted by the publisher.

families are now circumcising their girls at extremely young ages, before outside organizations have a chance to get suspicious and take action against them. Many Maasai, particularly those who live near urban areas, no longer announce their circumcision ceremonies. In some cases, the main circumcision ceremony takes place days after the surgery. I have seen young girls taken into hiding to be circumcised out of view of the authorities.

Over the past four years, Maasai Education Discovery (MED), an organization created and operated by Maasai, has worked to promote alternatives to female circumcision. Unlike many non-Maasai anti-PGM activists, we have not threatened to prosecute those who practice female circumcision. Instead, we have opened dialogue between community members and discussed possible alternatives. We have also encouraged young girls to speak out about their true feelings on the practice. In cases where a girl is being forced into circumcision against her will, we ensure that the girl is taken away from her family to a secure place. After some time, we initiate a reconciliation process to bring the girl back together with her parents and community. These strategies work.

MED also has initiated a program to involve the men. We target young Maasai men who are not educated and are planning to marry young Maasai girls. Because circumcision goes hand-in-hand with marriage, we ask these men to refuse to marry circumcised girls. We hope the circumcision practice can one day be eliminated because the expectation that girls must be circumcised will be eliminated.

Because of the negativity surrounding discussion of the practice, many Maasai are not willing to talk about the practice in public. Many of us who have been formally educated and exposed to the Western world understand that female circumcision, particularly the surgical part of the ceremony, must end. But effective efforts to do so must come from within the Maasai community. Maasai women and men must be educated about the dangers in order for them to find workable alternatives to a practice that has been a significant part of Maasai culture for generations.

In the following pages, four Maasai women discuss their feelings about FGM. International activists must listen to them.

Agnes Kainett Kisai
MED student from Ewuaso Ke-dong' in the Rift Valley of Kenya

The type of circumcision that the Maasai perform is called clitoridectomy, in which the entire clitoris or part of the clitoris, and at times the adjacent labia, is removed. The primary reason female circumcision is practiced among the Maasai is that it is considered a rite of passage. Circumcision is a cultural practice in the Maasai community, not a religious practice. It elevates a girl from childhood to the status of adulthood, and is necessary for a girl to be considered a complete woman. Another important belief among the Maasai is that the rite has an ability to reduce the woman's desire for sex, making her less likely to engage in pre-marital sex or adultery.

Being a Maasai woman who knows the effects of PGM, I feel obliged to tell about the harm that is brought to the girl. Excessive bleeding can occur during the practice and can lead to death. Today, because the procedure often has to take place in hiding, female circumcision is mostly performed using shared and un-sterilized objects, which can lead to HIV/AIDS and tetanus, and damage organs including the vaginal walls. Inflammation of the cells around the circumcision area also occurs shortly after the operation. The long-term effects of FGM include chronic infections of the reproductive parts, pain during sexual intercourse, and difficulties in childbirth.

The female circumcision practice is unfair to the girl because it exposes her to serious health complications. It is also mostly done against her wishes and becomes a violation of her rights. In the Maasai community, once a girl undergoes circumcision, she can start a family. This belief has contributed greatly to the practice of early marriage among the Maasai.

My parents, though they are illiterate, are against female circumcision—an unusual position for any typical Maasai. Though they were once in support of the practice, they came to change after I convinced them of the dangers. Being Christian and members of a denomination that does not allow the practice also encouraged them a great deal. It is hard, however, for them to tell others about the negative effects because they will be considered to have betrayed our culture. The Maasai people value our culture. Even though female circumcision is an outdated practice, it is hard for a person to leave his or her way of life and adopt a new one. If this change has to happen, it will happen gradually.

Eunice Sitatian Kaeio
MED student from Narok in the Rift Valley of Kenya

Female circumcision is a rite of passage among the Maasai that marks change from childhood to adulthood. Though some groups such as the Christian Church, educators, and some non-governmental organizations have made an effort to abolish this practice, the Maasai, according to my mother, are stubborn. She says, "Female circumcision is our culture. Why should we be forced to abandon it when we were born into it? Abandoning our culture would be annoying our ancestors. It would bring a curse to the entire community."

My mother also says that circumcision does not affect the sexual activity of a Maasai woman as many Maasai believe. Their heavy workloads, especially during times of nomadic moves, affect them more. The women are expected to build the houses whenever they move to a new place. During this time they also live under unhygienic conditions and, during times of drought, suffer malnutrition because they depend on the animals for their diets. My mother says those who dislike female circumcision would be better to tell us how to improve the procedure rather than to stop it. Why should we be forced to adopt a culture that is not ours?

In my own view, female circumcision should be abolished. To start with, it causes a lot of pain to the initiates. Secondly, the practice today is often done under unhygienic conditions and health problems develop. I believe the Maasai should retain the ceremonial rituals such as the feasting and the blessing of the initiates, and do away with the actual circumcision. Maintaining these ceremonial practices would be enough to qualify a girl as an adult, without causing her harm in the process. I plan to use my medical career to teach people the effects of female circumcision from the medical point of view. I think my community would respond better to a Maasai daughter than to a foreigner. I was circumcised when I was younger, before I understood the dangers. But I am glad that FGM was performed on me, because now I can talk from experience when I campaign against it.

Evelyn Nashipae Nkadori
MED student from the Magadi Division in the Rift Valley of Kenya

Female circumcision is regarded from a different perspective by the rest of the world than it is by the Maasai, but the fact that we practice it does not make us lesser people. According to our traditions and practices, it is meant to have a positive rather than a negative effect on the girl. It is supposed to reduce a woman's desire for sex and reduce immorality. Another thing is that traditionally, it is a rite of passage. It marks the end of childhood and the beginning of adulthood. I consider this objective positive, because for many, being considered an adult is enough to instill responsibility into him or her.

Although female circumcision does have some positive effects, I do not encourage it. In fact, I am campaigning to encourage Maasai families say no to FGM. The procedure is torture to the woman, and it is unnecessary. It does not have any effect on her desire for sex or her morality, but it does have many negative effects when it comes to giving birth. Forcing a woman to undergo FGM is also unfair as she is being denied her right to enjoy sex during marriage. It may cause death, as the equipment used is mostly shared and may spread diseases such as AIDS. A poorly performed procedure causes excessive bleeding, which causes death or anemia.

Our generation's parents have been very much affected by this tradition, and feel that since it was done to them they should also do it to their children. In some cases, Christianity has changed this attitude. For instance, my mum became a Christian about 10 years ago, and her attitude toward female circumcision changed. As a result, I was not circumcised. I am the new face of the Maasai girl and I will do all I can to help educate my community and my people positively and to ensure that I am a person who will be regarded as a source of hope in my community. Gradually we will be able to eliminate this outdated cultural practice.

Phideline Nasieku
MED student from Narok in the Rift Valley of Kenya

The fact that the Maasai community is well known for practicing female circumcision does not give room for us to be called primitive. We have always had reasons behind the practice.

In the Maasai community, circumcision is a rite of passage. It is a clear step between childhood and adulthood. Once a woman undergoes circumcision, she is ready for marriage. Maasai believe that the practice helps reduce immorality among girls because they are not allowed to engage in conjugal duties before they undergo circumcision. Boys are circumcised for similar reasons.

The Maasai believe that circumcision further helps improve people's morality because it reduces sexual urge, preventing cases of girls engaging in sex before marriage and giving birth out of wedlock. The Maasai do not perform the practice to harm people, but rather out of love and care for their people, because they are truly concerned about their people's morality.

The circumcision ceremony takes place in early morning. The girl first bathes with cold water, and then the operation is carried out. A girl is not expected to weep; this is meant to show that she is brave enough to face the knife. This gives her fame and respect from the community at large and she becomes a role model for the younger girls to emulate.

Female circumcision is a time-honored practice from the Maasai point of view, but it should be stopped for the betterment of the Maasai girls. Despite the Maasai's objectives in performing female circumcision, the disadvantages of the practice are increasing. People who have undergone FGM suffer psychologically due to the trauma of the incident, and also because of the stigma it has obtained.

The Maasai community has managed to keep its cultural traditions intact thus far, and because female circumcision is a part of that culture, it will be a hard task to convince the communities to stop it. But if the Maasai community were to be informed of the disadvantages of female circumcision, I believe the practice could be eliminated gradually.

Because my parents are Christian, I was not circumcised. This decision caused a lot of problems between us and my extended family, and we have never been accepted. Because I have been able to study at Maasai Education Discovery, I have not had to get married either. If it were not for my schooling, I would have been married by now.

Being a Maasai child, I understand our weaknesses and strengths. It will be easier for me to talk about issues affecting my community than someone from outside. I believe in being a role model for my younger sisters. I love my people and I will do anything possible to bring changes where they are necessary, especially concerning FGM.

Ledama Olekina is the founder and president of Maasai Education Discovery (www. maasaieducationdiscovery.org).

Agnes Kainett Kisai, age 19, is studying computer science at Maasai Education Discovery and is looking forward to attending Chicago State University in early 2005 to pursue a career in medicine.

Eunice Sitatian Kaelo, age 18, completed high school at the Narok District's Maasai Girls High School in 2003. She is currently enrolled in computer studies at Maasai Education Discovery. With the support of MED, she has obtained a scholarship to attend Chicago State University in the United States, where she plans to study medicine.

Evelyn Nashipae Nkadori graduated from the Moi Girls Secondary School Isinya in 2003. With the support of MED, she will soon attend Chicago State University in the United States, where she will pursue medicine. She is the first-born in a family of five.

Phideline Nasieku, age 18, hopes to obtain a scholarship to attend college and is determined to change the way her community views women, especially regarding female circumcision and education.

Our Silence About Race: America's Persistent Divide

By Barack Obama

The following is a transcript of the remarks of Democratic Illinois Sen. Barack Obama, delivered March 18, 2008, in Philadelphia at the Constitution Center. In it, Obama addresses the role race has played in the presidential campaign. He also responds to criticism of the Rev. Jeremiah Wright, an unpaid campaign adviser and pastor at Obama's Chicago church. Wright has made inflammatory remarks about the United States and has accused the country of bringing on the Sept. 11 attacks by spreading terrorism.

We the people, in order to form a more perfect union ..."—221 years ago, in a hall that still stands across the street, a group of men gathered and, with these simple words, launched America's improbable experiment in democracy. Farmers and scholars, statesmen and patriots who had traveled across an ocean to escape tyranny and persecution finally made real their declaration of independence at a Philadelphia convention that lasted through the spring of 1787.

The document they produced was eventually signed but ultimately unfinished. It was stained by this nation's original sin of slavery, a question that divided the colonies and brought the convention to a stalemate until the founders chose to allow the slave trade to continue for at least 20 more years, and to leave any final resolution to future generations.

Of course, the answer to the slavery question was already embedded within our Constitution—a Constitution that had at its very core the ideal of equal citizenship under the law; a Constitution that promised its people liberty and justice and a union that could be and should be perfected over time.

And yet words on a parchment would not be enough to deliver slaves from bondage, or provide men and women of every color and creed their full rights and obligations as citizens of the United States. What would be needed were Americans in successive generations who were willing to do their part—through protests and struggles, on the streets and in the courts, through a civil war and civil disobedience, and always at great risk—to narrow that gap between the promise of our ideals and the reality of their time.

This was one of the tasks we set forth at the beginning of this presidential campaign—to continue the long march of those who came before us, a march for a more just, more equal, more free, more caring and more prosperous America. I chose to run for president at this moment in history because I believe deeply that we cannot solve the challenges of our time unless we solve them together, unless we perfect our union by understanding that we may have different stories, but we hold common hopes; that we may not look the same and we may not have come from the same place, but we all want to move in the same direction—toward a better future for our children and our grandchildren.

This belief comes from my unyielding faith in the decency and generosity of the American people. But it also comes from my own story.

I am the son of a black man from Kenya and a white woman from Kansas. I was raised with the help of a white grandfather who survived a Depression to serve in Patton's Army during World War II and a white grandmother who worked on a bomber assembly line at Fort Leavenworth while he was overseas. I've gone to some of the best schools in America and lived in one of the world's poorest nations. I am married to a black American who carries within her the blood of slaves and slaveowners—an inheritance we pass on to our two precious daughters. I have brothers, sisters, nieces, nephews, uncles and cousins of every race and every hue, scattered across three continents, and for as long as I live, I will never forget that in no other country on Earth is my story even possible.

It's a story that hasn't made me the most conventional of candidates. But it is a story that has seared into my genetic makeup the idea that this nation is more than the sum of its parts—that out of many, we are truly one.

Throughout the first year of this campaign, against all predictions to the contrary, we saw how hungry the American people were for this message of unity. Despite the temptation to view my candidacy through a purely racial lens, we won commanding victories in states with some of the whitest populations in the country. In South Carolina, where the Confederate flag still flies, we built a powerful coalition of African-Americans and white Americans.

This is not to say that race has not been an issue in this campaign. At various stages in the campaign, some commentators have deemed me either "too black" or "not black enough." We saw racial tensions bubble to the surface during the week before the South Carolina primary. The press has scoured every single exit poll for the latest evidence of racial polarization, not just in terms of white and black, but black and brown as well.

And yet, it has only been in the last couple of weeks that the discussion of race in this campaign has taken a particularly divisive turn.

On one end of the spectrum, we've heard the implication that my candidacy is somehow an exercise in affirmative action; that it's based solely on the desire of wide-eyed liberals to purchase racial reconciliation on the cheap. On the other end, we've heard my former pastor, Jeremiah Wright, use incendiary language to express views that have the potential not only to widen the racial divide, but views that denigrate both the greatness and the goodness of our nation, and that rightly offend white and black alike.

I have already condemned, in unequivocal terms, the statements of Reverend Wright that have caused such controversy and, in some cases, pain. For some, nagging questions remain. Did I know him to be an occasionally fierce critic of American domestic and foreign policy? Of course. Did I ever hear him make remarks that could be considered controversial while I sat in the church? Yes. Did I strongly disagree with many of his political views? Absolutely—just as I'm sure many of you have heard remarks from your pastors, priests, or rabbis with which you strongly disagreed.

But the remarks that have caused this recent firestorm weren't simply controversial. They weren't simply a religious leader's efforts to speak out against perceived injustice. Instead, they expressed a profoundly distorted view of this country—a view that sees white racism as endemic, and that elevates what is wrong with America above all that we know is right with America; a view that sees the conflicts in the Middle East as rooted primarily in the actions of stalwart allies like Israel, instead of emanating from the perverse and hateful ideologies of radical Islam.

As such, Reverend Wright's comments were not only wrong but divisive, divisive at a time when we need unity; racially charged at a time when we need to come together to solve a set of monumental problems—two wars, a terrorist threat, a falling economy, a chronic health care crisis and potentially devastating climate change—problems that are neither black or white or Latino or Asian, but rather problems that confront us all.

Given my background, my politics, and my professed values and ideals, there will no doubt be those for whom my statements of condemnation are not enough. Why associate myself with Reverend Wright in the first place, they may ask? Why not join another church? And I confess that if all that I knew of Reverend Wright were the snippets of those sermons that have run in an endless loop on the television sets and YouTube, or if Trinity United Church of Christ conformed to the caricatures being peddled by some commentators, there is no doubt that I would react in much the same way.

But the truth is, that isn't all that I know of the man. The man I met more than 20 years ago is a man who helped introduce me to my Christian faith, a man who spoke to me about our obligations to love one another, to care for the sick and lift up the poor. He is a man who served his country as a United States Marine; who has studied and lectured at some of the finest universities and seminaries in the country, and who for over 30 years has led a church that serves the community by doing God's work here on Earth—by housing the homeless, ministering to the needy, providing day care services and scholarships and prison ministries, and reaching out to those suffering from HIV/AIDS.

In my first book, Dreams From My Father, I describe the experience of my first service at Trinity:

"People began to shout, to rise from their seats and clap and cry out, a forceful wind carrying the reverend's voice up into the rafters. And in that single note—hope!—I heard something else: At the foot of that cross, inside the thousands of churches across the city, I imagined the stories of ordinary black people merging with the stories of David and Goliath, Moses and Pharaoh, the Christians in the lion's den, Ezekiel's field of dry bones. Those stories—of survival and freedom and hope—became our stories, my story. The blood that spilled was our blood, the tears our tears, until this black church, on this bright day, seemed once more a vessel carrying the story of a people into future generations and into a larger world. Our trials and triumphs became at once unique and universal, black and more than black. In chronicling our journey, the stories and songs gave us a meaning to reclaim memories that we didn't need to feel shame about—memories that all people might study and cherish, and with which we could start to rebuild."

That has been my experience at Trinity. Like other predominantly black churches across the country, Trinity embodies the black community in its entirety—the doctor and the welfare mom, the model student and the former gang-banger. Like other black churches, Trinity's services are full of raucous laughter and sometimes bawdy humor. They are full of dancing and clapping and screaming and shouting that may seem jarring to the untrained ear. The church contains in full the kindness and cruelty, the fierce intelligence and the shocking ignorance, the struggles and successes, the love and, yes, the bitterness and biases that make up the black experience in America.

And this helps explain, perhaps, my relationship with Reverend Wright. As imperfect as he may be, he has been like family to me. He strengthened my faith, officiated my wedding, and baptized my children. Not once in my conversations with him have I heard him talk about any ethnic group in derogatory terms, or treat whites with whom he interacted with anything but courtesy and respect. He contains within him the contradictions—the good and the bad—of the community that he has served diligently for so many years.

I can no more disown him than I can disown the black community. I can no more disown him than I can disown my white grandmother—a woman who helped raise me, a woman who sacrificed again and again for me, a woman who loves me as much as she loves anything in this world, but a woman who once confessed her fear of black men who passed her by on the street, and who on more than one occasion has uttered racial or ethnic stereotypes that made me cringe.

These people are a part of me. And they are part of America, this country that I love.

Some will see this as an attempt to justify or excuse comments that are simply inexcusable. I can assure you it is not. I suppose the politically safe thing to do would be to move on from this episode and just hope that it fades into the woodwork. We can dismiss Reverend Wright as a crank or a demagogue, just as some have dismissed Geraldine Ferraro, in the aftermath of her recent statements, as harboring some deep-seated bias.

But race is an issue that I believe this nation cannot afford to ignore right now. We would be making the same mistake that Reverend Wright made in his offending sermons about America—to simplify and stereotype and amplify the negative to the point that it distorts reality.

The fact is that the comments that have been made and the issues that have surfaced over the last few weeks reflect the complexities of race in this country that we've never really worked through—a part of our union that we have not yet made perfect. And if we walk away now, if we simply retreat into our respective corners, we will never be able to come together and solve challenges like health care or education or the need to find good jobs for every American.

Understanding this reality requires a reminder of how we arrived at this point. As William Faulkner once wrote, "The past isn't dead and buried. In fact, it isn't even past." We do not need to recite here the history of racial injustice in this country. But we do need to remind ourselves that so many of the disparities that exist between the African-American community and the larger American community today can be traced directly to inequalities passed on from an earlier generation that suffered under the brutal legacy of slavery and Jim Crow.

Segregated schools were and are inferior schools; we still haven't fixed them, 50 years after Brown v. Board of Education. And the inferior education they provided, then and now, helps explain the pervasive achievement gap between today's black and white students.

Legalized discrimination—where blacks were prevented, often through violence, from owning property, or loans were not granted to African-American business owners, or black homeowners could not access FHA mortgages, or blacks were excluded from unions or the police force or the fire department—meant that black families could not amass any meaningful wealth to bequeath to future generations. That history helps explain the wealth and income gap between blacks and whites, and the concentrated pockets of poverty that persist in so many of today's urban and rural communities.

A lack of economic opportunity among black men, and the shame and frustration that came from not being able to provide for one's family contributed to the erosion of black families—a problem that welfare policies for many years may have worsened. And the lack of basic services in so many urban black neighborhoods—parks for kids to play in, police walking the beat, regular garbage pickup, building code enforcement—all helped create a cycle of violence, blight and neglect that continues to haunt us.

This is the reality in which Reverend Wright and other African-Americans of his generation grew up. They came of age in the late '50s and early '60s, a time when segregation was still the law of the land and opportunity was systematically constricted. What's remarkable is not how many failed in the face of discrimination, but how many men and women overcame the odds; how many were able to make a way out of no way, for those like me who would come after them.

For all those who scratched and clawed their way to get a piece of the American Dream, there were many who didn't make it—those who were ultimately defeated, in one way or another, by discrimination. That legacy of defeat was passed on to future generations—those young men and, increasingly, young women who we see standing on street corners or languishing in our prisons, without hope or prospects for the future. Even for those blacks who did make it, questions of race and racism continue to define their worldview in fundamental ways. For the men and women of Reverend Wright's generation, the memories of humiliation and doubt and fear have not gone away; nor has the anger and the bitterness of those years. That anger may not get expressed in public, in front of white co-workers or white friends. But it does find voice in the barbershop or the beauty shop or around the kitchen table. At times, that anger is exploited by politicians, to gin up votes along racial lines, or to make up for a politician's own failings.

And occasionally it finds voice in the church on Sunday morning, in the pulpit and in the pews. The fact that so many people are surprised to hear that anger in some of Reverend Wright's sermons simply reminds us of the old truism that the most segregated hour of American life occurs on Sunday morning. That anger is not always productive; indeed, all too often it distracts attention from solving real problems; it keeps us from squarely facing our own complicity within the African-American community in our condition, and prevents the African-American community from forging the alliances it needs to bring about real change. But the anger is real; it is powerful. And to simply wish it away, to condemn it without understanding its roots, only serves to widen the chasm of misunderstanding that exists between the races.

In fact, a similar anger exists within segments of the white community. Most working- and middle-class white Americans don't feel that they have been particularly privileged by their race. Their experience is the immigrant experience—as far as they're concerned, no one handed them anything. They built it from scratch. They've worked hard all their lives, many times only to see their jobs shipped overseas or their pensions dumped after a lifetime of labor. They are anxious about their futures, and they feel their dreams slipping away. And in an era of stagnant wages and global competition, opportunity comes to be seen as a zero sum game, in which your dreams come at my expense. So when they are told to bus their children to a school across town; when they hear an African-American is getting an advantage in landing a good job or a spot in a good college because of an injustice that they themselves never committed; when they're told that their fears about crime in urban neighborhoods are somehow prejudiced, resentment builds over time.

Like the anger within the black community, these resentments aren't always expressed in polite company. But they have helped shape the political landscape for at least a generation. Anger over welfare and affirmative action helped forge the Reagan Coalition. Politicians routinely exploited fears of crime for their own electoral ends. Talk show hosts and conservative commentators built entire careers unmasking bogus claims of racism while dismissing legitimate discussions of racial injustice and inequality as mere political correctness or reverse racism.

Just as black anger often proved counterproductive, so have these white resentments distracted attention from the real culprits of the middle class squeeze—a corporate culture rife with inside dealing, questionable accounting practices and short-term greed; a Washington dominated by lobbyists and special interests; economic policies that favor the few over the many. And yet, to wish away the resentments of white Americans, to label them as misguided or even racist, without recognizing they are grounded in legitimate concerns—this too widens the racial divide and blocks the path to understanding.

This is where we are right now. It's a racial stalemate we've been stuck in for years. Contrary to the claims of some of my critics, black and white, I have never been so naïve as to believe that we can get beyond our racial divisions in a single election cycle, or with a single candidacy—particularly a candidacy as imperfect as my own.

But I have asserted a firm conviction—a conviction rooted in my faith in God and my faith in the American people—that, working together, we can move beyond some of our old racial wounds, and that in fact we have no choice if we are to continue on the path of a more perfect union.

For the African-American community, that path means embracing the burdens of our past without becoming victims of our past. It means continuing to insist on a full measure of justice in every aspect of American life. But it also means binding our particular grievances—for better health care and better schools and better jobs—to the larger aspirations of all Americans: the white woman struggling to break the glass ceiling, the white man who has been laid off, the immigrant trying to feed his family. And it means taking full responsibility for our own lives—by demanding more from our fathers, and spending more time with our children, and reading to them, and teaching them that while they may face challenges and discrimination in their own lives, they must never succumb to despair or cynicism; they must always believe that they can write their own destiny.

Ironically, this quintessentially American—and yes, conservative—notion of self-help found frequent expression in Reverend Wright's sermons. But what my former pastor too often failed to understand is that embarking on a program of self-help also requires a belief that society can change.

The profound mistake of Reverend Wright's sermons is not that he spoke about racism in our society. It's that he spoke as if our society was static; as if no progress had been made; as if this country—a country that has made it possible for one of his own members to run for the highest office in the land and build a coalition of white and black, Latino and Asian, rich and poor, young and old—is still irrevocably bound to a tragic past. But what we know—what we have seen—is that America can change. That is the true genius of this nation. What we have already achieved gives us hope—the audacity to hope—for what we can and must achieve tomorrow.

In the white community, the path to a more perfect union means acknowledging that what ails the African-American community does not just exist in the minds of black people; that the legacy of discrimination—and current incidents of discrimination, while less overt than in the past—are real and must be addressed, not just with words, but with deeds, by investing in our schools and our communities; by enforcing our civil rights laws and ensuring fairness in our criminal justice system; by providing this generation with ladders of opportunity that were unavailable for previous generations. It requires all Americans to realize that your dreams do not have to come at the expense of my dreams; that investing in the health, welfare and education of black and brown and white children will ultimately help all of America prosper.

In the end, then, what is called for is nothing more and nothing less than what all the world's great religions demand—that we do unto others as we would have them do unto us. Let us be our brother's keeper, scripture tells us. Let us be our sister's keeper. Let us find that common stake we all have in one another, and let our politics reflect that spirit as well.

For we have a choice in this country. We can accept a politics that breeds division and conflict and cynicism. We can tackle race only as spectacle—as we did in the O.J. trial—or in the wake of tragedy—as we did in the aftermath of Katrina—or as fodder for the nightly news. We can play Reverend Wright's sermons on every channel, every day and talk about them from now until the election, and make the only question in this campaign whether or not the American people think that I somehow believe or sympathize with his most offensive words. We can pounce on some gaffe by a Hillary supporter as evidence that she's playing the race card, or we can speculate on whether white men will all flock to John McCain in the general election regardless of his policies.

We can do that.

But if we do, I can tell you that in the next election, we'll be talking about some other distraction. And then another one. And then another one. And nothing will change.

That is one option. Or, at this moment, in this election, we can come together and say, "Not this time." This time, we want to talk about the crumbling schools that are stealing the future of black children and white children and Asian children and Hispanic children and Native American children. This time, we want to reject the cynicism that tells us that

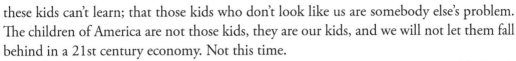

these kids can't learn; that those kids who don't look like us are somebody else's problem. The children of America are not those kids, they are our kids, and we will not let them fall behind in a 21st century economy. Not this time.

This time we want to talk about how the lines in the emergency room are filled with whites and blacks and Hispanics who do not have health care, who don't have the power on their own to overcome the special interests in Washington, but who can take them on if we do it together.

This time, we want to talk about the shuttered mills that once provided a decent life for men and women of every race, and the homes for sale that once belonged to Americans from every religion, every region, every walk of life. This time, we want to talk about the fact that the real problem is not that someone who doesn't look like you might take your job; it's that the corporation you work for will ship it overseas for nothing more than a profit.

This time, we want to talk about the men and women of every color and creed who serve together and fight together and bleed together under the same proud flag. We want to talk about how to bring them home from a war that should have never been authorized and should have never been waged. And we want to talk about how we'll show our patriotism by caring for them and their families, and giving them the benefits that they have earned.

I would not be running for President if I didn't believe with all my heart that this is what the vast majority of Americans want for this country. This union may never be perfect, but generation after generation has shown that it can always be perfected. And today, whenever I find myself feeling doubtful or cynical about this possibility, what gives me the most hope is the next generation—the young people whose attitudes and beliefs and openness to change have already made history in this election.

There is one story in particularly that I'd like to leave you with today—a story I told when I had the great honor of speaking on Dr. King's birthday at his home church, Ebenezer Baptist, in Atlanta.

There is a young, 23-year-old white woman named Ashley Baia who organized for our campaign in Florence, S.C. She had been working to organize a mostly African-American community since the beginning of this campaign, and one day she was at a roundtable discussion where everyone went around telling their story and why they were there.

And Ashley said that when she was 9 years old, her mother got cancer. And because she had to miss days of work, she was let go and lost her health care. They had to file for bankruptcy, and that's when Ashley decided that she had to do something to help her mom.

She knew that food was one of their most expensive costs, and so Ashley convinced her mother that what she really liked and really wanted to eat more than anything else was mustard and relish sandwiches—because that was the cheapest way to eat. That's the mind of a 9-year-old.

She did this for a year until her mom got better. So she told everyone at the roundtable that the reason she joined our campaign was so that she could help the millions of other children in the country who want and need to help their parents, too.

Now, Ashley might have made a different choice. Perhaps somebody told her along the way that the source of her mother's problems were blacks who were on welfare and too lazy to work, or Hispanics who were coming into the country illegally. But she didn't. She sought out allies in her fight against injustice.

Anyway, Ashley finishes her story and then goes around the room and asks everyone else why they're supporting the campaign. They all have different stories and different reasons. Many bring up a specific issue. And finally they come to this elderly black man who's been sitting there quietly the entire time. And Ashley asks him why he's there. And he does not bring up a specific issue. He does not say health care or the economy. He does not say education or the war. He does not say that he was there because of Barack Obama. He simply says to everyone in the room, "I am here because of Ashley."

"I'm here because of Ashley." By itself, that single moment of recognition between that young white girl and that old black man is not enough. It is not enough to give health care to the sick, or jobs to the jobless, or education to our children.

But it is where we start. It is where our union grows stronger. And as so many generations have come to realize over the course of the 221 years since a band of patriots signed that document right here in Philadelphia, that is where the perfection begins.

CPSIA information can be obtained
at www.ICGtesting.com
Printed in the USA
BVHW010722030219
539337BV00009B/371/P